Comics as Culture

Comics as Culture

M. Thomas Inge

University Press of Mississippi
JACKSON AND LONDON

The paper in this book meets the guidelines for permanence
and durability of the Committee on Production Guidelines
for Book Longevity of the Council on Library Resources.

Title page illustration © King Features.
Reprinted by special permission of King Features Syndicate,
Inc.

Designed by John Langston and Sally Horne.

The University Press of Mississippi and M. Thomas Inge
thank the following publishers and artists for granting
permission to reprint material in this book:

King Features Syndicate; *Appalachian Journal* for "The
Appalachian Backgrounds of Billy De Beck's Snuffy Smith,"
AJ, 4 (Winter 1977), pp. 120-32; Gale Research Inc. for
"Winsor McCay," *Dictionary of Literary Biography, Vol. 22:
American Writers for Children, 1900-1960* (1983), pp. 252-59;
Journal of Popular Culture for "Introduction" to In-Depth
Section "The Comics as Culture," *JPC*, 12 (Spring 1979), pp.
631-39; Oxford University Press for "What's So Funny about
the Comics," from *American Humor* by Arthur Power
Dudden, Copyright © 1987 by Arthur Power Dudden,
Reprinted by permission of Oxford University Press, Inc.;
Studies in American Humor for "The *New Yorker* Cartoon
and Modern Graphic Humor," 3 (Spring 1984), pp. 61-72;
Mort Walker for *The Lexicon of Comicana* (Port Chester,
NY: Museum of Cartoon Art, 1980), Copyright © Mort
Walker; Robert Crumb for "Keep on Truckin'" (from a 1972
XYZ Comics) and "Mr. Sketchum" from a 1970 *Hydrogen
Bomb Funnies*; DC Comics, Inc. for the cover of Action
Comics No. 1 and Superman, "Superman is a trademark of
DC Comics Inc. All rights reserved. Used with permission";
William Gaines for EC Publications, "Lost in the
Microcosm," *Weird Science* (May 1950), "My World," *Weird
Science* (November-December 1953), "He Walked Among
Us," *Weird Science* (May-June 1952), "The Reformers,"
Weird Science (July-August 1953); Editors Press Service for
Mutt and Jeff by Bud Fisher; Will Eisner for *Spirit*; Marvel
Entertainment Group, Inc. for Spider-Man: TM © 1989,
Marvel Entertainment Group, Inc., All rights reserved; *The
New Yorker* for drawings by Charles Addams, © 1940, 1968,
Peter Arno, © 1941, 1969, Carl Rose, © 1928, 1956; North
American Syndicate for *Andy Capp*, Courtesy of
Syndication International, Distributed by NAS, Inc.;
Okefenokee Glee and Perloo Society for *Pogo*; Rosemary
Thurber for "Touché" and "All Right Have It Your way,"
Copyright © 1945 James Thurber, Copyright © 1973 Helen
Thurber and Rosemary A. Thurber, From *The Thurber
Carnival*, published by Harper & Row; Tribune Media
Services for *Terry and the Pirates*, Milton Caniff self-
portrait, *Smokey Stover* 1940, Wallet Family Tree from
Gasoline Alley 1988, *Little Orphan Annie*, *Gumps* panel, and
Chester Gould self-portrait; Charles Schulz for *Peanuts*, The
Peanuts cartoons are copyrighted by United Feature
Syndicate, Inc. and may not be reprinted without
permission; United Media for *Nancy*, copyrighted by UFS,
Inc. and may not be reprinted without permission and for
the portrait of Bushmiller, *Out Our Way*, *Captain Easy and
Wash Tubbs*, copyrighted by NEA, Inc. and may not be
reprinted without permission; Virginia Commonwealth
University for sketches from the "Billy DeBeck Library,"
Special Collections and Archives Department, James Branch
Cabell Library, Virginia Commonwealth University; and
Toni Mendez for *Steve Canyon* by Milton Caniff.

Library of Congress Cataloging-in-Publication Data

Inge, M. Thomas.
    Comics as culture / M. Thomas Inge.
        p. cm.
    Includes bibliographical references.
    ISBN 0-87805-407-3 (alk. paper). — ISBN 0-87805-408-1
(pbk. : alk. paper)
    1. Comic books, strips, etc.—United States—History
and criticism.   2. United States—Popular culture.
3. American literature—History and criticism.   I. Title.
PN6725.I54   1990
741.5′0973—dc20   89-37375
                                                                    CIP

British Library Cataloguing-in-Publication data available

For Will Eisner
master creator, mentor,
and friend

Contents

Acknowledgments

Some of the material in these chapters was published in a different form in essays for the *Appalachian Journal, Journal of Popular Culture,* and *Studies in American Humor.* Four of the chapters substantially appeared in books: "What's So Funny About the Comics?" in *American Humor,* ed. Arthur P. Dudden (Oxford University Press, 1987); "Fantasy and Reality in Winsor McCay's *Little Nemo*" in Volume 22 of the *Dictionary of Literary Biography* (Bruccoli Clarke/Gale Research, 1983); "Faulkner Reads the Funny Papers," in *Faulkner & Humor,* ed. Doreen Fowler and Ann J. Abadie (University Press of Mississippi, 1986); and "*Peanuts* and American Culture" in *The Graphic Art of Charles Schulz* (Oakland Museum, 1985). "American Industrial Culture and the Comic Book" was read at a symposium on "Reading in America, 1840-1940" at the Strong Museum in Rochester, New York, and "Charlie Chaplin and the Comics" was prepared for the colloquy held in celebration of the centennial of the birth of Charles Chaplin in Paris. Portions of the bibliographic essays were published in my *Handbook of American Popular Culture,* 2nd edition (Greenwood Press, 1990), and my *Handbook of American Popular Literature* (Greenwood Press, 1988). Permission to include previously published material in this book is gratefully acknowledged. Thanks also to Bill Blackbeard, my main authority in all things historical and factual, and the others who have trusted in me and the importance of things comic: Ruth Brent, Louis Budd, Lucy Caswell, Pavla Duplinska, John D. Lyle, Larry Mintz, Judith O'Sullivan, Robert Overstreet, Ladell Payne, Jack Salzman, Tony Silver, Barbara Sirota, Kathryn Van Spanckeren, and Sharon Weinstein, as well as the three stooges, Tonette, Scott, and Michael.

Introduction: Comics as Culture

The comic strip may be defined as an open-ended dramatic narrative about a recurring set of characters, told in a series of drawings, often including dialogue in balloons and a narrative text, and published serially in newspapers. The daily and Sunday comic strips are part of the reading habits of more than one hundred million people of all educational and social levels. During the first half of this century, surveys have indicated that sixty percent of newspaper readers consider the comic page the priority feature in their reading. Along with jazz, the comic strip as we know it perhaps represents America's major indigenous contribution to world culture.

Comic books, on the other hand, originally an offshoot of the comic strip, are regarded with considerable suspicion by parents, educators, psychiatrists, and moral reformers. More than one critic has called them crude, vulgar, and ultimately corrupting. They have been investigated by governmental committees and subjected to severe censorship. Yet even in today's uncertain market, more than two hundred million copies are sold a year, and the comic book collecting business has become an important area of investment with its own price guide and publications to facilitate exchange and trade.

Any phenomenon which plays so heavily on the sensibility of the American populace deserves study purely for sociological reasons if for no other. The comics serve as revealing reflectors of popular attitudes, tastes, and mores. Because comic strips appear in daily newspapers, a publication designed for family consumption, the syndicates, editors, and publishers submit strips to the severest kind of scrutiny and control to be sure that no parent, political bloc, or advertiser whose support they

Mort Walker, *Beetle Bailey*, April 8, 1982.
© King Features Syndicate, Inc.

Harold Gray, *Little Orphan Annie*, July 10 and 13, 1935. These two sequences from a 1935 story reflect Harold Gray's view of benign American Capitalism and economic isolationism. If the first kind of generosity seldom happened, the last attitude has been all-too-characteristic of American foreign policy.
© Tribune Media Services.

court will take offense. In the thirties conservative Harold Gray once had to redraw a *Little Orphan Annie* sequence because of its attack on one of Franklin Delano Roosevelt's New Deal programs, and the liberal slanted *Pogo* strip by Walt Kelly was often banned in the fifties in southern newspapers because of its satiric thrusts at school segregationists.

Examine the comics in any daily newspaper and each will be found to support some commonly accepted notion or standard of society. *Blondie, Archie, Mary Worth, Li'l Abner,* and *Gasoline Alley* in different ways support the idea that the family is the basic social unit. *Judge Parker, Rex Morgan, Mark Trail,* and *Gil Thorpe* support the concepts of decency and fair play among the professions. While *The Wizard of Id, B.C., Peanuts, Funky Winkerbean, Doonesbury, Bloom County,* and *Shoe* are overtly satirical, they also provide a rational standard against which the aberrations they portray can be measured and found laughable. Why is Andy Capp, who drinks heavily, gambles, and commits adultery, permitted to violate these social taboos on the pages of the funny papers? Possibly because he is British and Americans are willing to forgive such behavior

Reggie Smythe, *Andy Capp.* Unlike most comic strip husbands, Andy Capp refuses to work, drinks to an excess, stays out all night, and chases other women. One reason for the popularity of this British strip may be Andy's willingness to recognize his human failings and accept himself for the miserable sinner that he is.
Courtesy of Syndication International. Distributed by NAS, Inc.

Robert Crumb, *Mr. Sketchum*, 1970. Robert Crumb is a brilliant innovator in comic art who has spawned an entire school of imitators and has had a pronounced impact on popular iconography. As in this comic book page, Crumb often reflects a radical stance beyond any political ideology.
© Robert Crumb.

on the part of Europeans. It is little wonder that Andy has such a large following—he is a stubbornly unpredictable and incorrigible individualist among many repetitious and mindless Caspar Milquetoasts. In the last decade, I should note, a few strips have daringly dealt with such hitherto forbidden topics as homosexuality, pre-marital sex, unmarried teen-age mothers, and mental retardation, but with trepidation and frequent local censorship.

Comic books are submitted for approval prior to publication to the Comics Code Authority, which exercises the most severe censorship applied to any mass media. Guidelines prohibit displays of sex, adultery, divorce, drugs, corrupt authority, or unpunished crimes. Submission to the authority requires a medium mainly irrelevant to reality; thus characters escape into a world of fantasy, dominated by super-heroes, a world in which both might and right are on the side of morality. When needed to support his country in time of war, however, no superhero has ever dared to refuse. The recent development of adult comic books and graphic novels, it should be noted, as well as alternative methods of publication and distribution, have greatly eroded the influence of the Authority.

The underground press comic strips and books of the 1960s and 1970s, which came into being partly to defy the restrictions of the Comics Code Authority, ironically failed to escape the basically political nature of American comic art. The defiance of American materialism by Robert Crumb, however, approaches anarchy, the rejection of society's sexual taboos by S. Clay Wilson is absolute, and the doomsday vision of Spain Rodriguez predicts the total destruction of civilization. These are radical stances beyond the pales of political ideology, but the underground cartoonists had the incredible luxury of unrestricted artistic freedom. This freedom has yielded brilliant results in the work of Art Spiegelman and Harvey Pekar, both of whom emerged from the underground comic book movement. Spiegelman's impressive retelling of the Holocaust in animal fable form *Maus*, haunting and moving in its intelligence and sincerity, brought a nomination for a National Book Critics Circle Award in 1987, the first comic book to be so honored, and Harvey Pekar's philosophic disquisitions on the nature of mundane life in Cleveland collected in *American Splendor* and *More American Splendor* in 1986 and 1987, have made him an influential

Superman.
© DC Comics Inc.

force on the national cultural scene. These are obviously comic books with a serious purpose and something important to say about modern human life and history.

The comics also derive from popular patterns, themes, and symbols of Western culture. Chester Gould credited Sherlock Holmes as the inspiration for Dick Tracy (compare the shape of their noses), and Superman was partly based on Philip Wylie's 1930 novel *Gladiator*. *Bringing Up Father*, better known as "Maggie and Jiggs," by George McManus was inspired by a popular play, *The Rising Generation*, and Philip Nowlan based *Buck Rogers* on his own short story "Armageddon 2419." Dick Tracy's gallery of grotesque villians draws on the gothic tradition and follows the medieval concept that the outward appearance reflects the inner character. Flash Gordon, Prince Valiant, Captain Marvel, and the Fantastic Four draw on the heroic tradition to which Hercules, Samson, King Arthur, Beowulf, Davy Crockett, and Paul Bunyan belong.

If the comics have absorbed much of Western tradition, they have also had their influence on popular language and culture. Word coinages deriving from comic strips, and still found in

Alex Raymond, *Flash Gordon*, 1937 (detail).
© King Features Syndicate, Inc.

general currency, include *jeep, baloney, yard-bird, horsefeathers, google-eyed,* and *twenty-three skidoo.* There are Rube Goldberg contraptions and Mickey Mouse college courses. Certain foods are inextricably associated with certain characters: Popeye's spinach, Wimpy's hamburgers, Jiggs' corned beef and cabbage, and Dagwood's incredible sandwiches. Buster Brown clothes and shoes can still be bought, and the Prince Valiant haircut has been popular at times. While Charlie Brown did not invent the expletive "Good Grief!" it will be a long time before anyone can use the phrase without automatically associating it with Charles Schulz's diminutive loser in the game of life.

Perhaps a major reason for recognizing and studying the comics is the fact that they are one of the few native American art forms. Literature, drama, music, film, and the other forms of popular culture were largely established in Europe and most American practitioners (with perhaps the exception of film) have followed the patterns and standards established by foreign masters—Joyce in the novel, Ibsen in the drama, or the Beatles in popular music. In the comic strip and comic book, however, Americans

Chic Young, *Dagwood*. Dagwood prepares to make one of his famous sandwiches, a facsimile of which is found on many luncheon menus today.
© King Features Syndicate, Inc.

Milton Caniff, *Steve Canyon*, January 19, 1946. This is the first page of Caniff's new strip after he had ceased to draw *Terry and the Pirates*. The adventures of this soldier of fortune suited the tastes of a post-war America entering the Cold War.
© Milton Caniff.

have defined the forms, expanded their aesthetic possibilities, and become the first masters of their unique visual and narrative potential. Winsor McCay, George Herriman, Alex Raymond, Hal Foster, Roy Crane, Milton Caniff, Will Eisner, and Harvey Kurtzman are just a few of the internationally recognized geniuses of the comic strip, and all are Americans.

In a great variety of ways, the comics have influenced the general culture of the United States and the world. Pablo Picasso was supplied with American funny papers in France by his friend Gertrude Stein, and he drew inspiration from them for much of his work, such as *The Dream and the Lie of Franco* (1937). When samples of George Herriman's brilliant *Krazy Kat* pages circulated in France, they were recognized as early examples of dada art, and a few great modern masters, such as George B. Luks and Lyonel Feininger, produced comic pages early in their careers. The pop art movement of the 1960s witnessed the wholesale

appropriation of the forms, symbols, and style of comic art for the individual aesthetic intentions of a number of contemporary artists such as Andy Warhol, Roy Lichtenstein, Mel Ramos, Claes Oldenburg, and Ray Yoshida, among others. They saw the iconography of comic art as an appropriate idiom for communicating their contemporary visions. Comic imagery is liable to crop up in the most unlikely places. In Crystal City, Texas, the "Spinach Capital of the World," there stands a statue of Popeye, erected by a grateful community. The command module of the crew Apollo 10 answered to "Charlie Brown," while the LEM was named "Snoopy." Blondie has helped sell margarine in Norway, and in France Mandrake the Magician once promoted Renault automobiles. The Phantom is the subject of a series of highly popular novels published in ten languages throughout all of Europe.

In addition to their sociological value and their cultural significance, the comics are also of importance unto themselves, as a form of

George McManus, *Bringing Up Father*, 1940 (detail). This is a striking example of the kind of architectural detail McManus gave his strip about an Irish nouveau riche couple, Maggie and Jiggs, attempting to adjust to the world of the wealthy. Jiggs continually slips back into his working class origins.
© King Features Syndicate, Inc.

creative expression apart from their relationship to other forms of art. This is the most difficult area to write about because we lack the critical vocabulary and have only begun to define the structural and stylistic principles behind successful comic art. Instead we tend to rely on terms borrowed from other areas of creative expression.

For example, we can talk about the comics as a form of communication and how they can be used as propaganda, in advertising, for the dissemination of information, or as instructional aids. Reading teachers have only recently begun to realize the effectiveness of comic books in teaching reluctant or unresponsive children to read—fascinated by the pictures and the story being portrayed, they are led to study the words to figure out what is happening. Contrary to the notion that comic book reading serves as a cop out and escape from reading "real" books, young readers are often led to novels and plays after reading the comic book adaptations, in the same way adults want to read a book after viewing the movie version of it (a trend so popular that now a book is often not written until after the film version has been released).

We can talk about the comics as graphic art,

Alex Raymond and Dashiell Hammett, *Secret Agent X-9*, May 15, 1934. Hardboiled detective writer Hammett was hired to write the story line for this detective comic strip, drawn in anticipation of *film noir* style by master artist Alex Raymond, creator of *Flash Gordon*.
© King Features Syndicate, Inc.

Wallet Family Tree

Gasoline Alley

ADA b AUG.8,1988

ADAM m TEEKA TOK NOV. 26, 1986

ADAM EVE b APR 21,1960

GRETCHEN b APR 13,1978

ROVER BUMP ADOPTED DEC. 1, 1983

CLOVIA m SLIM SKINNER MAY 31, 1977

GABRIEL b JUN. 27,1966

NUBBIN b JAN. 1,1954

JUDY m GIDEON GRUBB MAY 4, 1961

CORKY m HOPE HASSEL OCT. 1, 1949

CLOVIA b MAY 15,1949

THOMAS WALTER "CHIPPER" b APR. 1, 1945

CORKY b MAY 2,1928

JUDY LEFT IN WALT'S CAR FEB. 28,1935

(ALLISON) SKEEZIX LEFT ON WALT'S DOORSTEP FEB. 14, 1921 b FEB. 9,1921

SKEEZIX m NINA CLOCK JUN. 28,1944

AVERY

WALTER WEATHERBY WALLET m PHYLLIS BLOSSOM JUN. 24,1926

DOC

SCANCARELLI   WALT   BILL

Jim Scancarelli, *Wallet Family Tree*, 1988. *Gasoline Alley*, originated by Frank King and drawn subsequently by Dick Moores and Jim Scancarelli, is the only comic strip in which the characters have aged along with its readers.
© Tribune Media Services, Inc.

and clearly the visual attraction is the first thing that captures our attention. The comic artist must confront and solve the same problems of spatial relationships, balance, and form that every artist must face, and nearly all modern artistic movements and styles have either been anticipated by or reflected in the comics. In the case of pop art, they inspired a whole school of painting.

Narration or storytelling is also a main function of the comics. They are meant to be read, as opposed to traditional narrative art meant to be viewed and interpreted. While they have never competed with the classics, they have seriously altered popular reading habits by attracting readers away from pulp magazines, dime novels, and cheap tabloids (only detective

and science fiction have withstood the competition and survived). The total work of some cartoonists constitutes something like a novel on the pattern of Balzac's human comedy or Faulkner's Yoknapatawpha County cycle. *Little Orphan Annie* follows the picaresque pattern of *Adventures of Huckleberry Finn*, and *Gasoline Alley* anatomizes an entire midwestern community much in the tradition of Sherwood Anderson's *Winesburg, Ohio* or Sinclair Lewis's *Main Street* (especially with the recent emphasis by Dick Moores and his successor Jim Scancarelli on the provincial grotesque).

It has been suggested that the comics are closest to drama in that both rely on the dramatic conventions of character, dialogue, scene, gesture, compressed time, and stage

Will Eisner, *The Spirit*, November 30, 1947, splash page. Eisner's *The Spirit*, a 1940s comic book supplement for newspapers, demonstrated a striking use of angle, framing, lighting, and mood characteristic of the cinema, and captured the style and spirit of *film noir.*
© Will Eisner.

devices, but probably the motion picture is closer. Will Eisner, distinguished for his visual innovations in comic art, has stated that "comics are movies on paper." Eisner's work in *The Spirit* has always demonstrated a brilliant use of angle shots, framing, lighting, mood, and detail characteristics of the film medium. When William Friedkin, producer of *The French Connection, The Exorcist*, and other films, announced his intention to do a film version of *The Spirit* for television, he paid tribute to Eisner's influence on his own work: "Look at the dramatic use of montage, of light and sound. See the dynamic framing that Eisner employs,

and the deep vibrant colors. Many film directors have been influenced by *The Spirit*, myself included." Displaying an Eisner cover with a man being chased by an elevated train, Friedkin noted, "This is where I got ideas for the chase in *The French Connection*." Federico Fellini, Orson Wells, Alain Resnais, and George Lucas are other film makers who have acknowledged their indebtedness to the comics for cinematic concepts and techniques. In fact, many standard techniques were first employed in the comics— montage (before Eisenstein), angle shots, panning, closeups, cutting, framing, etc.

Yet none of these relationships and functions

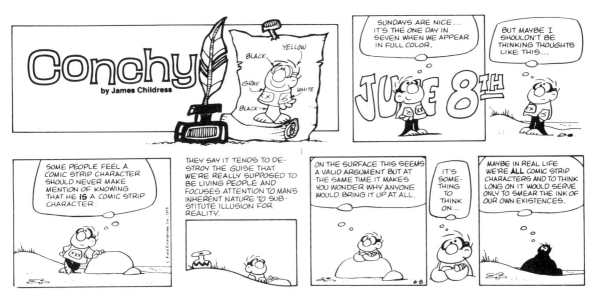

James Childress, *Conchy*, June 8, 1975. A little known strip, *Conchy* was distinguished by its deep philosophical examinations of society and human nature. Childress in this page uses the conventions of the comic strip to make a metaphoric comment on illusion and reality and creates a kind of self-reflexive meta-comic. © James Childress.

discussed so far elucidate comic art for the distinctive and separate medium it happens to be. Text, artwork, and meaning cannot be judged independently of the whole work. Word and picture interact in the best examples without one dominating the other, and quite literally the medium is the message. There has been nothing else quite like comic art on the cultural scene since the invention of the novel for potential in creative challenge and imaginative opportunity.

Historical studies, biographies, critical appreciations, anthologies, encyclopedias, and periodicals on the subjects of comic art and artists have begun to proliferate in recent years (see the bibliographic essays at the end of this book). Partly this has resulted from publishers wishing to tap the lucrative nostalgia market, but in many cases because individuals have begun to recognize the importance of documenting this part of our national heritage. The study of comics has become a part of high school, college, and university curricula throughout the country and abroad, and numerous museums have hosted major exhibitions of original comic art. At least five research centers now exist in the United States and are available to scholars: the San Francisco Academy of Comic Art; the Museum of Cartoon Art in Rye/Port Chester, New York; the Library for Communication and Graphic Arts at Ohio State University in Columbus; the Russel B. Nye Collection of Popular Culture at Michigan State University in East Lansing; and the Cartoon Art Museum in San Francisco.

Those who hesitate to accept comic art as a significant form of expression might remember that Shakespeare was once merely a contributor to Elizabethan popular culture who spoke to the pit as well as the gallery (and ultimately the ages), and it took decades for the elite to grant his work the respectability it deserved. Perhaps the day will come when some of our major comic artists will be granted the place they deserve in the pantheon of American culture. It is to that end that this volume is dedicated.

These chapters address collectively and are unified by their concern with the various ways comic strips and comic books reflect larger cultural trends. Relations between literature, language, technology, art, and the comics are explored in general chapters and discussions of specific major artists. But the comics are not important because of these connections. My intent is to suggest ways the comics also deal with the larger aesthetic and philosophic issues mainstream culture has always defined in its arts and humanities. The comics are another form of legitimate culture quite capable of confronting the major questions of mankind, but they do it with a gentler spirit that leads to laughter at the moment of recognition. The comics are well and deservedly loved, but they should also be respected for what they have contributed to the visual and narrative arts of the world.

Comics as Culture

"Guess if I'm careful I'll get along."

"By Jove! it is slippery."

"Oh, hang these slanting pavements!"

"A man does have to have command of his feet on these bad spots."

"Steady does it!"

"Oh dear me! I hope no one is looking!"

"Now which way is he coming, anyhow?"

"Excuse me!" "I beg your pardon!"

"Happy thought! What's the use of walking."

"———!"

"It's a mighty hard winter, anyhow."

"If ever I go out on a day like this again—"

A. B. Frost, *A Slippery Day*, 1883. Such sequential cartoons as this in popular humor magazines of the nineteenth century were precursors to the comic strip. Frost was best known as the illustrator of the Uncle Remus books by Joel Chandler Harris.

1

What's so Funny about the Comics?

Historians of the comic strip have traced its origin back to a number of sources in western art and culture—the pictorial narrative of the medieval Bayeux tapestry, the eighteenth-century print series of such artists as William Hogarth and Thomas Rowlandson, the illustrated European broadsheet, the illustrated novels and children's books, and European and American humorous periodicals.[1] Usually the interest in such cultural geneological research is to dignify and make respectable what is considered a low-brow form of entertainment, and while it may reflect the influence of all of these antecedents, the comic strip as we know it is a distinct form of artistic expression primarily American in its origin and development.

Any effort at definition must take into account a number of characteristics, such as its use of an open-ended dramatic narrative essentially without beginning or end about a recurring set of characters on whom the reader is always dropping in *in medias res*. Relationships have been established before we arrive, and they continue with or without our attention, even beyond the life of the comic strip in a world seldom bound by or conscious of time, except in such stories in which characters age as in *Gasoline Alley* or in such an intentionally anachronistic strip as *B.C.* The story is told or the daily joke made through a balance of narrative text and visual action, although the proper aesthetic balance remains to be determined, with allowances to be made for the totally visual story like *Henry* and the heavily textual Sunday page *Prince Valiant*. Dialogue is contained in seeming puffs of smoke called balloons, a feature which goes back to medieval art and early political cartoons, and the strips are published serially in daily newspapers, to be followed by readers in much the same way as the public followed the novels serialized in nineteenth-century periodicals.

Ernie Bushmiller, *Nancy*, December 19, 1947.
© United Feature Syndicate.

Above: Carl Anderson, *Henry*, March 18, 1947. Henry is one of the few comic strip characters who never speaks and depends on purely visual humor. © King Features Syndicate, Inc.

At right: Harold R. Foster, *Prince Valiant*, May 13, 1956 (detail). Foster revived the power of medieval romance for the modern reader. © King Features Syndicate, Inc.

Alexander Anderson, *Ograbme, or The Snapping-turtle*, 1813. Early political cartoons, such as this one about the Embargo of 1813, used the balloon with dialogue, later a basic feature of the comic strip.

Roy Crane, *Captain Easy and Wash Tubbs*, 1937 (detail). Crane's work is instructive in learning how to create effective photographs. His use of light and shadows was technically remarkable.
© Newspaper Enterprise Association.

The comic strip draws on many conventions associated with the theatre, such as dialogue, dramatic gesture, background or scene, compressed time, a view of the action framed by a rectangular structure, and a reliance on props and various stage devices. It also anticipated most of the techniques associated with the film, such as montage (before Eisenstein), angle shots, panning, cutting, framing, and the close-up.[2] Beginning photographers and film makers are often referred to such well-designed and highly visual strips as *Buz Sawyer* and *Steve Canyon* for rudimentary lessons in effective framing and angle shots. Yet the comic strip remains quite unlike the play or the film in that it is usually the product of one artist (or a writer and artist team) who must fulfill simultaneously the roles of scriptwriter, scene designer, director, and producer. The actors must be brought to life in the flat space of a printed page, engage our interest such that we want to return to them on a daily basis, and take less than a minute of our reading time. Working in the context of these characteristics establishes the challenge to the comic artist and contributes to the particular features of an art form very unlike any of its related forms in literature and the fine arts.

While any effort to identify the first comic strip is open to challenge, the artist who helped establish many of its basic features was Richard Felton Outcault in his depiction of the adventures of a street urchin in the low-class immigrant section of the city called *The Yellow Kid*. First produced for the *New York World* in 1895 as a single panel cartoon, Outcault's focus on a central character (clad in a yellow shift with dialogue printed across it) and his move to a progressive series of panels with balloon dialogue essentially defined the art form.[3] Despite the enormous popularity of *The Yellow Kid*, its use of the coarse reality of urban life would not prove to be staple fare for American comic strips, even though such writers as Stephen Crane, Frank Norris, and Theodore Dreiser were bringing naturalistic views of city life into the mainstream of American literature. It would be two decades before the tensions of urban existence fully entered the comics, and even then it was in the safe Midwestern worlds of Sidney Smith's *The Gumps* in 1917 and Frank King's *Gasoline Alley* in 1918, both of which emphasized the pathos of lower middle-class life and the impact of industrialism and technology on the ordinary family. By and large, however, critical realism was never to be a common attitude among comic artists.

What would prove to be an abiding presence in the comic strip was the American sense of humor. Most of the popular titles that came in the wake of the Kid for three decades were primarily characterized by humor and fantasy.

"If I gits married I got ter hustle if I wants ter keep de wolf away furninst me door."

"I'm stuck on der perleece, an' I tink I could do it, 'cause bein' a cop is dead easy."

"Composin' music dese days is easy; all yer have ter do is ter buy Gilbert and Sullivan and de 'Chimes of Normandy' an' yez kin rite an opera."

"I might earn some money on Park Row by shakin' de bones."

"I tink I could give parlor entertainments fer de '400' or play fer de Patriarchs' ball."

"If some pretty girl wot has got a good altogether will pose fer me I'll paint a nood. I'll ask ballet girl; she's a peach."

"It costs too much to be a real sport an' win prizes at de horse show"—

—"but I tink I would be a good jockey an' a prize winner fer some one else."

"If I could jist git in ter de fish business I could make money an' live on me stock."

"Dis is one ting I wouldn't do; I would much radder work."

Richard Felton Outcault, *The Yellow Kid*, 1896.

Sidney Smith, *The Gumps*, May 23, 1922 (detail).
© Tribune Media Services.

Ernie Bushmiller, self portrait, 1942. Bushmiller was
a master of minimalism in his strips featuring Fritzi
Ritz, Nancy, and Sluggo.
© United Feature Syndicate.

These included Rudolph Dirks' *The Katzenjam-mer Kids* whose hijinks on an island which was an absurd world unto itself would continue for over eighty years under other hands and titles; Frederick Burr Opper's wonderfully wacky creations *Happy Hooligan, Maude the Mule,* and the eternally polite *Alphonse and Gaston*; Outcault's *Buster Brown,* a naughty Lord Fauntleroy whose continual "Resolutions" provided a kind of penance for Outcault's illiterate, dirty Yellow Kid; Winsor McCay's dream fantasy *Little Nemo in Slumberland,* the most beautifully drawn and aesthetically pleasing Sunday page ever to grace the weekly color supplements; Bud Fisher's *Mutt and Jeff,* the first daily comic strip featuring the first successful comic team outside vaudeville with a breezy style all their own; George Herriman's *Krazy Kat,* a classic in abstract absurdist fantasy and a uniquely lyrical love poem; Cliff Sterret's *Polly and Her Pals,* a family situation comedy drawn in an oddly out of kilter style reflecting elements of cubism and surrealism;

with most sincere regards
R. F. Outcault

Richard Felton Outcault. Outcault, father of the comic strip, signed this photograph with a sketch of Buster Brown and Tige, which would date it after 1902. From the author's collection.

George McManus's *Bringing Up Father* whose featured players Maggie and Jiggs became a part of marital comic folklore; Billy De Beck's inspired portrayals of the sporting life and the Appalachian mountaineer in *Barney Google and Snuffy Smith*; Elzie Segar's *Thimble Theatre* which, after a ten year run, introduced Popeye, our first and still most popular comic superhero;

and Frank Willard's *Moon Mullins*, a farce about boarding house life which has far outlasted the existence of the boarding house.

These were the years in which the terms *comics* and *funnies* naturally, suitably, and inseparably became identified with this new form of entertainment so outrageously popular that the world sometimes seemed to wait on

Cliff Sterrett, self-portrait, 1942.
© King Features Syndicate, Inc.

developments in certain titles (the stock market once suspended operations to see if Uncle Bim got married in *The Gumps*), and many a newspaper would owe its very survival to the popularity of these attractive features. Then after three decades of fun and frolic, several new elements entered the funnies with the introduction of adventure and dramatic suspense. These had appeared to a certain degree

as early as 1906 in *Hairbreadth Harry*, an inventive burlesque of melodrama by C. W. Kahles. The adventure comic strip was established, however, in 1924 by Roy Crane in his vividly rendered *Wash Tubbs* and by Harold Gray whose *Little Orphan Annie* was a successful combination of gothic characterization, exotic suspense, and homespun right-wing philosophy, which gave us our favorite picaro outside Huckleberry Finn (Annie also achieved an independent stage and screen life).

The adventure strip would not become a dominant genre, however, until 1929 when Richard W. Calkins and Phil Nowlan introduced *Buck Rogers*, the first science fiction strip, and Edgar Rice Burroughs' classic primitive hero *Tarzan* was given his first translation into comic strip form (most admirably drawn in the early days by Harold Foster and later by Burne Hogarth). Directly on their heels the 1930s and 1940s would witness a great expansion in this category: Chester Gould's gothic morality play in the police detective mode *Dick Tracy*, Vincent Hamlin's combination of advanced technology and prehistory in *Alley Oop*, Milton Caniff's masterfully drawn and effectively plotted tales in *Terry and the Pirates* and his postwar *Steve Canyon*, Alex Raymond's futuristic visions and space fiction in *Flash Gordon*, Lee Falk's men of magic and mystery *Mandrake the Magician* (drawn by Phil Davis) and *The Phantom* (drawn by Ray Moore), Fred Harman's nicely stylized western story *Red Ryder*, Frank Striker's

Roy Crane, *Captain Easy and Wash Tubbs* (detail). Crane's first adventure strip was always full of two-fisted conflict.
© Newspaper Enterprise Association.

What's so Funny about the Comics?   9

Milton Caniff, self-portrait. Caniff is surrounded by characters from *Terry and the Pirates*.
© Tribune Media Services.

masked cowboy *The Lone Ranger* (drawn by Charles Flanders), Harold Foster's grand contribution to the Arthurian romance *Prince Valiant*, Alfred Andriola's well crafted detective stories in *Charlie Chan* and *Kerry Drake*, Roy Crane's second contribution to the tradition with a World War II setting *Buz Sawyer*, and Will Eisner's gently satiric and impressively rendered masterpiece of crime fiction *The Spirit*. Because of their use of mystery and suspense, the soap opera strips also belong in the adventure category. The best known of these are Allen Saunders and Dale Connor's *Mary Worth*, the matronly Miss Lonelyhearts of the Geritol set; writer Nicholas Dallis's several professionally oriented melodramas *Rex Morgan, M.D.*, *Judge Parker*, and *Apartment 3-G*; and Stanley Drake's fashionplate love story *The Heart of Juliet Jones*.

During the 1950s and 1960s satire flourished and dominated the comic strips, although it was consistently present at least from 1930 when Chic Young's *Blondie* satirized at first the flappers and playboys of the jazz age and subsequently the institution of marriage in what

was for decades the most popular comic strip in the world.[4] Al Capp's hillbilly comedy of 1934, *Li'l Abner* (with little of the authentic Southern humor Billy De Beck had used in *Snuffy Smith*),[5] evolved into an influential forum for ridiculing the hypocrisies and absurdities of the larger social and political trends of the nation. Just as Capp used the denizens of Dogpatch as vehicles for his satire, other artists of post-war America would follow his example and use even more imaginative vehicles, such as the fantasy world of children in *Peanuts* by Charles Schulz, the ancient form of the animal fable by the master of comic mimicry Walt Kelly in *Pogo*, an anachronistic military life in *Beetle Bailey* by Mort Walker, a fantasy world of prehistoric man by Johnny Hart in *B.C.*, and the absurd world of a medieval kingdom in *The Wizard of Id* by Hart and Brant Parker. During the 1970s, this trend would continue in such strips as Dik Browne's *Hagar the Horrible*, which relied on a farcical recreation of life among Viking plunderers, but it would also move in interesting new directions. Russel Myer's *Broom Hilda*, a wacky ancient witch, lives in a totally abstract

Chic Young, *Blondie*, February 17, 1933. The rich playboy, Dagwood, marries his flapper sweetheart, only to find himself disinherited. Their domestic bliss leads to one of the most popular family-oriented strips in the history of the comics.
© King Features Syndicate, Inc.

world in the imaginative tradition of George Herriman's *Krazy Kat*, while Garry Trudeau's *Doonesbury* moved into the realistic world of the radical student generation of the last two decades. Jeff MacNelly's *Shoe*, Jim Davis's *Garfield*, Berke Breathed's *Bloom County*, and Bill Watterson's *Calvin and Hobbes* all return to animals as effective ways of reflecting on the eccentricities of human behavior.

Because of the strong development of strips of a serious cast devoted to adventure and melodrama, and the efforts of artists to render these stories in a more life-like style, critics and historians of comic art have never been satisfied with the use of the word *comics*, and have found even more objectionable the word *funnies*. It is true, they say, that in the beginning comic strips were devoted to humorous stories, activities, and situations, but the development of realistic adventure strips calls for another less narrow term. In answer to this concern, commentators have suggested alternative terms such as visual narratives, pictorial fiction, or sequential art, none of which have gained widespread acceptance. Equally unsuccessful have been efforts to coin names for the field of study of the comics—such as Jerry Bails' *panelology* or Fred Stewart's *bildegraphics*.[6]

The use of the word *comic*, as in the plural noun *comics* or as an adjective in *comic art*, is perfectly appropriate and suitable, however, for this popular form of creative expression, in spite of the great range of topical categories which have developed including domestic drama, sci-

ence fiction, western and detective stories, medieval romance, war and crime stories, adventure in exotic places, fantasy, satire, situation comedy, and slapstick humor. Not all things "comic" are necessarily funny or laughable. Comedy implies an attitude towards life, an attitude that trusts in man's potential for redemption and salvation, as in Dante's *Divine Comedy* or Shakespeare's *Hamlet*. Since comic strips always conclude with resolutions in favor of morality and a trust in the larger scheme of truth and justice, they too affirm a comic view of the social and universal order. While *Krazy Kat* and *Smokey Stover* may appear absurd, they do not reflect on the world around them as being irrational or devoid of meaning, as in the drama of the absurd. Comic art is supportive, affirmative, and rejects notions of situational ethics or existential despair. For this reason, modern social concerns such as homosexuality, premarital sex, and abortion seldom enter the funnies, and when they do, as in recent episodes of *Doonesbury* and *Mary Worth*, they rest uncomfortably and can not easily be treated with the full complexity these ambiguous issues require.

Most of the popular adventure and suspense titles also reflect a satiric stance on the part of the author/artist—this includes the grotesque villains of Chester Gould's *Dick Tracy*; the romantic, and often adolescent adventures of the characters in Milton Caniff's stories, *Terry and the Pirates* and *Steve Canyon*; the exotic and exaggerated antics of such supporting char-

Bill Holman, *Smokey Stover*, 1940.
© Tribune Media Services.

acters as Wash Tubbs, Roscoe Sweeney, and Pepper Sawyer in the works of Roy Crane; the smug cynicism of Dr. Keith Cavell and the exaggerated villains in *Rex Morgan, M.D.*; the arrested adolescent love play of Sam Driver and Abbey Spencer in *Judge Parker*; or the inherent sense of literary and visual parody that invests the world of Will Eisner's *The Spirit*. Such strips as *Li'l Abner*, *Pogo*, *Peanuts*, and *Doonesbury* have never been alone in their overt satire and witty criticisms of the status quo.

To satirize life and institutions is to believe in a better mode of conduct which people fail to live up to, and humor may serve as a gentle but sometimes bitter or angry corrective. From the self-conscious parody of the super-hero in C.C. Beck's Captain Marvel to Stan Lee's neurotic and insecure Peter Parker, Spider-Man's alter ego, comic books also partake of the pervasive spirit of satire. The underground comic books such as *Zap*, *Fritz the Cat*, the *Fabulous Furry Freak Brothers*, and *Wonder Wart-Hog*, were

almost exclusively devoted to debunking not only society but the very forms of comic art itself. When a contemporary comic artist like Art Spiegelman wants to treat the Holocaust, he resorts to the satiric tradition of animal fable and the imagery of funny animal comic books and animated cartoons in his work-in-progress *Maus*, the effect of which is to make the subject all the more terrifying because of the incongruity between theme and visual imagery.

In its depictions of characters, physical objects, and landscape, all comic art draws upon and clearly belongs to the tradition of caricature and comic exaggeration. There is no such thing as realism to be found in the comics, either in the photographic sense or the sentimental sense of a Norman Rockwell. Even comic strips which have been praised for their authentic detail and meticulous draftsmanship, such as *Terry and the Pirates*, *Buz Sawyer*, *Prince Valiant*, or *Scorchy Smith* as drawn by Noel Sickles, do not for all their obvious qualities succeed in bringing to the flat printed page any sense of

Milton Caniff, *Terry and the Pirates*, December 29, 1946. This is the last *Terry* page drawn by Caniff before he began *Steve Canyon*.
© Tribune Media Services.

Stan Lee and Larry Lieber, *Spider-Man*, April 27, 1989. In meta-comic style, Spider-Man plays with the idea of being a comic strip character and thus satirizes the conventions of comic art.
© Marvel Entertainment Group, Inc.

dimensional reality or visual depth. Early efforts at 3-D comic books went the way of similar efforts in film the first time around. Realism is incompatible with comic art, whose virtues reside in the distinctive and inimitable drawing styles and points of view of the individual comic artists. *Steve Canyon* and *Buz Sawyer* are not better than *Smilin' Jack* because they are more realistic but because Caniff and Crane are better artists and stylists than Zack Mosely. *Dick Tracy* does not continue to hold our attention and interest because of its use of authentic police methods, a point in which Chester Gould took pride, but because of its grotesque villains (with ugly exteriors to match their warped souls), stylized violence (long before Arthur Penn's film *Bonnie and Clyde*), and an uncompromising belief in evil and incorrigibility. It is interesting to note that some of

the most popular and enduring strips—*Krazy Kat*, *Peanuts*, *Pogo*, *Li'l Abner*, or *Nancy*—have intentionally opted for the abstract, the non-representational, and the art of caricature through either exaggeration or over-simplification.

The comics also belong in the major divisions or patterns of American mainstream humor. The three major comic strips set in the South—*Li'l Abner*, *Snuffy Smith* (without Barney Google), and *Pogo*—all owe allegiance to the lively school of Southern frontier humor in the nineteenth century whose authors used regional dialects, folk humor, and outrageous actions to puncture the pretensions and hypocrisies of polite society. Some of Snuffy Smith's antics, in fact, were directly inspired by Billy De Beck's readings in the Sut Lovingood yarns of George Washington Harris, and surely in his study of Georgia

Chester Gould, self-portrait, 1942.
© Tribune Media Services.

Rube Goldberg, self-portrait, 1942.

impact of reality by providing a comic distance on life's dangers, disasters, and tragedies, and enable us to laugh at ourselves as the pretentious creatures we happen to be. The comics are a unique form of cultural expression which we have come neither to understand nor appreciate. When we do, the comics will be found to be one of those humanistic forces which add quality to life and enable us to believe in man's potential through the saving grace of comedy.

1. See, for example, Stephen Becker, *Comic Art in America* (New York: Simon and Schuster, 1959), pp. 1-4; Pierre Couperie, et al., *A History of the Comic Strip* (New York: Crown Publishers, 1968), pp. 7-19; David Kunzle, *The Early Comic Strip* (Berkeley: Univ. of California Press, 1973); and Maurice Horn, ed., *The World Encyclopedia of Comics* (New York: Chelsea House, 1976), pp. 9-10, 37-38.
2. John L. Fell, *Film and the Narrative Tradition* (Norman: Univ. of Oklahoma Press, 1974), pp. 89-121.
3. Horn, pp. 711-12.
4. Horn, pp. 118-119.
5. See the chapter on Billy De Beck later in this volume.
6. See Jerry G. Bails, *Collector's Guide: The First Heroic Age* (Detroit: Panelologist Publications, 1969), p. 8, and the subtitle of the journal begun by Fred Stewart in 1978, *Cartonaggio: A Journal of Bildegraphics*.
7. Murray Robinson, "Pogo's Papa," *Collier's*, 129 (8 March 1952), 20-21, 64-65.

dialects before creating Pogo, Walt Kelly must have encountered the Uncle Remus stories of Joel Chandler Harris.[7]

The wise fool who speaks more truth than he knows, from Benjamin Franklin's Poor Richard to Will Rogers and Archie Bunker, has his counterparts in Li'l Abner, Pogo, and Popeye. The timid soul or the little man trapped in the complexities of modern existence, as represented by Thurber's Walter Mitty, Charlie Chaplin's tramp, or Woody Allen's on-screen character, has his comic strip existence in a multitude of characters, including Andy Gump, Krazy Kat, Casper Milquetoast, Skeezix Wallet, Dagwood Bumstead, Mickey Mouse, Charlie Brown, Jiggs, Beetle Bailey, Ziggy, and the "Perfessor" in *Shoe*. The school of zany anarchy and irreverent ridicule to which S.J. Perelman, the Marx Brothers, and Robert Benchley belonged finds its practitioners in the comic strip work of George Herriman, Bill Holman (*Smokey Stover*), Rube Goldberg, and Milt Gross, the last in fact bridging the two worlds of literature and the comics with his columns and books using Yiddish-dialect humor and his screwball comic strips such as *Nize Baby, Count Screwloose*, and *That's My Pop!*

What's so funny about the comics? Everything. They clearly belong to the great body of humor which Americans cherish in their oral traditions, literature, stage entertainments, film, radio, and television. They soften the

Elzie Crisler Segar, *Thimble Theatre*, January 1, 1934 (detail).
© King Features Syndicate, Inc.

From Mort Walker, *The Lexicon of Comicana* (Port Chester, NY: Museum of Cartoon Art, 1980).
© Mort Walker.

2

Comics and American Language

Many parents, educators, and moral reformers have continued to express a grave concern over the allegedly harmful influence of popular culture on the minds of children. While primarily concerned with ethics and bad examples, they have as frequently warned of the possible evils of bad grammar and incorrect usage. As far back as 1884, the Boston Public Library banned Mark Twain's masterpiece, *Adventures of Huckleberry Finn*, for fear of the influence of Huck's bad grammar and dialect on the speaking habits of young readers, with no apparent regard for the high ethical standards of the novel's theme and meaning.

The medium under attack is less often literature, however, than motion pictures, television, and that most maligned stepchild of the narrative and pictorial arts, the comics. As one harsh critic has put it, "I despise the comics . . . because they have no subtlety and certainly no beauty. They oversimplify everything. For a good description they substitute a bad drawing. They reduce the wonders of language to crude monosyllables, and narration to nothing more than a printed film. I detest their lack of style and morals, their appeal to illiteracy, and their bad grammar. I execrate their tiresome harshness, their easy sensations, their imbecilic laughter."[1]

Perhaps some parents were put at ease by the research and findings of professor George E. Hill published during the 1940s in several articles for the scholarly journals in education. After studying sixteen daily comic strips for one month, he found that 80% of the vocabulary was composed of simple primary-school words and only 5% were slang, misspelled, or onomatopoeic words. Of the 130 different slang words he found, the worst of the lot were *chee, darn, dawgoned, heck, godfrey, gosh, nope, nuts, phooie, punk, rats,* and *shux.* (The strips that erred the most in word distortions, incidentally, were Ham Fisher's super-patriotic *Joe Palooka,* followed by *Mickey Mouse,* and *Popeye.*) With a sigh of relief, I am sure, Professor Hill reported that the reading of comics would not "do any serious harm to a child's vocabulary attainments. Most of the words used would, in fact, tend to help him build vocabulary meanings."[2]

The comics, however, not only serve to introduce the child to reading and give him his first taste of independent comprehension; they have also enriched the English language in unnumerable ways through popular phrases, word coinages, and the revival of archaic usages. As H. L. Mencken noted in *The American Language,* "the comic-strip artist . . . has been a very diligent maker of terse and dramatic words. In his grim comments upon the horrible calamities which befall his characters he not only employs many ancients of English speech, *e.g., slam, bang, quack, meeou, smash,* and *bump,* but also invents novelties of his own, *e.g., zowie, bam, socko, yurp, plop, wow, wam, glug, oof, ulk, whap, bing, flooie,* and *grr.*"[3] Were Mencken alive, he might add the more recent onomatopoeic coinages of Stan Lee's Marvel comic books, such as *Thtup!, Fzoppp!, Skiak!,* and *Ptoom!*

The very first American color comic, Richard Felton Outcault's *The Yellow Kid,* gave rise to the epithet "yellow journalism" it has been said

ONOMATOPOEIA

Cartoonists are especially fond of ONOMATOPOEIA (words that imitate natural sounds). Comic strips are literally strewn with PLOPS, BLAMS, ZOTS, OOFS, SWOOSHES and ZOOMS. What's more, they take great pride in interpreting new sounds all the time. Listening outside a cartoonist's studio you would constantly hear him vocalizing the piece of action at hand . . . a bat hitting a ball, FWAT! . . . a foot kicking a garbage pail, K-CHUNKKK! He will try many sounds before he settles on the one that satisfies him. Then he will add more meaning to the sound by animating the lettering.

From Mort Walker, *The Lexicon of Comicana* (Port Chester, NY: Museum of Cartoon Art, 1980). © Mort Walker.

because it appeared in Hearst's New York *World*, a newspaper noted for its sensationalism, exaggeration, and vulgarity. Several titles of strips and panels, and phrases often repeated within them, have become commonplace parts of speech, such as *Believe It or Not* by Robert Ripley, *Off the Record* by Ed Reed, *They'll Do It Every Time* by Jimmy Hatlo, *When a Feller Needs a Friend* by Clare Briggs, *Life's Darkest Moment* by H. T. Webster, *It's Papa Who Pays* by Jimmy Murphy, and *Them Days is Gone Forever* by Al Posen. J. R. Williams contributed three, *Heroes are Made—Not Born*, *Why Mothers Get Gray*, and *Born 30 Years Too Soon*; as did Milt Gross—*He Done Her Wrong*, *I Could Write a Book*, and *Then the*

Fun Began.

One popular phrase has followed an interesting route during the last few decades. When Charles Schulz published *Happiness is a Warm Puppy* in 1962, it gave rise to a multitude of imitative maxims and sentimental definitions, resulting in 1970 in the memorable quotation from an otherwise easily forgettable novel, Eric Segal's *Love Story*, "Love means never having to say you're sorry." Then that phrase inspired the equally trite comic panel by Kim Grove, *Love Is. . . .* But Schulz's inspired idea should not be blamed for the mindless imitations it has spawned. Perhaps Schulz's most significant contribution to American English is his extremely useful phrase for any object or person that has

Mort Walker, *Beetle Bailey*, July 17, 1989.
© King Features Syndiate, Inc.

the effect of reducing anxiety, "security blanket," based on Linus's weapon against the world. The phrase is already so familiar that I can't recall the time when it wasn't used and wonder what we used in its place. How else could *Newsweek* have expressed it when they reported in the January 21, 1974 issue, "Ziegler instead is, by one in-house assessment, Mr. Nixon's 'security blanket'. . . ."?

When the Funk and Wagnalls Company determined in 1933 to list the ten most prolific creators of American slang, Mr. W. J. Funk

himself nominated cartoonist T. A. (Tad) Dorgan as the first on the list. Though best known now as the granddaddy of the sports cartoonists and congenial confidante of all the early great American comic artists, such as Rube Goldberg and George Herriman, Dorgan contributed an endless series of zany expletives, words, and phrases to the daily tongue of the American during this century's first three decades, such as *apple-sauce, ball-and-chain* (for wife), *cake-eater, Dumb Dora, dumbbell* (for a stupid person), *nobody home, you said it, the cat's*

BORN THIRTY YEARS TOO SOON

J. R. Williams, "Born Thirty Years Too Soon," *Out Our Way,* June 26, 1932.
© Newspaper Enterprise Association.

Charles Schulz, *Peanuts*, June 2, 1954.
© United Feature Syndicate, Inc.

pajamas, *hard-boiled*, *hot dog* (the frank-furter), *dogs* (for feet), *you tell him*, *drug-store cowboy*, and *twenty-three skidoo* (although the last was contested after his death in 1929). One of the most popular song hits of the period was based on a phrase found in one of Dorgan's strips, "Yes, we have no bananas," but equally memorable is his statement "Half the world are squirrels and the other half are nuts."[4]

Next to "Tad" Dorgan, perhaps the next most imaginative cartoonist-creator of new words was Billy De Beck. In selecting a last name for his pop-eyed little race-horse manager who brought him fame and fortune, he used Google, an archaic word meaning the throat or Adam's apple. Once Billy Rose had set the nation to singing "Barney Google with his goo goo googly eyes," the adjective *googly* entered the language

Tad Dorgan, *That's What They All Say*, 1912.

Tad Dorgan , *Tad's Favorite Indoor Sports*, June 25, 1916.

to mean protruding or rolling, and "goo goo eyes" became a popular phrase for amorous or possessive glances. Other clever coinages which are now credited to De Beck in contemporary dictionaries are *horsefeathers*, an expression of incredulity or disgust; the *heebie-jeebies*, meaning an uneasy or nervous feeling; *hotsy-totsy*, a synonym for *high-faluting*; and *yard-bird*, which began as a term for a rookie infantryman or raw recruit (when Barney served in the Army) and came finally to mean a prisoner or convict (which is the source of the great jazz musician Charlie "Yardbird" Parker's nickname, which he acquired after serving a prison sentence for narcotics addiction). Only De Beck's contemporaries will remember his expletive *Oskie-Wowow*, but when he called an unmarried sexpot girlfriend of Barney Google "Sweet

Billy De Beck, *Barney Google*, September 15, 1932 (detail). Google pursues one of his "hot mommas," a Mae West look-alike with a Southern accent.
© King Features Syndicate, Inc.

Comics and American Language   21

Elzie Crisler Segar, *Thimble Theater*, April 1, 1936 (detail) and August 3, 1936 (detail). The Jeep is introduced and explained in two 1936 sequences.
© King Features Syndicate, Inc.

Momma," although many readers became outraged at the sensational implications (Freud would have appreciated the unconscious significance of the name), it began a rage for "momma" phrases which we still have with us, such as "Red-hot Momma" and "Fat Momma." When De Beck introduced a scruffy little mountaineer into the comic strip named Snuffy Smith, the language took on a new dimension under the influence of the great Southern dialect comedians of the nineteenth century whom he carefully studied. Phrases such as *time's a-wastin'*, *jughaid*, *shifless skonk*, and *balls o' fire* became authentic-sounding contributions to the traditions of Appalachian culture.

The creator of the indestructible *Popeye*,

Elzie Crisler Segar, has two dictionary citations to his credit. Under *jeep* in Mitford M. Mathews' *Dictionary of Americanisms*, the following historic note appears:

> The history of this term is obscure. The word is apparently a fanciful coinage by Elzie Crisler Segar in a comic strip ("Popeye") where on March 16, 1936, he introduced Eugene the Jeep, a small animal of supernatural powers. The word has been used of various devices. Its application to the Army vehicle may have been a verbalizing of GP (general purpose) inspired by a knowledge of its earlier use in the comic strip.[5]

Although the noun goon, meaning a stupid person, a hoodlum, or a strong-arm thug, goes back as far as Chaucer (when the dialectal

Elzie Crisler Segar, *Thimble Theater*. The cast of characters, including Alice the Goon, are assembled.
© King Features Syndicate, Inc.

gooney or *gony* meant fool), *The American Heritage Dictionary* notes, "popularized by the comic-strip character Alice the *Goon*, created by E. C. Segar (1894-1938)."[6] Also the penchant of Popeye's sidekick, Wimpy, for hamburgers created a still current vogue for fast-food words ending in *-burger*.

There are numerous other examples of contributions of the American funnies to the language which will be mentioned here briefly. Although the origin of the word *palooka*, meaning an inferior prizefighter or a stupid but strong lout, is obscure, Ham Fisher's unsophisticated and naively honest *Joe Palooka* gave the word new dignity. Bud Fisher's *Mutt and Jeff* gained currency as apt names for tall and short couples (Fisher also popularized *fall guy, inside stuff, got his goat,* and *piker*), and Frederick Burr Opper's Alphonse and Gaston ("After you, my dear Alphonse." "No, after you my dear Gaston," etc.) became synonymous with overdone politeness. Rube Goldberg (whose name can be

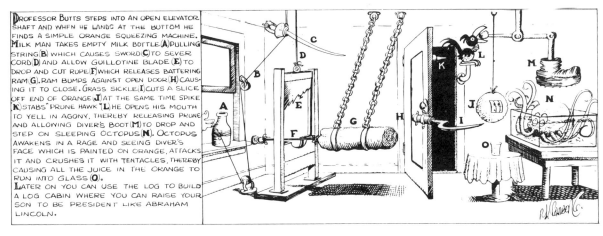

Rube Goldberg, *Inventions of Professor Lucifer Butts*, 1932. This is one of the inventions that got Rube Goldberg's name into the dictionary.
© King Features Syndicate, Inc.

Robert Crumb, *Keep on Truckin'*, 1972. This is a satiric effort to copyright and protect the phrase for which Crumb became famous after it had been appropriated for every conceivable kind of merchandise.
© Robert Crumb.

Bud Fisher, *Mutt and Jeff*. In the third panel, Mutt and Jeff perform one of the popular jitterbug steps known in the 1940s as "Truckin'" and the police follow suit.
© Editors Press Service.

found in the dictionary to signify intricate but useless contraptions designed to effect simple results, the designs for which constitute his most original cartoon work) popularized *Mike and Ike—they look alike, I'm the guy,* and the expletive *baloney!* David Breger's *G.I. Joe,* George Baker's *Sad Sack,* Bill Holman's *Foo* and *Notary Sujac* (from the fantastically absurd *Smokey Stover*), George McManns's *Let George do it,* Al Capp's *Kickapoo Joy Juice* and *Slobbovia,* Harold Gray's *Leapin' Lizards* and *Arf!* from Little Orphan Annie and Sandy, Bugs Bunny's *What's Up Doc?* and Fred Flintstone's *Yabadabadoo!* are further examples of innovative language. Before Archie Bunker called his wife *dingbat,* that was the name of the family comic strip (*The Dingbat Family*) in which George Herriman's immortal *Krazy Kat* first appeared (the word has been in use since the 1860s). Charles Schulz did not invent "Good Grief!", but we can't say it without thinking of Charlie Brown.

The influence of comic art on American speech has continued. The second supplemented edition of the *Dictionary of American Slang* by Harold Wentworth and Stuart Berg Flexner noted over nine different definitions for *Mickey Mouse* mainly as an adjective with reference to something easy, inferior, or inconsequential. Apparently during World War II, Mickey Mouse movies were documentaries shown to soldiers about the causes and cure for venereal disease or methods of hand-to-hand combat, but it was

in the world of entertainment that the rodent's name became applied to popular dance music that was sentimental and insincere or the result of trick effects (as in Disney's first animated Mickey shorts set to corny music). By the late 1950s, on college and university campuses, a Mickey Mouse course was an easy or snap course that required little work for a good grade. None of the uses listed are positive. There is no record of what Walt Disney thought about the perjorative uses to which his creature's name was put. Wentworth and Flexner's definition of *head comic* is extremely prejudiced: "Any of various underground comic books designed for teenagers and young adults, esp. to be read during the smoking of marijuana." This definition is wrong on all counts.[7] Robert L. Chapman's revision of Wentworth and Flexner listed *keep on trucking* without crediting the source, underground cartoonist Robert Crumb.[8] Actually Crumb was rejuvenating a verb for a

Walt Kelly, *Pogo*, 1971. Kelly coined the phrase here that became the byword of the conservation movement in America and has since found many other applications.
© Walt Kelly.

jitterbug step of the thirties and forties called *Trucking.*

Obviously the comics have added much color and spice to our everyday speech. For those still concerned about the corrupting influence of the comics on our language, they should take to heart Walt Kelly's wise maxim delivered to us through that great sage Pogo, words which capsulize the final truth about man, and civilization, and the ultimate reason for whatever evil and corruption that lurks in the world: "We have met the enemy, and he is us."

1. Cited in Pierre Couperie, et al., *A History of the Comic Strip* (New York: Crown Publishers, 1968), p. 103.

2. George E. Hill, "Word Distortions in Comic Strips," *Elementary School Journal*, 43 (May 1943), 520-525. See also Hill and M. Estelle Trent, "Children's Interest in Comic Strips," *Journal of Educational Research*, 34 (September 1940), 30-36, and Hill, "Taking the Comics Seriously," *Childhood Education*, 17 (May 1941), 413-414.

3. H. L. Mencken, *The American Language*, 4th ed. (New York: Alfred A. Knopf, 1936), p. 184.

4. Mencken, p. 560.

5. Mitford M. Mathews, ed., *A Dictionary of Americanisms on Historical Principles* (Chicago: University of Chicago Press, 1951), I, 901.

6. William Morris, ed., *The American Heritage Dictionary of the English Language*, (Boston: American Heritage/Houghton Mifflin, 1969), p. 568.

7. Harold Wentworth and Stuart Berg Flexner, *Dictionary of American Slang*, 2nd ed. (New York: Thomas Y. Crowell, 1980), pp. 338, 723, and 710.

8. Robert L. Chapman, ed., *New Dictionary of American Slang*, (New York: Harper & Row, 1986), p. 244.

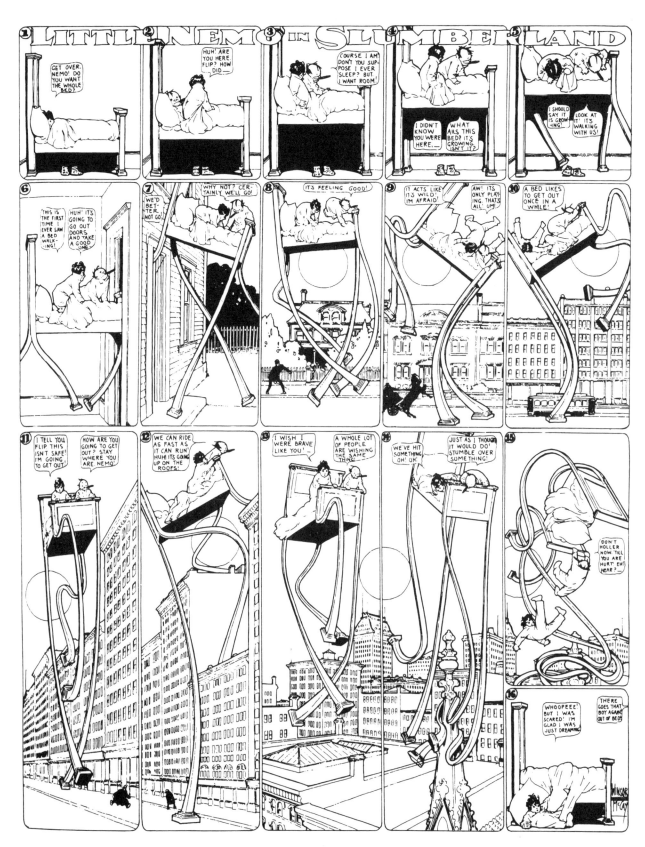

Winsor McCay, *Little Nemo in Slumberland*, July 26, 1908. This is the famous walking bed episode in which McCay anticipates surrealism.

Fantasy and Reality in Winsor McCay's *Little Nemo*

Winsor McCay, comic strip artist, illustrator, animator, and editorial cartoonist, is best remembered as the creator of *Little Nemo in Slumberland*, the most beautifully drawn and visually original comic strip produced in the United States. He also established animation as a film art form and had a distinguished career as an editorial cartoonist. Although he neither drew nor wrote any children's books, the imagery of *Little Nemo* and his other comic strips made him widely popular among the children of his time, and he had a profound impact on the

Winsor McCay, *Little Nemo in Slumberland* (detail).

art of subsequent book illustrators, especially Maurice Sendak, and animators such as Walt Disney.

Born in Spring Lake, Michigan, on September 26, 1871 (some accounts claim 1867 and others 1869), McCay was the only son of lumberman and real estate agent Robert McCay (1840-1915) and his wife Janett Murray McCay (1840-1927). In 1888 he studied art at Ypsilanti Normal College with John Goodison (1834-1892), a teacher who emphasized the importance of direct observation and a use of perspective based on geometric forms, both of which principles shaped McCay's later art. A year later, the family moved to Chicago. Unable to afford tuition at the Art Institute, he was hired to produce large woodcuts used to illustrate theatrical productions and traveling circuses, where perhaps he first learned the bold use of colors, the effect of heavy outlines, and the fanciful use of animal figures, qualities which would characterize his major work.

The young McCay came to Cincinnati as a painter-publicist for a carnival in 1889 and settled there to work as a poster painter and decorative artist for Kohl and Middleton's Vine Street Dime Museum, modeled after P. T. Barnum's famed freak show in New York. Undoubtedly his garish portrayals of bearded ladies, dog-faced boys, and cage-rattling geeks heightened his sense of the grotesque, which would also become a prominent part of his style. In 1891, he eloped with the teen-aged Maude Dufour (1878-1949) who would bear him two children, Robert Winsor McCay (the model for Little Nemo) in 1896 and a daughter, Marion, in 1897.

His work for the Museum attracted such attention that he was hired as a staff artist by the *Cincinnati Commercial Tribune* in 1898. By the late 19th century, illustrated journalism was an important part of the daily newspaper, as photographic reproduction was still in the experimental stage. In the tradition of the great reportorial artists for publications like *Harper's Weekly* and Frank Leslie's *Illustrated Newspaper* before the Civil War, the large city newspapers sent staff artists out to bring back lively renditions of accidents, fires, criminal trials, political and sports events, and prominent people. Illustrations were also needed for advertisements and fiction, as were political and sports cartoons. Like many other young American artists including Thomas Nast, Winslow Homer, and Thomas Hart Benton this was the school or academy where McCay brought his style to its maturity.

While in Cincinnati, along with his routine art work, McCay produced for the *Cincinnati Enquirer* his first Sunday color page, a series of 43 illustrations accompanying a verse text written by George Randolph Chester (1869-1924) under the weekly title *A Tale of the Jungle Imps* by Felix Fiddle. Partly a parody of Rudyard Kipling's *Just So Stories*, each episode describes a metamorphosis or adaptation an animal must make in order to survive, such as "How the Lion Got His Roar" and "How the Alligator Got

Winsor McCay, *A Tale of the Jungle Imps*, October 4, 1903.

His Big Mouth." Felix Fiddle is a detached Darwinian observer. The natives (the Jungle Imps), the animals, and the exotic locale brought out the best in McCay's talent for elaborate design and colorful patterns.

Apparently *The Jungle Imps* attracted the attention of James Gordon Bennett, Jr., publisher of the *New York Herald* and the *New York Evening Telegram*, and McCay was persuaded to move to New York late in 1903. For Bennett's papers he created two strikingly original comic features for children. *Little Sammy Sneeze*, begun in September of 1904, depicted the cataclysmic effect a little boy's irresistible sneezes have on the environment and proceedings around him. The feature was so popular that the Frederick A. Stokes publishing firm issued a reprint collection in 1905. *Hungry Henrietta*, which first appeared in January of 1905, described the effects of a devouring and insatiable infant.

McCay's most remarkable feature of these years, however, was the series under the title *Dream of the Rarebit Fiend*. Each page portrayed the nightmares of individuals addicted to eating rarebit cheese sandwiches before retiring. Despite the feature's use of fantasy, McCay

Winsor McCay, *Little Sammy Sneeze*, 1905. McCay plays with the conventions of the comic strip panel.

Winsor McCay, *Hungry Henrietta*, 1905.

Fantasy and Reality in McCay's *Little Nemo*   31

Winsor McCay, *Dream of the Rarebit Fiend*, 1905. The subject of death is dealt with from the point of view of the deceased, a striking example of McCay's innovative talent. Nothing like it has been done before or since in the comic strips.

set each dream in tl   emo's father or mother as the
twentieth-century A   d eaten the night before near
such morbid topics   n cake, peanuts, huckleberry pie,
such sensational sub   h ice cream, turkey dressing,
racial intermarriage   nce pie, sardines, and candy are
adults with an adult

of the mo   ge of October 15, 1905, demon-
ably to d   allegiance to the traditional
children   ranged panels of the Sunday
strips wi   cept that McCay breaks them
widely r   ts mainly. Already by the second,
in 1905 l   h pages, he begins to experi-
inspirec   methods of dividing the panels
Edwin   th an eye towards the total visual effect of the
animat   ole page. Already he experiments with per-
produc   ective and depth and toys with sequential
was A   ion to achieve an effect of motion. A running
drawn   rative, written in a stilted story-book style,
John B   at the bottom of each panel for the first 21
central   es. The commentary was an irrelevant gloss
carryin   he action, however, and played no integral
Cay des   t in the story. Realizing its uselessness,
progres   ay ceased this practice in March, 1906, and
rid of hi   eafter kept the use of dialogue and authorial
comes b   ription to an absolute minimum and made
'Glad Av   e Nemo into a more purely visual narrative
to Easy   orm.
him." Th   Cay demonstrated at the start an aware-
strips wo of dream psychology quite sophisticated for
strain in me. For example, each of the first five

   McCay use as a base one of the fundamental
Nemo in n fears: falling through space, being
Fiend ser ered under an avalanche of soft objects,
ically to p onto sharp objects or impalement, drow-
that and b nd having the solid ground collapse
readers of h one as in an earthquake. Only five
early twer earlier, Sigmund Freud had published his
to an eleg *The Interpretation of Dreams* (1900) and
imaginatio ened up an understanding of the sym-
dren's book portance of dreams and the subconscious
power and app hiatrist and artist alike. Freud conceived
Art Nouveau mc a middle ground between wish-denying
each full-page Sun nd wish-fulfilling fantasy, but McCay
color one further cha to have discovered this distinction
Nemo, a little boy repc dently. These define exactly the poles of
own son, Robert. artistic concern in *Little Nemo*, with
   In the beginning each pa test care and imagination being inves-
effort on Nemo's part to answ e dominating dream world of fantasy,
he come to Slumberland to play inal tumble from bed at the end of each
daughter of King Morpheus. Alwa g the disruptive concession to reality.
last panel, unforeseen circumstance one of the greatest satisfactions for the
general disaster which keeps Nemo fr as the opportunity to witness his
mission, and he awakes having fallen ou ish-fantasies come true before his
bed. In the first pages, in the fashion of th ectrifying color.
Rarebit Fiend series, the experiences are di he tousel-haired central character of these

Winsor McCay, *Little Nemo in Slumberland* (detail).

adventures was at first vague and ill-defined. Nemo would prove himself capable, however, of a certain amount of selflessness and self-sacrifice, grow more self-assured and self-confident, and ultimately prove himself capable of mastering the natural laws and psychic principles upon which Slumberland operates.

Upon Nemo's entrance into the gates of Slumberland in early March of 1906, he encounters the first character to become a regular part of the cast—Flip, described as "a bad and brazen brat," an "outcast relative of the Dawn family, arch enemies to Slumberland and its people." He is a competitor to Nemo for the affection of the King's daughter, even though his "big cigar and impudent face was shockingly frightful." His main mischief is to awaken Nemo from his sleep and thus remove him from Slumberland. When they blindfold Nemo the following Sunday so his antagonist will have no effect, Flip gets astride the old nightmare and asks his uncle Dawn to bring the sun, whereupon Nemo's beautiful chariot and the peacocks

drawing it fade away. With the passage of time, this little clown with the minstrel show grin functions less as a foe and more as a companion.

There is something appealing about Flip, who declares stubbornly on July 8, 1906, "I got as much right here as he has. I am not as purty as he [Nemo] is but I can fight." This is a courageous plea from an underdog not blessed with the handsomeness and natural advantages of Nemo from the bourgeois world of reality. Flip is a "Yellow Kid" from Hogan's Alley dropped into a Buster Brown land of good behavior and exemplary conduct, although he vehemently denies such an identification when he asserts, "I'm not one of those Sunday supplement-kids that play tricks on people. I only want a fair show in here" (November 4, 1906). Although Flip is an unwelcome third party most of the time, Nemo is compassionate towards him and on at least three occasions moves instinctively to save his life. As a cynical and practical realist, Flip offers an effective counterpart to the romantic and sentimental

Winsor McCay, *Little Nemo in Slumberland* (detail). Nemo walks on water.

and the [...]ling trinity [...]y who [...] Flip kid[...]s to make [...] his [...]hievous and [...] to join the [...] learned [...]lum[...]d in [...]he dancing missionary"; a young delinquent from the real world called "the professor"; the Candy Kid; and the ever present King Morpheus and his daughter, the Princess.

When one considers Nemo's selfless and occasionally sacrificial nature, and remembers that he saves Flip's life thrice and once even walked on water, one is tempted to engage in a little theological explication. This becomes almost unavoidable, however, on that one rare occasion that Nemo ventures into the harsh reality of early twentieth-century urban poverty in the episode from March 22 to April 26, 1908. Finding himself at the edge of Shanty Town, he is given a magic wand that can make his every

Winsor McCay, *Little Nemo in Slumberland*, April 26, 1908 (detail). Nemo as savior figure helping a sick child named Mary.

Fantasy and Reality in McCay's *Little Nemo*   35

Winsor McCay, *Little Nemo in Slumberland* (detail). McCay uses curvilinear perspective to encompass a view of stock yards.

wish come true. Like the good little soldier he is, rather than ask for toys or candy, Nemo goes about Shanty Town clothing the poor people in dandified finery, makes a blind woman see, restores a cripple's amputated leg, and on Easter Day of 1908 no less, Nemo transports a sick little girl named Mary from her ramshackle hovel into a lily-laden paradise. This ersatz Christ, however, falls short of his goal to "turn this place into a paradise," and after turning some blocks of shacks into palaces and a polluted lake into a lovely fountain, Nemo leaves the misery of the poor behind to take the formerly sick child on a tour of Slumberland. Perhaps McCay realized he had stumbled onto a form of reality that even pleasant dreams could not ameliorate. Turning rags into royal robes and tar shacks into the Taj Mahal hardly helped rectify the economic imbalance between progress and poverty. Even the sixteen billion dollars reward promised Mary for finding Nemo and intended for the rebuilding of Shanty Town finally disappears in a Flip-inspired parade riot, although the Princess promises to make Mary "very rich," at which point she disappears from the story. Nemo never wanders into Shanty Town again and restricts his savior impulses to a few adventurous rescues.

Aside from narrative, character, and meaning in *Little Nemo*, particularly noteworthy are the numerous technical innovations accomplished by McCay. McCay felt no compunctions about experimenting with the layout of a full Sunday page and expanding it into new aesthetic possibilities. The page became panoramic and

through perspective achieved amplitude and depth. His use of visual space was unlimited. Things shrunk or expanded as necessity required, yet all other things were kept in proper relationship to them. He employed architectural perspective in more accurate and inspiring a fashion than any comic artist before or since, whether he is providing a baroque palace as an incidental background, sending Nemo and his companions off to investigate the awesome interior of a massive palace, or portraying with incredible accuracy what New York must have looked like from hundreds of miles in the air from an airship. When classical perspective failed to allow him to encompass an extensive panorama or cityscape, he unhesitatingly moved to spherical or curvilinear perspective. While McCay reportedly worked very rapidly, most artists would have needed considerable time and careful forethought to accomplish such visual surprises.

Most readers were attracted to the mere color of the Sunday funnies, a welcome contrast to the drab columns of black and white in the rest of the newspaper. Before the turn of the century, printed illustrations in color were still a novelty, so much so that readers tended to like anything in the newspaper invested with the bright primary hues of red, green, blue, and yellow. McCay's use of color was no incidental matter, however. Rather than use colors merely to fill in the blank spaces between the black lines outlining the figures in a drawing, as is true with most comic strips, McCay was highly sensitive to what color could add to the effect of his art, and color functioned integrally with the other elements in a carefully calculated fashion. In many cases, objects and backgrounds were rendered fully in color with no reliance on a supporting black line or shading. For McCay, color served a purely aesthetic function in more accomplished a fashion than for any other artist in comics history.

In many of the *Little Nemo* pages, as well as the series *Dream of the Rarebit Fiend*, McCay was anticipating the techniques of film animation. All of them display an interest in action beyond the mere furthering of the narrative, and many scenes practically leap from the page. For example, the page for February 4, 1906, contains an experiment in slow motion—a series of drawings in which he traced the stages of a trapeze stunt performed by Nemo and his uncle with a technically accurate sense of realistic perspective and cinematic stop-action. Each panel has the appearance of a still from a motion picture film. All he needed were additional drawings between the ten portrayed scenes to fill out a complete sequence for an animated film. Such experiments were five-finger exercises for a developing interest of McCay's which would have considerable influence on the history of film.

In the same year that *Little Nemo* began, an American named J. Stuart Blackton created one of the first animated drawings on motion picture film—released by Vitagraph in 1906 as *Humorous Phases of Funny Faces*—in which chalk talk sketches moved and figures performed crude actions. Inspired by several flip-books brought home by his son, McCay proceeded to create single-handedly animation as we know it—fully developed three-dimensional figures acting out human actions, unlike Blackton's figures. It took him four years to complete the four thousand drawings, and to hand color each of the 35mm frames, for *Little Nemo* in 1911 as a part of McCay's artistic vaudeville act. The film had no plot and depicted characters from the comic strip cavorting and changing shapes. This was to be one of thousands of animated and live-action films based on comic strips, a popular practice lasting to the present as seen in such recent productions as *Superman, Popeye, Flash Gordon*, and *Batman*. Public enthusiasm over *Little Nemo* encouraged McCay to begin a second film released in 1912 called *The Story of a Mosquito* in which he methodically worked out an encounter between the insect and a drunken man. After Steve the mosquito feasts on the man's blood, he explodes through gluttony.

It is with the third film released in 1914 that McCay brought together the most appealing elements of animation and paved the way for Walt Disney, Paul Terry, Walter Lantz, and the

Winsor McCay, *Gertie the Dinosaur*, 1914 (still from animated film).

Winsor McCay, editorial cartoon. McCay's use of accurate architectural detail and of perspective carried over to his political art.

Winsor McCay, *Little Nemo in Slumberland* (detail).

numerous other creators of charming anthropomorphic animals to populate first the silver then the technicolor screen. This time he recreated an extinct animal, a dinosaur, and named her Gertie. Also originally designed to be a part of his vaudeville act in which McCay talked with the figure on the screen, Gertie responded to questions, ate trees and a pumpkin, drank up a good-sized lake, after throwing a mastadon into it, and cried when scolded. Gertie lives and breathes in this film, and what is most remarkable, she has a distinct personality the charm of which works on contemporary audiences as effectively as it did over seventy years ago. *Gertie, the Trained Dinosaur* caused such a sensation that many historians mistakenly dated the birth of American animation with the appearance of the film. While it was not the first, it demonstrated a concept that all subsequent animators would build on, from Disney's Mickey Mouse to Ralph Bakshi's Fritz the Cat.

McCay produced at least seven more films that we know about, the most noteworthy of which was *The Sinking of the Lusitania* in 1918, a recreation of the historic event which demonstrated, in spite of some impressive special effects, that animation could not replace the newsreel. Disturbed over the rapidly expanding commercialism of animation, rapidly produced to meet a deadline rather than to achieve an artistic effect, McCay abandoned the form after 1921. After 1913, except for a brief return to revive *Little Nemo in Slumberland* in 1924-1926, he also pretty much abandoned the comic strip.

Until his death on July 26, 1934, McCay devoted himself primarily to political cartoons and commercial illustration. While the cartoons are skillfully designed and executed, they were carefully tailored to suit the conservative and isolationist editorials of Arthur Brisbane (with which McCay no doubt agreed).

In his own time, McCay had the pleasure of seeing *Little Nemo in Slumberland* produced as an operetta in 1908 with music by Victor Herbert (including the famous "Whiffenpoof Song"). After his death, the strip was the source of a children's book with the same title by Edna Levin in 1941, and the pages have been collected and reprinted by fine art fanciers (the original drawings and published pages being much sought after by collectors). Numerous illustrators admit to the influence of his work, the most obvious being Maurice Sendak in his popular book, *In the Night Kitchen*. Sendak has written, "McCay and I served the same master, our child selves. We both draw not on the literal memory of childhood but on the emotional memory of its stress and urgency. And neither of us forgot our childhood dreams."[1] Like Sendak, McCay has incorporated the wonders and fears of childhood into enduring works of art and incomparable fantasy.

1. Maurice Sendak, *Caldecott & Co.: Notes on Books & Pictures* (New York: Farrar, Straus and Giroux, 1988), p. 78.

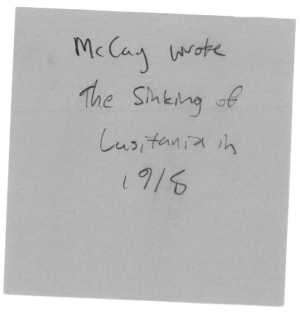

McCay wrote
The Sinking of
Lusitania in
1918

George Herriman, portrait. Herriman seldom appeared in photographs without his hat. From the author's collection.

Krazy Kat as American Dada Art

In October, 1921, a young American avant-garde poet and writer named Matthew Josephson joined the group of expatriates who had gathered in Paris for intellectual and aesthetic stimulation after World War I. He gravitated not towards the Americans but the unpredictable and zany Dadaists—Louis Aragon, Philippe Soupault, Tristan Tzara, and Paul Eluard. The Dada movement was at its height, and for inspiration the Dada artists were studying American popular culture, especially motion pictures, newspapers, and magazine advertisements, which they viewed as carriers of folklore. Aragon and Soupault, both of whom knew English, were engrossed in reading all the Nick Carter dime novels they could lay hands on. Among the "Americana" that Josephson brought with him was a large number of clippings of an American comic strip named *Krazy Kat* by George Herriman, which was very popular in the states. They were passed around and reportedly accepted by the gathered artists as examples of "pure American Dada humor."[1]

During his lifetime, Herriman probably remained unaware of his acceptance by the Dadaists and budding Surrealists (the latter especially had much to learn from him), and he was likely only vaguely aware of their existence. He had achieved the unconventional art and humor he practiced independently and without the philosophic posturing of the Dadaists. The similarities in their work demonstrate that cultural forces at both the avant-garde and popular levels have a way of achieving the same ends. What was there in Herriman's charming comic strip that would have appealed to them? To answer this question, it would be useful to put both the group and the artist into their cultural contexts.

The first few decades of this century was a time of great political and social unrest in the United States and most parts of the world. World War I was the single most important historic event, the aftermath of which was new alliances, new tensions, and disillusionment rather than the freedom, justice, and optimism that Woodrow Wilson thought would prevail. The Progressive Era had fostered widely accepted notions of humanitarianism, equality, and social justice, and Americans were fairly prosperous until the Depression set in. The increasing growth of cities and crowded urban life, however, brought a new set of social problems such as political corruption and poverty, and alienation spread at the local level. Some labor leaders and politicians voiced socialist and Marxist solutions to a growing disparity between progress and poverty, but the prevailing attitude was Jeffersonian in its nostalgic attempt to preserve the stability and virtues of small town life and neighborliness.

Although America attempted to shore itself up against many of the unsettling social and political forces at loose in the world, the war would permanently destroy the possibility of isolationism. In the world of culture and art, America had been given its first glimpse of the radical notions afoot before World War I when the famed Armory Show opened on February 17, 1913, in the 69th Regiment Armory building on Lexington Avenue at 25th Street in New

York. Here viewers were visibly disturbed by the post-impressionist paintings of Cézanne, Gauguin, and Van Gogh, as well as the work of several Americans—such as watercolorist John Marin, realist Edward Hopper, and cubist Charles Sheeler. The most shocking painting of all, the one the journalists and critics seized upon to represent the startling nature of the whole show was *Nude Descending a Staircase* by the twenty-six-year-old French-American Marcel Duchamp, one of the founders of the Dada movement. Then and for a long time thereafter, editorial cartoonists and comic artists would parody that particular painting whenever they wished to satirize most modern art movements; thus the painting gained prominence as an icon for an entire era of artistic

activity.

Some historians, in fact, would date the beginning of the Dada school from that very year of 1913 when Duchamp renounced painting and jammed a bicycle wheel upside down through a footstool to create his first "readymade," a manufactured physical object seized from the context of life and apparently meant to encourage in the viewer an aesthetic indifference. When invited in 1917 to contribute to an exhibition, Duchamp sent a plain white porcelain urinal with the name R. Mutt signed in paint on the side. Any contemporary viewer would have recognized the probable source of the last name as the funny papers. Cartoonist Bud Fisher had originated in 1907 a comic strip about an unsuccessful racetrack gambler named

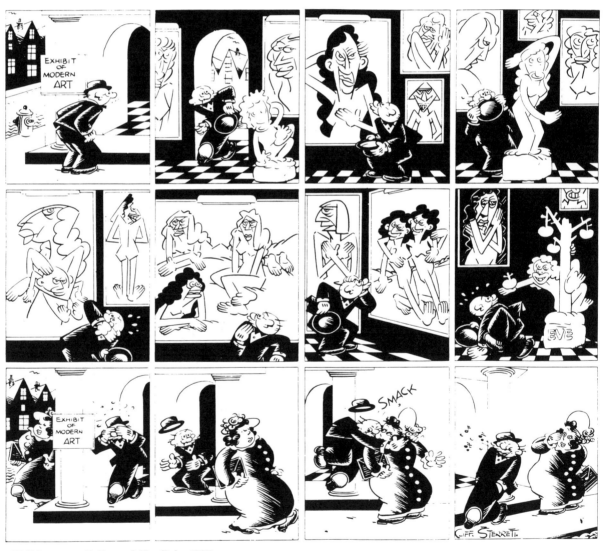

Cliff Sterrett, *Polly and Her Pals*, 1927.
© King Features Syndicate, Inc.

A. *Mutt*, at first designed to provide racing tips. It was enormously popular as the first continuously published daily comic strip, and Mutt's name was well known in 1917, even though the strip's title changed to *Mutt and Jeff* in 1916 to give equal billing to Mutt's partner (in line with its vaudeville team origins).

Other historians would note the starting point of Dadaism as 1916 in Zurich when the literary nightclub Cabaret Voltaire opened and the name was officially adopted by such artists as Tristan Tzara and Jean Arp. The movement soon went to Paris and from there to Germany, Holland, Italy, Russia, and Spain and involved some of the leading painters of the period—Man Ray, George Grosz, and Max Ernst among them. A poet named André Breton joined them, but when he discovered the works of Freud, he issued his *Manifesto of Surrealism* in 1924 and soon led the Dadaists toward a new movement emphasizing the systematic exploitation of dreams, unconscious imagery, and free association, a movement joined by Joan Miró, Salvador Dali, Pablo Picasso, René Magritte, and many others.

Dada was less a style of art than an intellectual attitude, a spiritual conviction, and a lifestyle. Dadaists "attempted to suppress the logical relationship between idea and statement, argued for absolute freedom, . . . with the admittedly destructive intent of perverting and demolishing the tenets of art, philosophy, and logic and replacing them with conscious madness as a protest against the insanity of war [World War I]."[2] As Max Ernst would put it, ". . . our aim was total subversion. A ghastly and senseless war had cheated us out of five years of our lives. We had seen all that had been held up to us as good, beautiful and true topple into an abyss of ridicule and shame. The work I produced in those days was not meant to please but make people scream."[3] Art itself was seen as a debased currency only for the connoisseur and the artist as an anachronistic prop of bourgeois society. Ironically, while they called for the collapse of society, that same society embraced their work and supported their efforts.

In rejecting bourgeois rationalism, Dadaists turned to the absurd and the primitive. Dada was senseless, more natural, and childlike. As Hugo Ball, organizer of the Cabaret Voltaire, noted, "Dada aimed to destroy the reasonable deceptions of man and recover the natural and unreasonable order. Dada wanted to replace the logical nonsense of the men of today by the illogically senseless."[4] Thus it was appropriate that the movement adopted as its name Dada, a child's word in French for hobbyhorse. While not a Dadaist, Giorgio De Chirico, who inspired the Surrealist movement in painting, shared this attitude: "To be truly immortal a work of art must go completely beyond the limits of the human: logic and common sense will have to be completely absent. In this way it will approach the dream state and mental attitude of a child. . . . In this case, there is no naivety, there is none of the native charm of the primitive artist; the work possesses a strangeness similar to that which is often created by the impressions of children—but consciously."[5]

While Surrealism would bring an emphasis on the systematic exploitation of the unconscious sources of creation, especially dreams and psychic automatism, it retained several elements in common with Dadaism. In order to free man from the constraints of logic and rationalism, and destroy the conventional ways of apprehending the world through preconceived patterns, it was necessary to disorient the spectator. As in Max Ernst's collage novels, composed of rearranged old engravings, the scenes disorient our perceptions and require an adjustment to their multiple images. All things appear transmutable. The familiar becomes something strange and unfathomable through incongruity and metamorphosis. We are deprived of a frame of reference.

George Herriman, *Krazy Kat* (detail).
© King Features Syndicate, Inc.

These then are exactly some of the major characteristics of the comic strip *Krazy Kat*: a childlike simplicity and sense of wonder, an aggrandizement of the unreasonable, a reversal of the logical order of things, a denial of common sense, a continuous transmutation of objects and landscapes, and a disorientation for the reader with regard to a rational frame of reference. It should be noted, however, that the artist in this case was not responding to the collapse of rationalism or the emotional impact of World War I, nor was he declaring war on the traditional standards of art and aesthetics. The truth is, we hardly know what he thought about society and politics, given the few documents, letters, or writings that remain, none of which are very helpful on that score. What we do have is the testimony of his work, over thirty years of the daily absurdist drama of Krazy and friends.

The creator of Krazy Kat, George Joseph Herriman, was born in New Orleans, Louisiana, August 22, 1880. There is some uncertainty about his racial background. Accounts by friends suggest he was either French or Greek, the latter especially for his adonis-like appearance. His 1944 death certificate identified him as "Caucasian." His birth certificate, however, on file with the City of New Orleans Bureau of Vital Records, listed his race as "Colored," and the 1880 federal census records noted that his parents were "mulatto." The latest biographical account of Herriman reports that he once confided in a friend that he was "Creole" and thought that he might have some

At left: George Herriman, self-portrait, *Judge* magazine, October 21, 1922. Below and bottom right: George Herriman, *The Dingbat Family*, July 26, 1910.

"Negro blood," but the source of this information is not identified.[6] The black writer, Ishmael Reed, thought that the birth certificate was sufficient evidence in 1972 for him to dedicate his novel *Mumbo Jumbo* to "George Herriman, Afro-American."[7] It is true that the term "colored" was applied to those of African descent in New Orleans, but it was also applied to a variety of mixed racial groups as well, so we may never learn the truth of his ethnic identity. The ambiguity does add, however, an interesting complexity to any interpretation of his work. Krazy Kat is a black cat after all.

Herriman's father, a tailor in New Orleans, moved to Los Angeles to open a barber shop, so George's childhood and early years were spent in California. His first sketches were printed in local newspapers, but sometime after 1900 he moved to New York and contributed to *Judge*, *Life*, and other publications. His first efforts at comic strip pages for the Sunday papers attracted the attention of newspaper czar William Randolph Hearst, who hired him for his Los Angeles staff first but returned him to New York in 1910. Herriman's first widely successful creation was a comic strip called *The Dingbat Family* (and later *The Family Upstairs*), a middle-class situation comedy in which the Dingbats are continually annoyed and frustrated by an eccentric, noisy family living in the apartment above but who are never seen. This

intriguing strip, while limited in the scope of its humor by the situation, remains an incisive study in urban paranoia, and the absurdity of some events are suggestive of the coming drama of Pirandello, who was at that moment working out his theories on the continent.

In some of the first daily pages of *The Dingbat Family* from June 20, 1910, a cat is a part of the family. At the bottom of the strip for July 26, 1910, the cat is hit by a rock thrown by a mouse, and in that act was the genesis of Krazy Kat and Ignatz the Mouse. Within a month, the cat and mouse had a strip of their own at the bottom of the Dingbat feature, and on July 2, 1911, the first full-sized and independent *Krazy Kat* strip to appear on a regular basis replaced the Dingbats who were sent on a vacation. By then the charming Krazy and Ignatz had developed a following of their own, and a coterie of admirers and loyal readers, including Hearst himself, would keep the comic strip in print until Herriman's death over thirty years later, after which the title was appropriately retired.

Although Herriman was at work well before the Armory Show of 1913 and the subsequent art movements, he anticipated a good many of the ideas and attitudes which would characterize their art. The world of *Krazy Kat* is a world of fantasy set against the Surreal and abstract landscapes of Herriman's imagination

approximating the real Coconino County in the state of Arizona. Herriman had returned to California to settle in Hollywood in 1922, and he loved to visit the Navajo country near Monument Valley, Arizona.

Within this world is acted out one of the strangest love stories of all time, itself a total reversal of the expected order of things and common sense. Krazy is totally in love with Ignatz the Mouse, not for the pleasure of pursuit or for food as in the real world but for pure affection. The sole passion of Ignatz, in another defiance of the usual, is to crease Krazy's skull with a brick, which Krazy accepts as a token of affection and proof of true love

George Herriman, *Krazy Kat*, October, 1915. © King Features Syndicate, Inc.

George Herriman, *Krazy Kat*, July 30, 1939.

returned. Presiding over this bittersweet situation in a final twist of absurdity is a dog, the benevolent Offissa Pup, himself in love with Krazy. He sees the bricks for the evil things they are intended to be and stands ready to jail Ignatz at the slightest provocation.

While such love triangles in which there is no returned affection have many parallels in world literature (Shakespeare made the most intricate use of this pattern in *Midsummer Night's Dream*), this one is made distinctive by the fact that Krazy's sex is ambiguous. Sometimes referred to as a "he" and others as a "she," when pressed on the point, Herriman refused to settle the issue. While both happened to be working on the lot of Hal Roach studios in Hollywood, the director Frank Capra once asked Herriman about Krazy Kat's gender. Capra reported his response in his autobiography:

> "You know," he mused, lighting his pipe, "I get dozens of letters asking me the same question. I don't know. I fooled around with it once; began to think the Kat is a girl—even drew up some strips with her being pregnant. It wasn't the Kat any longer; too much concerned with her own problems—like a soap opera. Know what I mean? Then I realized Krazy was something like a sprite, an elf. They have no sex. So the Kat can't be a he or a she. The Kat's a spirit—a pixie. . . ."[8]

The Kat was also confused by its own androgyny. In a daily strip of October, 1915, Krazy discusses with Ignatz a "serious quandary": "It is embarrassment which smacks of the connubial, Ignatz, dual matrimony in fact. . . . Y'see I don't know whether to take unto myself a wife or a husband." Ignatz's advice is to "take" neither but instead "Take care, take care."

In a sense then Krazy symbolizes a kind of

romanticism that is above the sensual and abides in an ideal world beyond the physical. Yet every chance he gets, Ignatz the realist attempts to puncture Krazy's romanticism and brings the literal into conjunction with the

ideal, a kind of disjunction and disorientation common to the paintings of the Surrealists. Krazy is usually impervious to Ignatz's brick of disillusionment. In one Sunday page when Krazy seeks the truth from Joe Stork about

George Herriman, *Krazy Kat*, January 15, 1928. © King Features Syndicate, Inc.

Words and Images

No object is so attached to its name that another cannot be found which suits it better:

There are objects that get by without a name:

Sometimes a word does no more than designate itself:

An object comes in contact with its image, an object comes in contact with its name. This object's image and name happen to come in contact with each other:

Sometimes the name of an object stands in for an image:

A word can take the place of an object in reality:

An image can take the place of a word in a proposition:

An object leads us to suppose there are others behind it:

Everything tends to suggest that there is little relation between an object and that which represents it:

The words used to designate two different objects do not show what can separate these objects from each other:

In a picture, words have the same substance as images:

Images and words are seen differently in a picture:

A nondescript form can replace the image of an object:

An object never does the same job as its name or its image:

Now, the visible outlines of objects in reality touch as if forming a mosaic:

Indefinite figures have as necessary and perfect a significance as precise ones:

Sometimes the names written in a picture designate precise things and the images indefinite things:

Or else the contrary:

René Magritte, *Words and Images*, December 15, 1929.

whether kittens are found under roses, he/she comes away believing a bigger fairy tale than before about how Joe played craps with Santa Claus to see who would go down the chimney first when Krazy was delivered. Ignatz tirelessly stands ready to throw one more brick at the impossibly gullible Kat.

Along with their lack of faith in rational discourse, the Dadaists had also distrusted language which they had seen abused by those intent on defending the status quo. Language was a barrier rather than a bridge to effective communication, words seem interchangeable rather than fixed and dependable points in a shifting universe. The Belgian Surrealist, René Magritte, made this point in his comic strip essay on "Words and Images" published in the December 15, 1929 issue of *La Révolution surréaliste*. As is true for comic strips, Magritte's pictures are more than simple illustrations of the text. They are an integral part of what he is trying to communicate, and both words and images reflect on each other. He even uses the comic strip convention of word balloons for his figures to speak. Magritte's intention, among others, is to distinguish between the thing (the signified), the name for that thing (the signifier), and the visual representation of

George Herriman, *Krazy Kat*, January 6, 1918.
© King Features Syndicate, Inc.

that thing. This is a point important in the study of semiotics as initiated in the lectures of Ferdinand de Saussure in Geneva in the first decade of the century.

In a less direct way, Herriman had made a similar point about the shifting nature of language over a decade earlier than Magritte in a daily *Krazy Kat* published January 6, 1918. Krazy asks Igntaz, "Why is lenguage, Ignatz?" "Language is that we may understand one another," replies Ignatz. The dialogue continues:

> K R A Z Y: "Can you unda-stend a Finn, or a Leplander, or a Oshkosher, huh?"
> I G N A T Z: "No."
> K R A Z Y: "Can a Finn or a Leplender, or a Oshkosher, unda-stend you?"
> I G N A T Z: "No."
> K R A Z Y: "Then *I* would say, lenguage is, that we may *mis*-unda-stend each udda."

As many sequences show, Herriman, like Magritte, knew that there was a difference between what we say and what we mean, between what we think we see and what we see. Like the Dadaists, the Surrealists, and semioticians, then, Herriman instinctively understood that language is not a stable and invariable element in human discourse but instead, more often than not, leads to misunderstanding rather than effective communication.

One of the most delightful aspects of *Krazy Kat* is Herriman's free and footloose way with the English language, as if to prove their point. To a certain degree Herriman belongs in the great American tradition of literary dialect,

originated by the frontier humorists of the Old Southwest and the Down East Yankee comedians and perfected by Joel Chandler Harris and Mark Twain. But Herriman's language is a bastardized, perhaps unique dialect drawing on all the varieties of English: Shakespearian and Elizabethan rhetoric, eighteenth-century malapropisms, Victorian and Dickensian usages, American deep South dialects of blacks and whites, Hollywood movie slang, and undefinable Herriman whimsy. Brooklyn Yiddish, Spanish, and a little French also appear. He has a way of playing with the meaning and sounds of words which reminds one of James Joyce, not merely for the sake of nonsense, as sometimes intended by the Dadaists, but for the sake of true pleasure in the flexibility of the English language. At its best, his language becomes pure poetry, just as his imagery becomes art.

The disorientation of the viewer through the transmutation of figures, landscape, and objects was a common practice of both Dadaists and Surrealists. It is also a prominent characteristic of Krazy Kat's comic strip environment, located in the Arizona desert. As Leslie Howard warned in the film *The Petrified Forest* (1936), set in the same desert, "These mesas are enchanted, and one must be prepared for the improbable." While the characters stand still, mountains in the background rise or fall, change colors or shape, or take on the appearance of large steam ships puffing across the horizon. Trees change their shape and variety, while flowers and cacti appear from nowhere. Adobe houses suddenly develop windows and doors, and walls change

George Herriman, *Krazy Kat*, March 12, 1933.
© King Features Syndicate, Inc.

George Herriman, *Krazy Kat*, June 6, 1941.
© King Features Syndicate, Inc.

their height, length, or direction. The laws of nature and physics are sometimes completely suspended only to be reactivated without warning. Even the moon, that usual symbol of fixity in the universe and dependable navigation point, turns upside down or changes in shape from a globe to something like an abandoned orange peel. It can develop rings, or even triangles and squares, suggesting that not only is it where we stand but the view of the perceiver that makes us see things differently. We seem to be in the presence of an enactment of Einstein's theory of relativity which suggests that there are no absolutes in time or space and that they vary in accordance with the speed at which a given object travels.

One contribution of the Dadaists to modern art is an awareness of the materials and conventions of the art practiced, be it painting, sculpture, photography, film, or poetry, such that it becomes self-reflexive. We are made aware that it is an artifice we are viewing, and the violation of conventions becomes a technique itself to further its own ends. The art form reflects on its own history and comments on itself, as in the recent films of Woody Allen. Herriman also played with the conventions of the comic strip in a self-reflective manner. Sometimes he would remind us that the characters are nothing but ink on paper by leaving a drawing unfinished, or he would allow the characters to draw each other with the drawings becoming a part of the fictive world occupied by the characters. In one complex Sunday page, Krazy reads in the newspaper and comments on the very same Sunday page we are at that moment reading ourselves. Such sequences serve to comment on the nature of reality, the relationship between reality and art, and the expectations we have as viewers. We often measure art against reality rather than allow art to develop its own world and reason for being. Herriman requires us to suspend our

George Herriman, *Krazy Kat*, February 23, 1941.
© King Features Syndicate, Inc.

expectations of comic art to remain within the strictures of tradition, common practice, and the limitations of the form.

Although *Krazy Kat* was drawn during the course of two world wars and a Depression, and Herriman witnessed some of the most tu-

George Herriman, *Krazy Kat*, January 25, 1939.
© King Features Syndicate, Inc.

George Herriman, *Krazy Kat*, June 11, 1939. © King Features Syndicate, Inc.

multuous decades of modern American history, national crises and current events only occasionally crept into Herriman's fantasy world. When he did deal with political and social issues, it was usually under the guise of fable and allegory. Popular culture, however—the latest fads in music, clothing, mass media, or popular belief—he often satirized, such as the intrusion of the telephone in private life, a popular song, or general interest in the occult and spiritualism.

There is much that is lighthearted and gay about Krazy's world, yet underlying the action is a deep-rooted sense of determinism and Naturalistic despair, not unlike the world view of Theodore Dreiser or the more extreme Dadaists. Fate, identified by Herriman as "she who deals her cards from the bottom," is a

George Herriman, *Krazy Kat*, April 16, 1922.
© King Features Syndicate, Inc.

frequent witness to all that transpires. Krazy can be viewed as another Sister Carrie afloat on Dreiser's sea of circumstance, but in a wooden crate and singing nevertheless a hopeful song, "There is a heppy lend, fur, fur a-way!" In his richly poetic language, Herriman once wrote,

"Be not harsh with 'Krazy.' He is but a shadow himself, caught in the web of this mortal skein. We call him 'cat,' we call him 'crazy' yet he is neither. At some time he will ride away to you, people of the twilight, his password will be the echoes of a vesper bell, his coach, a zephyr from

George Herriman, *Krazy Kat*, April 25, 1920.
© King Features Syndicate, Inc.

the West. Forgive him, for you will understand
him no better than we who linger on this side of
the pale."

If the Dada movement had a profound influence on modern art, *Krazy Kat* has had its
influence on modern American culture. In Herriman's own lifetime, John Allen Carpenter

wrote the music for a ballet based on *Krazy Kat*
which was performed in New York in 1922.
Pablo Picasso and William De Kooning reportedly were admirers of the comic strip,[9] and pop
artist Öyvind Fahlström has produced a series
of Performing Krazy Kat paintings with move-
able parts in tribute to Herriman. After

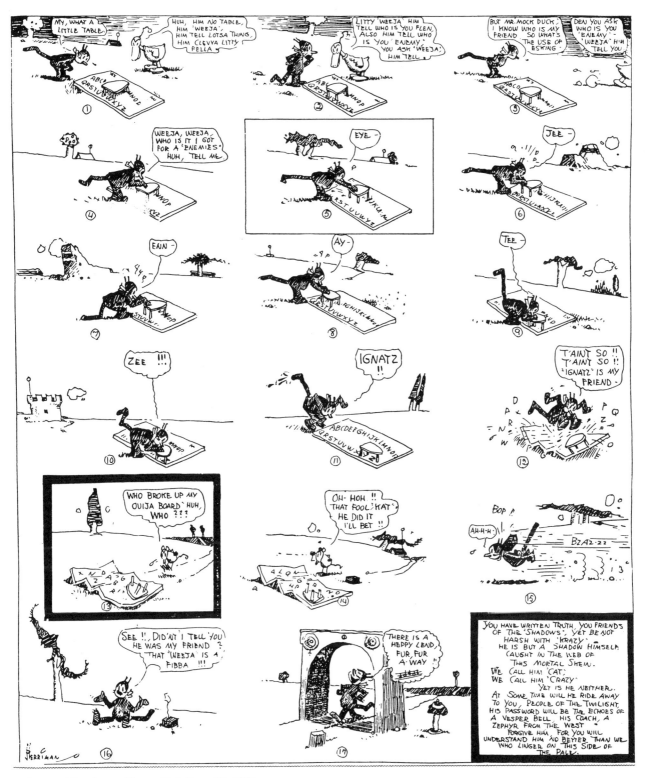

George Herriman, *Krazy Kat*, June 17, 1917.
© King Features Syndicate, Inc.

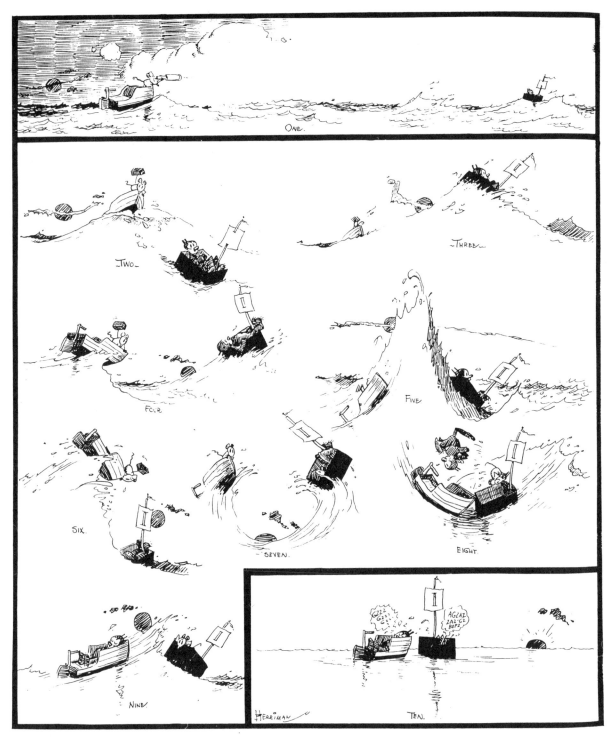

George Herriman, *Krazy Kat*, September 3, 1916.
© King Features Syndicate, Inc.

Herriman's death, poet e. e. cummings wrote an essay in appreciation of the cartoonist which recognized him as a kindred spirit,[10] and Jack Kerouac once cited *Krazy Kat* (along with the comic strips *Popeye* and *Captain Easy and Wash Tubbs*) as a source of inspiration for the Beat movement, itself the American literary counterpart to the Dada school of art. Among comic strip artists, the influence of *Krazy Kat* has been acknowledged by Walt Kelly in *Pogo*,

George Herriman, *Krazy Kat* (detail).
© King Features Syndicate, Inc.

to comic pages which delight through their visual variety and humorous whimsy. I would argue that once we have come to terms with the aesthetics of his accomplishment, we will find that to the world of comic art George Herriman was its Picasso in visual style and innovation, its Joyce in stretching the limitations of language, and its Beckett in staging the absurdities of life. With *Krazy Kat*, he reached a peak of achievement in the art of the comic strip which no one else has approached.

Charles Schulz in *Peanuts*, and Russell Myers in *Broom Hilda*, to name a few.

Whether we classify him as a Dadaist, a Surrealist, or entirely in a class by himself, one thing seems clear: Herriman is an artist of the most singular and exceptional type. Theme, structure, line, mass, color, design—all add up

1. Matthew Josephson, *Life Among the Surrealists: A Memoir* (New York: Holt, Rinehart and Winston, 1962), p. 124.
2. C. Hugh Holman, *A Handbook of Literature* (New York: Bobbs Merrill, 1980), p. 118.
3. Quoted in Uwe M. Schneede, *Surrealism* (New York: Harry N. Abrams, 1973), p. 11.
4. Quoted in Dawn Ades, *Dada and Surrealism* (Woodbury, N.Y.: Barron's, 1978), p. 16.
5. Quoted in the exhibition brochure, *Five Surrealists* (Washington, D.C.: National Gallery of Art, June 17–September 25, 1983), p. 4.
6. Patrick McDonnell, Karen O'Connell, and Georgia Riley de Havenon, *Krazy Kat: The Comic Art of George Herriman* (New York: Harry N. Abrams, 1986), p. 30.
7. Ishmael Reed, *Mumbo Jumbo* (Garden City, NY: Doubleday & Co., 1972), p. 12.
8. Frank Capra, *The Name Above the Title: An Autobiography* (New York: Macmillan Co., 1971), p. 40.
9. McDonnell, et al., p. 26.
10. George Herriman, *Krazy Kat* (New York: Henry Holt and Company, 1946), "Introduction."
11. Jack Kerouac, "The Origins of the Beat Generation," *Playboy* 6 (June 1959), 31-32.

CHARLIE CHAPLIN APPEARS TO-DAY. CHARLIE CHAPLIN

The Funny Wonder ½d

Vol. II.—No. 72.]   EVERY TUESDAY.   [WEEK ENDING AUGUST 7, 1915.

CHARLIE CHAPLIN, the Scream of the Earth (*the famous Essanay Comedian*).

1. Here he is, readers! Good old Charlie! Absolutely IT! A scream from start to finish. What's he doing now, eh? "'Twas here," says he, standing in a graceful posish. by an artistically designed coal-hole, with the faithful hound attached to his cane: "'Twas here I was to meet Maggie! Phwpsts!" But see! A rival approaches!

2. Then the rival, one Esmond MacSydeslyppe Hugo Balscadden O'Chuckitupp—the rival, we repeat, did a bit of dirty work. Fact! He held forth a tempting bone, and Charlie's faithful hound cast the eye of approval on same. Base rival! "Soon," says the chirpy Charlie, putting on another fag : "Soon she will be here. Oh, joy!"

3. But the hound, deciding to do the chew on the bone, legged it up the paving stones, taking Charlie's stick with him. And Charlie, with his visible means of support thus removed, did a graceful flop into said coal-hole just as the lovely Maggie appeared! "Charlie!" said she, with much spurnery, "What do you think you're doing?"

4. Ha! Enter the rival! "Don't you have anything to do with him, Maggie," says the rival : "He's absolutely sale price, he is. Marked down to one-and-nine-three-him! Come with me to some nook, where we may hold converse!"

5. So off they went to the nook, but Charlie was soon up and doing. Yes! He flopped along, soon coming upon the rival telling the tale of love to the beauteous one. "Ho!" says he. "Now to get a portion of my own back! Now for it!"

6. Well, the rival was just on the point of laying his riches at the damsel's dainty patent number two's, when Charlie, picking up a dustbin (full flavour) which happened to be handy, shoved it into his outstretched fins. Which did it—yes!

7. Up jumped the young person. Talk about the frozen eye! Wow! "Sir-r!" she said : "I did not come here to be entertained by such poltroonery. Please remove yourself forthwith. Your face causes me uneasiness! No explanations, please! Get hence and proceed to climb trees for mushrooms. All is over between us!" Or words to that effect. Then Charlie did the inward chuckle, and raised his hat with courtly grace.

8. And he did the affable and endearing chat that completely restored him to favour in the damsel's eyes. "Permit me to suggest," says this gallant old filbert, "a light lunch at the Café de Chancitt, with a jaunt on the merry old motor-'bus to follow. Having just received my quarterly allowance—not half—all is well. Let us proceed!" And they did proceed—some! More news next week, so look out!

Bertie Brown, *Charlie Chaplin*, August 7, 1915.

5

Charlie Chaplin and the Comics

Charlie Chaplin and the funny papers grew up together. Chaplin was born April 16, 1889 in an unfashionable neighborhood in London. Just six years later, on May 5, 1895, a color panel in the *New York World* by cartoonist Richard Felton Outcault called "At the Circus in Hogan's Alley" portrayed a group of ethnic slum children creating chaos in a back alley of New York. Among the children was a large-headed, big-eared child wearing a night-shirt, later to become yellow, who with the addition of words on his shirt would become known as "The Yellow Kid." With a change in format a year later, he would be the first continuing character in what we know as the comic strip. Both Charlie and the comic strip, therefore, had disreputable backgrounds, and just as the Yellow Kid appeared to be a mixture of Irish and Oriental elements, so Charlie was the product of a racial amalgam of French, Irish, and Gypsy descent. While the Kid was quickly becoming a popular symbol in American culture, young Charlie was struggling to survive the rigors of a poorhouse and an orphanage near London, but both would bank for their appeal on using their backgrounds as low-class urchins to attract the world's sympathy through pathos and comedy.

By the time Chaplin arrived at Keystone Studios in December of 1913 to begin his screen career, the American comic strip was in full bloom and had become one of the most popular features in the newspaper. After the Yellow Kid had demonstrated the enormous appeal and vitality of the form, on his heels had come a variety of comic and slapstick features, among them *The Katzenjammer Kids* (1897), *Happy*

Richard Felton Outcault, *Buster Brown*, 1902 (detail).

Hooligan (1900), *Buster Brown* (1902), *Little Nemo in Slumberland* (1905), *Mutt and Jeff* (1907), *Polly and Her Pals* (1912), and *Bringing Up Father* (1913). How aware the young Chaplin might have been of this development, we do not know. He is likely to have seen the funny papers during his extended tour of the United States and Canada in 1910-1912. We do know that he had to be aware of the British comic strip as a teenager since one of his early feature roles at the age of seventeen was as the star of a variety troupe called "Casey's Court," in which he parodied famous people. The name was borrowed from *Casey Court*, one of England's earliest and most popular comic paper panels which ran from 1902 to 1953. Modeled after *The Yellow Kid*, it featured the crowded shenanigans of back-street urchins vigorously involved in a variety of playful and sometimes harmful activities. In fact, in addition to his impersonations, Chaplin played the role of one of the central characters who is always bossing the other children around, Billy Baggs.[1]

Tramps and hobos had long been a part of the cartoon and comic strip tradition before Chaplin came along, represented most prominently in England in 1896 by Tom Browne's *Weary Willie and Tired Tim* and in America in 1900 by Frederick Burr Opper's Irish tramp *Happy Hooligan*. But Chaplin was to bring a definitive genius to the figure and raise it to heights of poetic and mythic power in his first year with

Mack Sennett at the Keystone company. That Chaplin had considered using the tramp figure earlier is suggested by the title of one of his childhood stage teams, "Bristol and Chaplin, the Millionaire Tramps." But once he had donned the baggy pants, the floppy shoes, the cane, the derby hat, and the little moustache for his second film, *Kid Auto Races at Venice* (February 1914), as Chaplin would later tell it, "The moment I was dressed, the clothes and make-up made me feel the character. By the time I walked on stage 'The Tramp' was fully born."[2] He would polish and revise the character through other roles until by 1915, he was featured in his own two-reel film *The Tramp*.

In his own comments on the Tramp, Chaplin put his finger on many of the elements which made the characterization so powerful and universally relevant. As he told Mack Sennett on the set, after first introducing the character to the director, "You know this fellow is many-sided, a tramp, a gentleman, a poet, a dreamer, a lonely fellow, always hopeful of romance and adventure. He would have you believe he is a scientist, a musician, a duke, a polo player. However, he is not above picking up cigarette butts or robbing a baby of its candy."[3] The Tramp, in other words, is a human being down and out on his luck but full of passion for life and hope that things will get better. He is imaginative and creative, and thus a romantic and an artist, who brings style to his meager existence and art to his struggle for survival. Yet when things become worse, he is willing to place practicality above sentiment and violate the usual social amenities. He is indeed complex and many-sided, thereby touching most human beings at one or more points in our character and makeup. There is a good deal in his nature that most of us identify with in our secret selves, apart from what we are in the actual worlds we inhabit.

In effect, Chaplin created the "little man" in American humor, the timid soul overcome by the difficulties of life, yet resilient and cheerful in the face of life's challenges and often wresting victory out of the jaws of defeat. The Tramp was the prototype for many comic figures to come, including James Thurber's Walter Mitty, Casper Milquetoast and Dagwood Bumstead of the comics, and Woody Allen's stand-up and on-screen persona. As I shall outline here, he was to influence several major comic strip figures of this century, but he was to have his own existence as a comic strip character as well.

Albert "Charlie" Pease, *Casey Court* (detail).

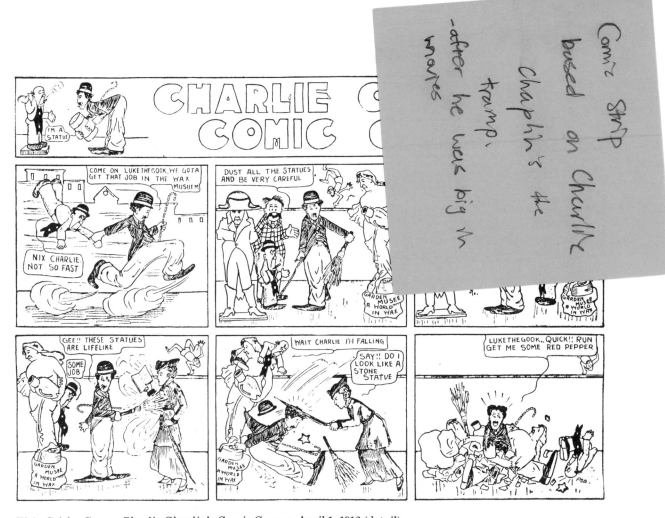

Elzie Crisler Segar, *Charlie Chaplin's Comic Capers*, April 1, 1916 (detail).

Once the figure of the Tramp had taken hold of the public imagination as it had by 1915, it was possible to market the image in hundreds of ways. Soon the stores were filled with "Charlie Chaplin lapel pins, hats, socks, ties, complete costumes, spoons, Christmas decorations, statuettes, buttons, paper dolls, games, playing cards, squirt rings, comics, dolls, and anything else on which his likeness could be reproduced."[4] So frequent were requests for licensing to the Essanay studios which had Chaplin under contract, that in 1915 Chaplin's half-brother, Sydney, stopped acting in order to handle his business affairs. Among the propositions to which they responded was an offer from publisher James Keeley of the *Chicago Record-Herald and Inter-Ocean* (later known as the *Chicago Herald*) to produce and distribute a comic strip based on the film character. Thus early in 1915, a daily and Sunday comic strip appeared called *Charlie Chaplin's Comic Capers*, at first in the home paper and within six months in papers throughout the nation.

That the strip succeeded at all during its first year is more a tribute to the power and appeal of the image than to the several nondescript and unknown staff artists who produced it. The jokes were usually weak efforts to capture what might have been an effective gag on screen, and the sequences sometimes mixed Chaplin the actor with the character of the Tramp. Then, in 1916 Keeley assigned a newcomer to the strip, a twenty-one-year-old cartoonist from Chester, Illinois, named Elzie Crisler Segar. Segar's humor was no better than that of his predecessors, but the comic art style began to improve during the eighteen months he drew the feature, from March 12, 1916 through September 16, 1917. Segar would go on to draw other strips until he began *Thimble Theatre* on December 27, 1919, where his genius would finally emerge with the appearance of a character named Popeye on January 17, 1929.[6] The best service provided by *Charlie Chaplin's Comic Capers* then was to be a proving ground for one of our most talented comic artists and the creator of

Pat Sullivan, *How Charlie Captured the Kaiser*, 1918
(still from animated film).

one of our most enduring comic strip characters.

Many newspapers and readers in general were not pleased with this portrayal of their best-loved film star, so the strip seldom ran for very long in any one paper. Although Chaplin left Essanay for the Mutual Company in February of 1916 and then the First National Circuit in June of 1917, the comic strip was allowed to continue until it abruptly disappeared in 1917. Bill Blackbeard speculates that Chaplin and his brother Sydney decided to stop the strip because of its poor quality,[7] and it was certainly adding nothing to the comedian's reputation. No other syndicate was ever granted a license to try again, thus ending Chaplin's career as a comic strip character, except for occasional guest appearances as a secondary character in other strips, especially those set in Hollywood.

No other live film actor has ever inspired a successful comic strip in America (unless we take into account some W. C. Fields look-alikes), but this was not the case in England, where almost from the start silent film comedians became popular figures in the comic strips. Not long after *Charlie Chaplin's Comic Capers* began in the *Chicago Herald*, the August 7, 1915 issue of the comic paper *Funny Wonder* published the first page of a strip simply called *Charlie Chaplin* drawn by the skillful and highly prolific artist Bertie Brown, who would become noted for his lively renditions of numerous film comedians. Brown's version would run for over a thousand issues on the cover of *Funny Wonder*, and the strip would not end until May 13, 1944. The most popular British comic paper, *Film Fun*, which would run for over forty years (1920-1962) and feature strips about Laurel and Hardy, Buster Keaton, Fatty Arbuckle, Harold Lloyd, Joe E. Brown, and a long list of others, never carried Chaplin because *Funny Wonder* had secured sole rights to the star's name, but both Sydney Chaplin and Jackie Coogan, Chaplin's co-star in *The Kid*, would have their own strips in *Film Fun*.[8] Other European countries also had their comic strip versions of Chaplin, mostly successful and probably most without the authorization of the actor. The figure of the Tramp was so widely known and beloved that he took on the aspects of a mythic figure created and owned by the folk imagination, thus many felt that they could do with the image what they pleased, as would IBM in this decade in their use of the figure to promote computers. Only the figure of Mickey Mouse would achieve a similar status in Chaplin's lifetime.

Without Chaplin, in fact, there is a question as to whether Mickey Mouse would have taken the form he did. The influence of Chaplin had already had an impact on the animated film before Mickey came along. Australian immigrant Pat Sullivan had begun a series of animated shorts based on the Tramp beginning with *How Charlie Captured the Kaiser* in 1918, but in 1919 he created his own character that would overshadow all the others on the cartoon screen, Felix the Cat. The chief animator for Sullivan, Otto Messmer, had studied Chaplin's movements for the earlier series, so he brought the Chaplin style to bear on Felix and invested him with not only the body movements but many of the Tramp's whimsical and philosophical dimensions, especially his lonely alienation and persistence in the face of hostility. In one 1922 short, *Felix in Hollywood*, the cat encounters Charlie while doing an imitation of the Tramp and is accused of plagiarism, an inside joke for those few who knew the cat's parentage.[9]

The story of Chaplin's influence on Mickey Mouse, who would dethrone Felix as king of the animated film characters in 1928, was often told by Disney himself. As a child, Disney had been a fan of Chaplin films and once entered an amateur night contest at a local theater in Kansas City imitating the Tramp in his father's clothes. Chaplin had remained his idol throughout his early years in animation, thus when he came to create what would be his most influential character, Disney recalled the Tramp.

George Corley, "Bouquet for Mickey Mouse," Portland (Oregon) *News*, March 16, 1931. The original caption reads: No less a star than Charlie Chaplin hands floral tribute to Mickey Mouse. In releasing his new picture, "City Lights," now showing at the United Artists, Charlie specified that a Mickey Mouse picture be shown on the same program with his picture.

"Mickey's a nice fellow who never does anybody any harm, who gets in scrapes through no fault of his own but always manages to come up grinning," Disney once said. "We thought of a tiny bit of a mouse that would have something of the wistfulness of Chaplin—a little fellow trying to do the best he could."[10] Mickey would not retain the Chaplin influence for very long as he became on the screen the voice of calm and rationality in a chaotic Donald Duck world and in the comic strips under the inspired hand of master artist Floyd Gottfredson, a rambunctious and aggressive adventurer. But the seed of inspiration for Mickey was partly sparked by the Chaplin genius.

When Disney's impact on the Hollywood scene became evident, Chaplin used to give him advice, especially recommending that he protect his independence by owning every picture he made. Chaplin would remain a fan of Mickey Mouse too during these years, but in 1931 when the popular Disney shorts threatened to undermine the market for live-action comedy shorts, Chaplin decided to maneuver Mickey to his side. When *City Lights* was released in January of that year, Chaplin announced that theaters should accompany all showings of his film with a Mickey Mouse cartoon. Who was helping whom was made clear in a cartoon by George Corley in the *Portland* (Oregon) *News* of March 16, 1931, which depicted Charlie giving one of the famous flowers from the film to Mickey in tribute.[11]

Before Mickey had reached the comic strips in 1930, another comic strip character had shown the Chaplin influence almost fifteen years earlier, George Herriman's *Krazy Kat*. In fact, the Kat was developed simultaneously in the light of the tramp's developing image. The main characters in *Krazy Kat*, a cat and a mouse, had developed as a byproduct of *The Family Upstairs*, a strip Herriman began in 1910, and on October 28, 1913, it had become an independent continuing feature. Less than four months later, the Tramp made his first appearance on the screen. Having grown up in Los Angeles, Herriman was a fan of the silent comedies, and he followed Chaplin's career closely. His devotion to the comedian was displayed most obviously in a comic strip called *Baron Bean*, begun January 5, 1916, about a member of European nobility down on his luck and usually broke in the American land of opportunity. Rather than use his wits to get ahead, he is always freeloading and taking advantage of others, in a sense a tramp dressed like an aristocrat. In his appearance, the Baron borrowed his cane and his facial features from Chaplin. Like the Tramp, Baron Bean maintains a sense of social decorum and dignity whether he is courting a lady or being tossed out of a tavern for stealing a meal, and much of the humor for both derives from the incongruity between their pretentious attitude and the stark reality of the world around them. Until it ceased January 22, 1919, *Baron Bean* remained a subtle tribute to the master comedian.

But *Krazy Kat* was to absorb the aesthetic spirit of Chaplin and transmute it into comic art of pure genius. The relations between the protagonists was one only Chaplin might have

George Herriman, *Baron Bean*, January 5, 1916 (detail).

done justice to in a film. Krazy loves Ignatz the mouse, whose sole passion is to sock Krazy against the head with a brick. Krazy receives them as tokens of affection, while Offisa Pup, in love with Krazy himself, looks on with paternalistic care to prevent the mouse from fulfilling his intentions. No one's love is requited, and the whole fanciful world around them is constantly shifting and informed with uncertainty and fatalism. In his/her abiding patience, faith in the possibility of love, courage against all odds, and unwillingness to accept defeat, Krazy has much in common with the Tramp.

We do not know if Chaplin was aware of his influence on Krazy, but one of the early artists named Carothers who drew a 1915 daily sequence of *Charlie Chaplin's Comic Capers* appears to have seen the connection. In an obvious tribute to Krazy Kat, he portrayed the Tramp on a movie set being hit several times by a brick like the ones made famous by Ignatz and connecting much like they did with the feline's delicate skull.[12] And the editor of *Motion Picture Classic* magazine must have seen the relationship too when he invited George Herriman to review *The Gold Rush* for the October, 1925 issue. Clearly banking on a thorough familiarity with over a decade of Chaplin's film work and writing in the language of Krazy Kat,

Herriman comments that under the spell of Chaplin's talent, "the magic of transmutation takes place—from the musty metal in the crucible—arises enchantment—witchery in large flat shoes, swishing a reed, a billycock hat doffed to the universe, a gracious salutation, and the world acknowledges it with the smile of a child." Herriman continued in his best Joycean language:

We have waited long to katch this sprite at play, so let no one stay our step while we have him—we will follow—whither he wills until he loses us in the mists and we flounder back to earth again. Rich man, poor man, beggar man, thief—leveled to a kommon denomination.

Why say that he made us laugh? Why say he made us cry? Why boast of his braveries?

A knight in armor on a horse aglitter with regal trappings never went into the fray for the love of his lady, or the advancement of chivalry with lighter heart than he. No social lion ever graced a banquet hall with more inspiring gentility—no friend ever stood by a pal with more self-sacrifice. No elf made more mischief—and, kould any maker of dreams have better awakened into the souls of a brace of buns stuck on the end of a pair of forks, the dance of a Pavlova. What chef kould have brewed a stew from a shoe, from which would arise such a gastronomic ecstasy—and what more perfect host than he—the white meat giving to his

George Herriman, *Krazy Kat* (detail), left; and Carothers, *Charlie Chaplin's Comic Capers*, 1915 (detail), above.

"guest," with the grand gesture. No favorite kourtier of a Stuart, or a Bourbon, kould have been more graciously served—and all this in a desolate kabin in the Klondike.

A king of Babylon konjuring a royal fete for his queen kould not have more bravely battled the bitter bite of disappointment of finding her seat empty at the feast.

What Midas better born to his wealth.

Let all the kobblers of earth fashion flat shoes, all awry—and all the tailors trim trousers as loose as gunny sacks, put all the reeds of the world into kanes, and let the hatter go mad making Derbies— then pour into them the genius of another Chaplin. . . .

And now Ignatz!! The BRICK!!![13]

It is interesting to note that in these passages, Herriman used some of the same descriptive epithets he applied to Krazy Kat—Chaplin is a "sprite" and an "elf"—thus suggesting in his own mind an identification between his Kat and the Tramp. Herriman's warm appreciation for Chaplin's artistry suggests that one genius easily recognizes that of another.

The example of Chaplin's Tramp would have a shaping influence on numerous other comic strip characters over the years, the most popular recent one being Charles Schulz's diminutive loser in life, Charlie Brown in *Peanuts*. Both figures are known by the same familiar first name, Charlie, and reflect a similar view of the sadness and disappointment that underlies the comic in existence. As a child, Schulz frequently attended the Saturday afternoon matinees at the movie theaters in St. Paul, Minnesota, where undoubtedly he viewed Chaplin shorts and feature films, which seem to have taught him a lesson about the nature of humor. As he explained it after having drawn *Peanuts* for 35 years:

Happiness does not create humor. There's nothing funny about being happy. Sadness creates humor. Krazy Kat getting hit on the head by a brick from Ignatz Mouse is funny. All the sad things that happen to Charlie Chaplin are funny. It's funny because it's not happening to us.[14]

Charlie Chaplin and the Comics   65

In this statement, Schulz not only identifies his work with that of Herriman and Chaplin but locates the sources of the special comic pathos that informs the world of Charlie Brown in *Peanuts*.

Schulz has said that "Charlie Brown is supposed to represent what is sometimes called 'everyman,' " and he continued:

> Readers are generally sympathetic toward a lead character who is rather gentle, sometimes put upon, and not always the brightest person. . . . In the case of *Peanuts*, I like to have Charlie Brown eventually be the focal point of almost every story. No matter what happens to any of the other characters, somehow Charlie Brown is involved at the end and usually is the one who brings disaster upon one of his friends or receives the brunt of the blow. Charlie Brown has to be the one who suffers, because he is a caricature of the average person. Most of us are much more acquainted with losing than we are with winning. Winning is great, but it isn't funny.[15]

Quite unconsciously, Schulz is echoing something Chaplin once wrote when he noted that his art was directed towards the interests and sensibilities of the "Average Man":

> He is a rather undersized, pathetic figure, this average man, not able to afford very elegant clothes, but trying his best to appear decent and proper, slightly bowed with a sense of his own limitations and almost resigned to the fact that fate never intended him for a Don Juan or a captain of industry. . . . His fortunes always drag a little behind his expectations and fulfillment lies always just out of his reach. . . . And in spite of the most painful and obvious shortcomings, he manages to acquit himself fairly well.[16]

This might as easily have been written about Charlie Brown as the Tramp, so well does it fit Schulz's eternally hopeful average man. Both artists realized the value of creating characters with whom the majority of the people can sympathize and identify.

Would we have Krazy Kat, Mickey Mouse, and Charlie Brown as we know them without the model of Charlie Chaplin's Tramp? Perhaps they were inevitable as reflections of the American character and psyche, but surely Chaplin helped Herriman, Disney, and Schulz discover the wellsprings of comedy more easily by his brilliant practice. We have little evidence that Chaplin read the comics regularly or that he saw the reflections of his own genius at work in the pages of the funny papers. But in 1953, while writing a foreword to a collection of Al

Capp's strip *Li'l Abner*, having just left the United States permanently to reside in Switzerland, he noted:

> In a troubled world such as the one in which we live, comic strips have become a powerful force to divert the public: to such a degree, in fact, that newspaper circulation depends largely upon their popularity. A comic artist is, therefore, lost if he does not reflect the public mind and appeal to the masses.[17]

Thus Chaplin recognized that cartoonists and film comedians were both involved in a form of "art" designed both to relieve the cares of the world and speak as well to the emotional needs and daily problems of the larger public. Their work on paper and film will remain as eloquent testimony to the success of their talents. The Tramp, Krazy, Mickey, and Charlie Brown continue to exercise a strong hold on the popular imagination.

1. Chaplin makes the connection himself in the caption on pages 54-55 of *My Life in Pictures* (New York: Grosset & Dunlap, 1975). Also see the entry on *Casey Court* by Denis Gifford in Maurice Horn, ed., *The World Encyclopedia of Comics* (New York: Chelsea House, 1976), pp. 161-162.
2. Chaplin, *My Life in Pictures*, p. 76.
3. Charles Chaplin, *My Autobiography* (New York: Pocket Books, 1966), p. 150.
4. Wes D. Gehring, *Charlie Chaplin: A Bio-Bibliography* (Westport, Conn.: Greenwood Press, 1983), p. 61.
5. Bill Blackbeard in Horn, p. 166.
6. Ibid., p. 166 and 606-607. Five anthologies of *Charlie Chaplin's Comic Capers* were published by M. A. Donohue & Co. of Chicago, all in 1917: *Charlie Chaplin's Comic Capers*, Series 1, No. 315; *Charlie Chaplin in the Movies*, No. 316; *Charlie Chaplin Up in the Air*, No. 317; *Charlie Chaplin in the Army*, No. 318; and *Charlie Chaplin's Funny Stunts*, No. 380. The first four contain reprints of black-and-white daily strips mainly by Segar and the last Sunday pages in color entirely by Segar. My gratitude to Bill Blackbeard for providing sample copies of this material on deposit in the San Francisco Academy of Comic Art.
7. Blackbeard in Horn, p. 166.
8. Denis Gifford, *Encyclopedia of Comic Characters* (Essex: Longman, 1987), p. 46; Gifford in Horn, p. 135; Graham King and Ron Saxby, *The Wonderful World of Film Fun* (London: Clarkes New Press, 1985).

9. Horn, pp. 246-247, 641; Denis Gifford, *The Great Cartoon Stars: A Who's Who* (London: Jupiter Books, 1979), p. 24; Gehring, p. 76.

10. Bob Thomas, *Walt Disney: An American Original* (New York: Simon and Schuster, 1976), pp. 38, 108.

11. Thomas, pp. 113-114; Richard Hollis, *Walt Disney's Mickey Mouse* (New York: Harper & Row, 1986), p. 25; Bernard C. Shine, *Walt Disney's Mickey Mouse Memorabilia* (New York: Harry N. Abrams, 1986), pp. 15-16.

12. The sequence appears in the first reprint volume *Charlie Chaplin's Comic Capers*, Series 1, No. 315 (Chicago: M. A. Donohue & Co., 1917), page unnumbered.

13. George Herriman, " 'The Gold Rush' as Seen by Krazy Kat," *Motion Picture Classic*, 22 (October 1925), 43, 80.

14. Charles M. Schulz, *You Don't Look 35, Charlie Brown!* (New York: Holt, Rinehart and Winston, 1985), p. [178].

15. Charles M. Schulz, *Peanuts Jubilee: My Life and Art with Charlie Brown and Others* (New York: Ballantine Books, 1976), pp. 83-84.

16. Charles Chaplin, "In Defense of Myself," *Collier's*, November 11, 1922, reprinted in Gehring, pp. 111-112.

17. Charles Chaplin, "Foreword," in Al Capp, *The World of Li'l Abner* (New York: Ballantine Books with Farrar, Straus and Young, 1953), p. [xi].

Billy De Beck, sketch of Snuffy Smith inside back
cover on endpaper, George Washington Harris, *Sut
Lovingood Yarns* (1867), De Beck library.
Courtesy James Branch Cabell Library, Virginia
Commonwealth University

Justin Howard, "Sut Lovingood's Daddy
Acting Horse," *Sut Lovingood Yarns* by
George Washington Harris (New York: Dick
& Fitzgerald, 1867).

6

Sut Lovingood and Snuffy Smith

Billy De Beck's reputation as one of America's most talented and accomplished comic strip artists during the 1920s and 1930s derives from his creation of a bulb-nosed, pop-eyed, dumpy little bummer and sometime race-horse owner named Barney Google. The daily and Sunday comic strip panels he occupied, however, were invaded in 1934 by an equally dumpy and scruffy little mountaineer named Snuffy Smith, and slowly the hillbilly individualist stole Barney's popularity until the strip title became "Barney Google and Snuffy Smith," and after De Beck's death in 1942 just "Snuffy Smith" under the hand of his assistant Fred Lasswell, who today still draws the strip. Anyone who has read

extensively in the literature of Appalachia has probably been struck upon encountering Snuffy Smith, Lowizie, and their nephew Jughaid with what seem to be familiar language and situations. This is more than coincidence, as this chapter will demonstrate.

William Morgan De Beck was born in Chicago on April 15, 1890 of French, Irish, and Welsh descent (the family name originally was spelled De Becque). Following high school, he briefly attended the Academy of Fine Arts before working as a staff artist and cartoonist for several mid-western newspapers and joining the staff of the *Chicago Herald* in 1916. When William Randolph Hearst bought the *Chicago*

Billy De Beck, *Barney Google*, 1923 (detail).
© King Features Syndicate, Inc.

Herald in 1919, he moved De Beck to New York where he created "Barney Google" and achieved immediate fame and fortune, which was intensified in July, 1922, when Barney acquired a race horse named Spark Plug. Millions of dollars worth of Barney Google and Spark Plug statues, games, and toys were sold. Billy Rose celebrated the characters in a song which sold hundreds of thousands of copies and started America singing, "Barney Google with his goo goo googly eyes," and three "Barney Google" musicals toured the country for two years. As reported earlier, De Beck had a genuine penchant for creating clever catch-phrases which swept the country, such as "the Heebie-Jeebies," "horse-feathers," "Oskie-Wowow," and during the war "yard bird," many of which can be found in the dictionary. When he called a sensational sexpot girlfriend of Barney's "Sweet Momma," it inspired other "momma" phrases, such as "Red-hot Momma" and "Fat Momma." After De Beck married in 1927, he first lived in Paris for two years before finally settling in alternate residences in Great Neck, Long Island, and Palm Beach, Florida.

It was in 1934 that Barney Google became a combination manager, promoter, and nurse-maid to a witless wrestler named Sully. When they got into trouble and had to hide out for a while, they headed into the Southern hills. This was when they met Snuffy Smith, whose Appalachian world would draw De Beck more and more deeply into its language, folklore, and customs. This was no accidental excursion for the artist into a foreign environment for a brief respite from the city sporting life which Barney loved. It was, instead, the result of a newfound fascination over things having to do with the life and culture of the mountaineer.

What first sparked De Beck's interest is not known. We do know, however, that in preparation for the new episodes he traveled through the mountains of Virginia and Kentucky, talked to the natives, made numerous sketches, and read everything he could lay hands on that treated mountaineer life. Just how extensive and thorough the reading was has not been generally known, but it can be documented by an examination of his working library which was contributed to the special collections of Virginia Commonwealth University.

De Beck, it turns out, did an exhaustive job of familiarizing himself with the literature of Appalachia, both fiction and nonfiction. Without attempting a complete checklist, the library

Billy De Beck, sketch of mountain woman on blank page opposite page 3 in Frances L. Goodrich, *Mountain Homespun* (1931), in De Beck library. Courtesy James Branch Cabell Library, Virginia Commonwealth University.

contains extensive mountaineer fiction by Mary Noailes Murfree, John Trotwood Moore, Lucy Furman, Charles Neville Buck, Rose Butterham, John Fox, Jr., Jean Thomas, Maristan Chapman, Percy Mackaye, and Harry Harrison Kroll. The frontier humorists are represented by George Washington Harris and William Tappan Thompson; the dialect comedians by Artemus Ward, Petroleum V. Nasby, and Henry Hiram Riley; and there are several anthologies of humorous sketches, including Henry Watterson's popular collection of 1883, *Oddities in Southern Life and Character*. There are also selected books of nonfiction describing the folklore and folk customs of Appalachia, including Francis L. Goodrich's *Mountain Homespun* (1931), Muriel Early Sheppard's *Cabins in the Laurel* (1935), Horace Kephart's *Our Southern Highlands* (1922), and several of Vance

Billy De Beck, sketch on cover of Charles Neville Buck, *Hazard of the Hills* (1932), in De Beck Library. Courtesy James Branch Cabell Library, Virginia Commonwealth University.

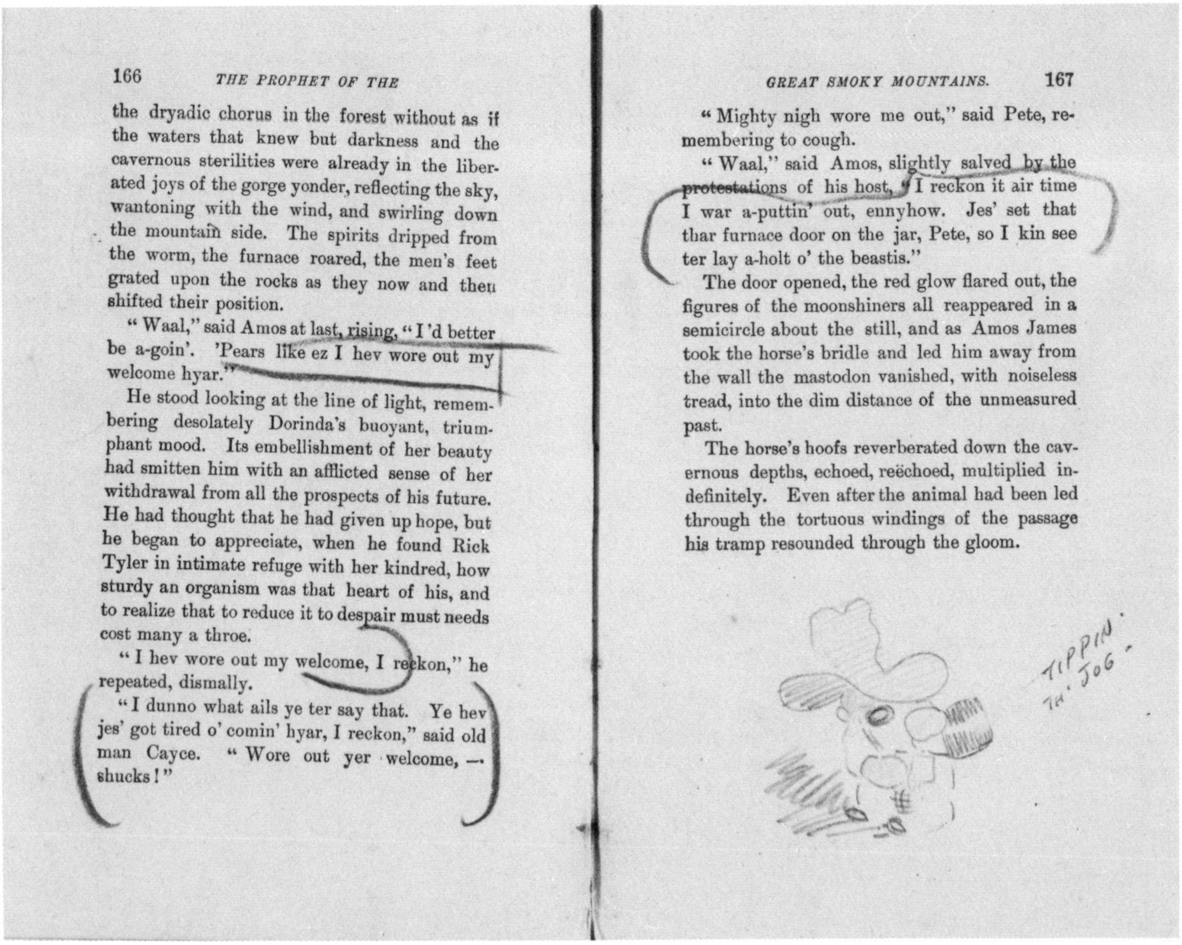
166 *THE PROPHET OF THE*

the dryadic chorus in the forest without as if the waters that knew but darkness and the cavernous sterilities were already in the liberated joys of the gorge yonder, reflecting the sky, wantoning with the wind, and swirling down the mountain side. The spirits dripped from the worm, the furnace roared, the men's feet grated upon the rocks as they now and then shifted their position.

"Waal," said Amos at last, rising, "I 'd better be a-goin'. 'Pears like ez I hev wore out my welcome hyar."

He stood looking at the line of light, remembering desolately Dorinda's buoyant, triumphant mood. Its embellishment of her beauty had smitten him with an afflicted sense of her withdrawal from all the prospects of his future. He had thought that he had given up hope, but he began to appreciate, when he found Rick Tyler in intimate refuge with her kindred, how sturdy an organism was that heart of his, and to realize that to reduce it to despair must needs cost many a throe.

"I hev wore out my welcome, I reckon," he repeated, dismally.

"I dunno what ails ye ter say that. Ye hev jes' got tired o' comin' hyar, I reckon," said old man Cayce. "Wore out yer welcome, — shucks!"

GREAT SMOKY MOUNTAINS. 167

"Mighty nigh wore me out," said Pete, remembering to cough.

"Waal," said Amos, slightly salved by the protestations of his host, "I reckon it air time I war a-puttin' out, ennyhow. Jes' set that thar furnace door on the jar, Pete, so I kin see ter lay a-holt o' the beastis."

The door opened, the red glow flared out, the figures of the moonshiners all reappeared in a semicircle about the still, and as Amos James took the horse's bridle and led him away from the wall the mastodon vanished, with noiseless tread, into the dim distance of the unmeasured past.

The horse's hoofs reverberated down the cavernous depths, echoed, reëchoed, multiplied indefinitely. Even after the animal had been led through the tortuous windings of the passage his tramp resounded through the gloom.

Billy De Beck, color sketch of Snuffy Smith "tippin' th' jug," on page 167 of Mary Noailles Murfree, *The Prophet of the Great Smoky Mountains* (1885), De Beck library.
Courtesy James Branch Cabell Library, Virginia Commonwealth University.

Randolph's works including *The Ozarks* (1931), *Ozark Mountain Folks* (1932), and *From an Ozark Holler* (1933).

At least one of these authors, Vance Randolph, was aware of the influence of his books on Snuffy Smith. Inside the copy of *From an Ozark Holler* are two letters to De Beck from Randolph. The first is a short and terse note dated January 25, 1939, from Galena, Missouri:

> Dear Mr. De Beck:
> A Texan named Wood writes me that you read some of his Ozark rhymes, and sent him a signed cartoon.
> Well by God you can send me a signed cartoon, too—a good big one! You certainly have used a lot of my Ozark stuff in "Barney Google."
> Cordially,
> Vance Randolph

The second letter dated February 1, 1939, acknowledges receipt of the cartoon: "I'm mighty proud to have a De Beck drawing, and it certainly impresses my fellow villagers. They never heard of my books, but they all know your pictures." Randolph goes on to invite De Beck to visit him to see his collection of Ozark Humor, some of it "Much better than the items you so flatteringly crib out of my books."

Nearly all of these books are annotated, some lightly and others extensively, oftentimes with original pencil sketches and cartoons. Opposite page 3 of *Mountain Homespun* by Goodrich is a sensitive pencil portrait of a mountain woman dated 1935, the cover of Charles Neville Buck's *Hazard of the Hills* contains a characteristic De Beck comic mountaineer portrait, and page 167 of Miss Murfree's *The Prophet of the Great*

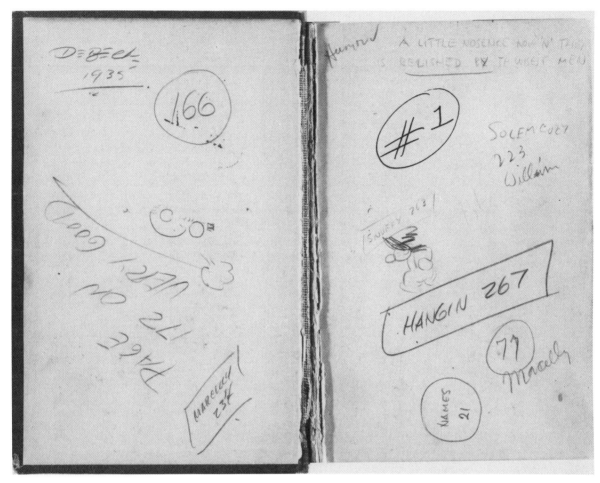

Billy De Beck, sketches and notes inside front cover on endpapers of George Washington Harris, *Sut Lovingood Yarns* (1867), De Beck library.
Courtesy James Branch Cabell Library, Virginia Commonwealth University.

Smoky Mountains has a color sketch of Snuffy Smith demonstrating the custom of "tippin' th' jug."

The two authors, however, whose works are most heavily annotated, and obviously most influential on De Beck's conception of the life and language of the mountaineer, are Mary Noailes Murfree and George Washington Harris. Both authors defined for American literature the character of the Tennessee mountaineer, Harris through his early nineteenth-century humorous sketches about Sut Lovingood, Murfree through her late nineteenth-century local color stories about the quaint customs and superstitions of the hill people. In the latter's books hundreds of examples of dialogue caught De Beck's attention and he marked them heavily, like this passage from page 13 of *Down the Ravine:*

"Ef that thar child don't quit that fool way o' stickin' her head a-twixt the rails ter watch fur her brother, she'll git catched thar some day like a peeg in a pen, an' git her neck brok."

Such passages were likely to appear in a modified form in one of the scenarios acted out by the inhabitants of Snuffy Smith's mountain community.

The single book that most struck De Beck's imagination and fired his fancy was an 1867 edition of the collected *Sut Lovingood's Yarns*, purchased in 1935. There isn't a page in the book not heavily annotated, including inside the front cover, where De Beck noted "Page 172 on very good" and quoted the book's epigraph "A little nonsense, now and then, Is relished by the wisest men," amidst many page references and sketches. The book was ranked #1 in his library and is so marked on the spine. Above a rough sketch of Snuffy is a reference to page 263, where the following passage is found that inspired the drawing:

> I seed ole Doltin cumin waddlin outen the courthous', wif a paper in his han, an' a big stick onder his arm, lookin to'ards the doggery wif his mouf puss'd up, an' his brows draw'd down.

Inside the back cover, almost as if in tribute to the comic genius of an artist of another century, De Beck sketched a perfectly detailed and deftly rendered miniature portrait of his contribution to the tradition of Sut Lovingood, Snuffy Smith.

While neither the full impact nor influence of

Harris's Sut Lovingood stories on Snuffy Smith can be explored here (that would require a lengthy dissertation), a few beginning observations can be made, especially with regard to the use of dialect. An examination of selected Sunday pages published during the early years of the Snuffy Smith adventures, between 1934 and 1939, indicates that De Beck borrowed heavily from Harris for his dialect spellings. A selective list of common dialect spellings includes *axes* for asks, *ary* for any, *atter* for after, *'caze* for because, *daid* for dead, *ez* for as, *enuff* for enough, *fer* for for, *fust* for first, *fit* for fought, *gonter* for going to, *hit* for it, *haid* for head, *hev* for have, *hyar* for here, *jes* for just, *kin* for can, *kivers* for covers, *mought* for might, *orter* for ought to, *propitty* for property, *pitcher*

Barney Google

Billy De Beck, *Barney Google*, September 16, 1934.
© King Features Syndicate.

for picture, *rale* for real, *sich* for such, *sez* for says, *sot* for set, *taters* for potatoes, *thet* for that, *ter* for to, *widder* for widow, *wun* for one, *wif* for with, and *yere* for here. Like Harris, De Beck would mix sound dialect with eye dialect for no rhyme or reason.

One of Harris's major contributions to literary humor was his remarkable facility for some of the most richly metaphoric and figurative language found in American prose. A major source of metaphors was the animal life with which the Tennessee mountaineer was intimately familiar. While De Beck lacked Harris's touch of genius in this regard, he made many interesting efforts as in the following:

> Foolin with him air like makin' faces at a rattlesnake —Hit mought be satisfyin ter the feelin's, but hit ain't safe. (Sunday page dated January 13, 1935)

> Her face air th' color o' hawk meat an' she's bellerin' lak some crazy onsettled creature. (October 13, 1935)

> Mah stummick air growlin' wusser'n a houn dorg caught in a b'ar trap. (December 15, 1935)

A widder man air ez lonesum ez a b'ar in a holler tree. (January 19, 1936)

Some of those would surely elicit the admiration of Sut Lovingood, under whose influence they were undoubtedly written. It is not at all surprising that on August 4, 1937, a character named Sut Turner turned up in a Sunday page.

In at least one regard, De Beck outstripped Harris, and that is in his ability to coin new dialect phrases which had the ring of Appalachian authenticity at the same time that they captured the fancy of the wider American reading public. Among such phrases are "Daider'n a door-knob," "Time's a-wastin," "A little tetched in th' haid," "Shif'less skonk," "Bodacious idjit," and "Ef that don't take th' rag off'n th' bush."

De Beck, of course, not only draws heavily on the Sut Lovingood tales but on the whole corpus of Appalachian literature for his motifs, stories, themes, and anecdotes. I will mention just a few noticed in selected Sunday pages of 1934-1939. Ghosts and spirits are frequent sources of humor in the comic strip, although they usually have a natural explanation, as in

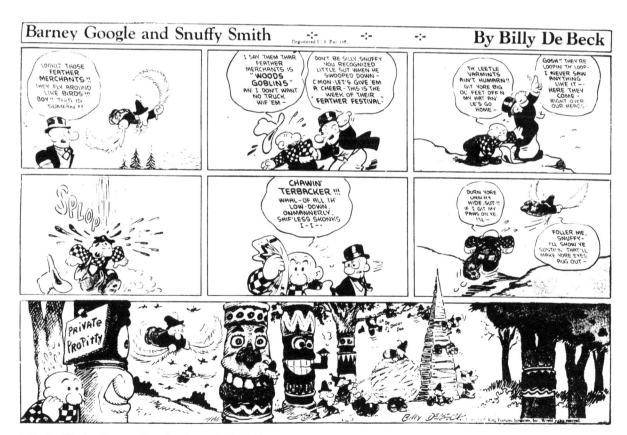

Billy De Beck, *Barney Google*, August 16, 1939.
© King Features Syndicate, Inc.

Barney Google

Billy De Beck, *Barney Google*, October 6, 1935.
© King Features Syndicate, Inc.

the page of September 16, 1934. De Beck did not hesitate, however, to enter entirely into the realm of the supernatural, as he did in one of the most delightful of Snuffy's adventures. The narrative, which began in June, 1939, and ran on for two months, concerned the encounters of Barney Google and Snuffy Smith with a whole tribe of devilish dwarfs and mischievous wood goblins called Feather Merchants, familiar figures in the world of folk mythology and folk tales. Family feuds of the Hatfield and McCoy variety, usually with the typical star-crossed lovers of both families involved, frequently provide a basis for humorous tales which more often than not avoids a tragic ending. A rich variety of both literary and oral folk sources appear to have been merged in telling the tale of Hobo Snow and Fanny Parker on January 6,

1935, a prologue to the further adventures of Widder Snow that followed in subsequent weeks.

While seeming to be a form of artistic expression ephemeral to the dominant society's lasting culture, comic art has often served as a method of preserving and reshaping the concerns of the folk culture into a popular and highly influential mode of expression. It would be revealing to investigate the sources of all the hillbilly comic strips, such as Al Capp's *Li'l Abner*, Bob Lubbers' *Long Sam*, or Ray Gotto's *Ozark Ike*, to determine the extent to which they serve as purveyors of the frontier humor tradition. In any case, it would appear right and proper that we consider Snuffy Smith a legitimate addition to the canon of Appalachian-inspired art and literature.

Barney Google

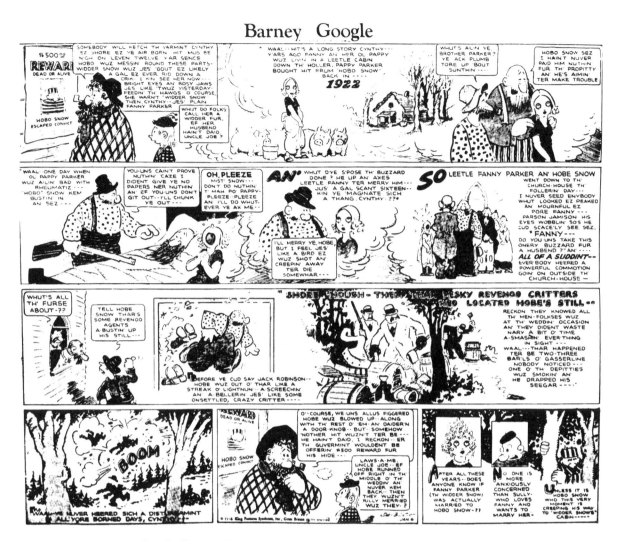

Billy De Beck, *Barney Google*, January 6, 1935.
© King Features Syndicate, Inc.

Elzie Crisler Segar, *Thimble
Theater*, January 17, 1929.
© King Features Syndicate, Inc.
The first appearance of Popeye.

7

Faulkner Reads the Funny Papers

In assessing the work of a great writer of the twentieth century, it can be informative to examine the cultural context in which the author lived and worked. No writer works entirely in a vacuum, and a work of literature relates to and is influenced by the things the writer reads, sees, and experiences. Since this century has witnessed the complex development of a massive media environment and new forms of popular culture that reach people at all social and economic levels in all regions, it is necessary to examine not only the classics and so-called "high" culture of a writer's time but the popular and mass culture as well.

Of all the popular arts, the comic strip is considered the most inconsequential. Produced by a daily deadline, read quickly and thrown out with the trash, and considered primarily to be a childish amusement, little appreciation has been accorded this uniquely American derived art form, even though at certain points in the history of journalism, the comics have spelled the financial success or failure of a newspaper. Some fine works of the imagination and visual artistry have appeared in the comics in the course of their development, but they have been lost to cultural history because of their impermanent format. There is evidence that William Faulkner—himself once an aspiring cartoonist—had a fondness for the funny papers that is reflected in his fiction.

Through the tutoring of his mother, young William Faulkner learned to read the newspapers before he entered school, and the Memphis *Commercial Appeal* was among them.[1] A major Southern daily since its begin-

ning in 1839, the *Commercial Appeal* carried then a Sunday color Comic Section featuring such strips as *The Katzenjammer Kids* by Rudolph Dirks, *Happy Hooligan* by Fredrick Burr Opper, *Little Jimmy* by James Swinnerton, *Buster Brown* by Richard Felton Outcault, *Foxy Grandpa* by "Bunny" (Carl Edward Schultze), and other favorites of the time. As daily comic strips became available (Bud Fisher's *Mutt and Jeff* beginning on November 15, 1907 was the first regularly published daily comic strip), these were added to the columns of the daily issues of the *Commercial Appeal*. Another source of the comics could have been the Hearst *Chicago American*, which was advertised in the October 30, 1902 issue of the Oxford *Eagle* as available through local newsdealers by subscription and containing on Sundays "A Humorous Weekly Printed in Colors." Most of America's favorite strips were available to Faulkner throughout his life, and his references to at least two specific titles in his fiction, as well as allusions to several others, demonstrate that he paid them some attention.

It is also important to note that from the start it seemed that as a child, Faulkner had an interest in drawing, which almost certainly would have led his eyes to the bright colorful pages of the funnies. He gave his first grade teacher a watercolor sketch and once spent his time during a sermon in the Baptist church drawing a carefully detailed train in the hymnal, a subject which he repeated in his first grade reader. His artistic abilities attracted the attention of his teachers who would send him to the blackboard when an illustration was needed.[2]

He once astonished his mother when he had rushed home to tell about a new sprinkler wagon he had seen in the streets of Oxford, but unable to describe it in words, he produced a highly detailed drawing of the machine.[3]

While he had always had his mind set on becoming a writer, he also illustrated some of his own childhood stories and apparently entertained the idea of a professional career in art. When he was fourteen, he submitted an entry to a *St. Nicholas* magazine drawing contest, and he drew cartoons for classmates as well as for an eleventh-grade yearbook that remained unpublished. After leaving school and on trips away from home, Faulkner's letters to family and friends often included drawings, and while in training with the RAF in Canada in 1918, his class notebook included precise renderings of the trainer planes and sketches of other cadets, officers, and scenes both real and imagined. In the 1920s, he produced several illustrated hand-lettered booklets including a 1920 set of poems called *The Lilacs*, the 1920 play *Marionettes*, and the 1926 chivalric allegory *Mayday* written for Helen Baird, a woman he was courting. During the time he spent in New York City in 1921, Faulkner planned to take some art classes and hoped to earn money from his art while perfecting his skills as a writer. Long after he gave up his artistic ambitions, he would entertain close friends and family with cartoons, caricatures, and sketches.[4]

The only Faulkner drawings to see print during his lifetime, at least that we know about, were the 21 cartoons and sketches he produced primarily for local publication—14 for five editions of the University of Mississippi yearbook, *Ole Miss*, issued between 1917 and 1922, 4 for the university humor magazine *The Scream* in 1925, and 3 for the May 1925 issue of *The Double Dealer* in New Orleans. These are not the drawings of an amateur but rather those of an artist who knows how to control a line for maximum effect, to suggest in a few lines a more complex scene or idea, and to suggest through controlled caricature the humorous side of the people around him, swept up in the latest fashions, fads, and attitudes encouraged by the Jazz Age. They are carefully balanced in design, make effective use of blacks and whites, and are restrained in style. Faulkner had full control of his pen and ink.

The artist who influenced Faulkner's work most profoundly was Aubrey Beardsley (1872-1898) whose sensually shocking illustra-

SOCIAL ACTIVITIES

William Faulkner, *Ole Miss*, 1919-1920.

tions in the 1890s came to symbolize the Decadent Movement in England. Beardsley is mentioned in at least three of Faulkner's novels—*Soldiers' Pay, Light in August,* and *Absalom, Absalom!* In the most thorough analysis of this influence, Addison C. Bross suggested that Faulkner was attracted by Beardsley's "playful whimsy, his extravagant grotesqueness, his eternal suggestiveness—often erotic, often hinting at perversity, but always suave, always self-contained. A Beardsley drawing seems to hide, just beyond the observer's awareness, a sinister and abominably fascinating story."[5]

In several of his *Old Miss* drawings, particularly the border decoration for his poem "Nocturne" in the 1920-21 volume and the introductory illustration for the "Social Activities" section in the 1919-20 volume, the evidence of Beardsley's influence is fairly obvious, especially in the second where Faulkner appropriates the earlier writer's trademark—the candelabrum. It is in the fiction, however, rather than the drawings that the full ethos of Beardsley was to have its effect, such as the

John Held, Jr., cartoon.

William Faulkner, *Ole Miss*, 1916-1917.

hints of corruption, sensuality, and decadence, or in the use of the grotesque.[6]

The other artist with whom Faulkner himself has been compared in his style was mentioned by Faulkner himself in a passage in *Mosquitoes*. Julius Kauffman is speaking but the sarcasm about college students affecting the latest attitudes and aping the Jazz Age stereotypes was probably shared by the writer himself:

> A few years ago a so-called commercial artist . . . named John Held began to caricature college life, cloistered and otherwise, in the magazines; ever since then college life, cloistered and otherwise, has been busy caricaturing John Held.[7]

John Held, Jr., was probably one of the most widely recognized cartoonists of the 1920s. His thin, flat-chested, unconventional women gave full visual form to what became known as the flappers, and his pseudo-sophisticated, booze-drinking, racoon-coated men gave new meaning to the Joe College caricature. Faulkner could have caught his work in *Life*, *Vanity Fair*, the *New Yorker*, or any number of popular maga-

zines of the period, or even in his Hearst syndicated newspaper comic strip feature *Oh! Margy!* If F. Scott Fitzgerald was the literary spokesman for the Jazz Age, Held was its illustrator, so it was a most appropriate collaboration when he did the drawings for Fitzgerald's *Tales of the Jazz Age* in 1922. Hardly any artist since Held who has set out to portray the Roaring Twenties was able to escape his influence, Faulkner included. Held's thin and nervous line, the angular attitudes of his figures, his ability to capture the energy of dance and music, and the inherent satire of his detached point of view—all of these are characteristic of Faulkner's cartoons as well.[8]

In addition to Held, there are other popular cartoonists of the time who might easily have had an influence on Faulkner's style. One was George McManus, best known for his classic tale of the nouveau riche, *Bringing Up Father* (beginning in 1913), in which Maggie tried to rise above her origin as a washerwoman after winning the Irish sweepstakes while Jiggs continually slipped back into the former world of

Faulkner Reads the Funny Papers   81

Through the Dim Haze of Memory Comes
KLASSY KUT KOLLEGE KLOTHES
ENGRAVED BY JOHN HELD JR AN OLD ALUMNUS

CLASSES

John Held, Jr., block print, top. Directly above,
William Faulkner, *Ole Miss*, 1919-1920.

his cronies in Dinty Moore's tavern for a serving of corn-beef and cabbage. McManus achieved a clean line in his comic strip panels with stylized fashions, Art Nouveau backgrounds, and neatly detailed architecture, directions in which Faulkner seemed to be working.

Another was Cliff Sterrett, whose *Polly and Her Pals* (beginning in 1912) began as a type of college humor strip focusing on Maw and Paw Perkins, their attractive daughter Polly, and the dozens of collegiate suitors who pursue her affections. Sterrett began to experiment with the visual potential of comic art and was soon incorporating in the 1920s striking patterns of abstraction much in the style of cubism and surrealism. Faulkner too demonstrated an interest in such non-realistic patterns and a similar preference for design over characterization. Other cartoonists whose work bears artistic similarities with Faulkner's include Bud Fisher, whose classic adventures of the comic team *Mutt and Jeff* became the longest running daily

Bringing Up Father

At right, George McManus, *Bringing Up Father*, 1921.
© King Features Syndicate, Inc.
Below, William Faulkner, *Ole Miss*, 1920-1921.

Above, Cliff Sterrett, *Polly and Her Pals* (detail).
© King Features Syndicate, Inc.
At right, William Faulkner, *Ole Miss*, 1917-1918.
Below, Bud Fisher, *Mutt and Jeff* (detail).
© Editors Press Service.

Billy De Beck, *Barney Google* (detail).
© King Features Syndicate, Inc.

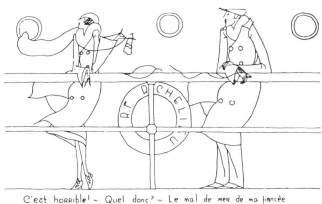

William Faulkner, *Ole Miss*, 1922.

American comic strip, and Billy De Beck, whose sporting life feature *Barney Google* (beginning in 1919) kept the nation involved in the picaresque adventures of this pint-sized hero.

Finally, however, it should be noted that none of these creative artists—Beardsley, Held, McManus, Sterrett, Fisher, or De Beck—is a direct source of imitation for Faulkner. The Mississippian may have observed and learned from them and others as well, but he was working in a vein that is distinctly his own. He was no copyist. His sense of design, his satirical point of view, his effective arrangement of blacks and symmetrical patterns, his ability to suggest with a few lines rather than include details—these might have matured into a comic style suitable for the humor magazines and funny papers of the time. If Faulkner was, as he described himself, a "failed poet," one might say that before that he was a "failed cartoonist."

It is in his fiction that the influence of popular comic art was to linger. One can see it in the early unpublished short story of 1925 called "Frankie and Johnny." Were it not for the fact that the chronology prohibits it, one might guess that Faulkner was inspired by the set of block prints called *The Saga of Frankie and Johnny* begun by a young John Held, Jr., in 1916 but not published until 1930.[9] Faulkner's version has recast and revised the American folk ballad in the form of a series of bold vignettes and rough prints much in the style of Held's unrefined woodcuts. The cast of characters has been expanded, the mother is the prostitute rather

than Frankie, and the ending has been changed, or rather we are not witness to Johnny's death which is likely to follow upon the tragic events.

Faulkner invests the story with a certain degree of psychological subtlety by focusing upon Frankie's relationship with her mother and Frankie's plight as the archetypical wronged woman likely to follow in her mother's footsteps.

John Held, Jr., block print, *The Saga of Frankie and Johnny*, 1930.

For the most part, however, the story is told through exaggerated caricature (such as the father who drowns saving the fat lady at the beach, a scene taken directly from hundreds of comic post card drawings of the period), and bittersweet comic detail (such as the prostitute mother whose sense of decency is offended by what people will think of her pregnant unwed daughter). The stereotypes of comic strip art—the domineering, strong-willed mother who never realizes the hypocrisy of her own actions, the dominated father who is all kind-hearted boast, the delicate heroine who can pack a mean punch in the style of Little Orphan Annie, and the posturing Johnny who sees himself as a bold Hairbreadth Harry who comes to Frankie's rescue—these are set in the naturalistic context of a *Maggie* by Stephen Crane or *Sister Carrie* by Theodore Dreiser. In the contrast and melodramatic juxtaposition lies the brilliance of Faulkner's story. Frankie says, "Gee, at times Johnny was worse than a movie," and she might as easily have said, "Johnny was worse than the funny papers."[10]

Also noteworthy is Faulkner's slightly stilted use of urban backstreet dialect and criminal slang, although such lines as "Beat it, Bum; or I'll slam you for a row," and "Hit me, baby, I like it,"[11] sound like dialogue from the later gangster films of the 1930s. Crane and Dreiser had made attempts at such language, but before Crane went public with *Maggie* in 1896 (an edition was printed privately in 1893), Richard Felton Outcault had already originated a form of urban slang in his comic feature begun on May 5, 1895, *Hogan's Alley*, where a street urchin, better known as *The Yellow Kid*, spoke in crude language by way of words printed on his yellow nightshirt. The influence of the character was such that parents and guardians of propriety soon brought such pressure and notoriety to bear on Outcault that he abandoned the feature in 1898 and created in 1902 the more proper *Buster Brown*, but *The Yellow Kid* lingered on into the new century in the form of book reprints, magazines, advertisements, games, and toys which Faulkner could have encountered as a child.

The one novel by Faulkner with a character whose name is most closely associated with comic strips is *Sanctuary*. Popeye Vitelli was, of course, partly modeled after the Memphis gangster Neal Karens Pumphrey, also known as "Popeye," who had subjected a young woman to much the same treatment accorded Temple

Richard Felton Outcault, *The Yellow Kid.*

Drake in *Sanctuary*.[12] Before then the adjective "popeyed," meaning open-eyed with surprise, expectation, and wonder, had been around a long time, at least as far back as the early nineteenth century in America (*A Dictionary of Americanisms on Historical Principles* by Mitford Mathews takes it back to 1824 in print), and Faulkner used it twice in application to the character Major Ayers in *Mosquitoes* in 1927 before there was a comic strip Popeye.[13] So we cannot argue that the only source of the name could be the comic strip, although other evidence suggests a connection.

Faulkner's Popeye first appeared in an unpublished short story written around the same time as *Sanctuary*, called "The Big Shot," where he is described in the style of a stark comic strip image: " . . . a slight man with a dead face and dead black hair and eyes and a delicate hooked little nose and no chin, crouching snarling behind the neat blue automatic. He was a little dead-looking bird in a tight black suit like a vaudeville actor of twenty years ago, with a savage falsetto voice like a choir-boy

. . . . "[14] An identification with a comic strip character even appears quite intentional here when two pages later Faulkner describes him as "a little cold, still, quiet man that looked like he might have had ink in his veins . . . . ."[15] Indeed, all comic strip characters have nothing but ink in their veins.

Faulkner continued to use these stylized caricature-like descriptions of Popeye in the opening pages of *Sanctuary:*

> He [Horace Benbow] saw, facing him across the spring, a man of under size, his hands in his coat pocket, a cigarette slanted from his chin. His suit was black, with a tight, high-waisted coat. . . . His face had a queer bloodless color, as though seen by electric light; against the sunny silence, in his slanted straw hat and his slightly akimbo arms, he had the vicarious quality of stamped tin . . . .
>
> Across the spring Popeye appeared to contemplate him with two knobs of soft black rubber . . . . The cigarette wreathed its faint plume across Popeye's face, one side of his face squinted against the smoke like a mask carved into two simultaneous expressions . . . . His skin had a dead, dark pallor. His nose was frankly aquiline, and he had no chin at all. His face just went away, like the wax of a doll set too near a hot fire and forgotten . . . .
>
> Popeye's eyes looked like rubber knobs, like they'd give to the touch and then recover with the whorled smudge of the thumb on them . . . . Ahead of him Popeye walked, his tight suit and stiff hat all angles, like a modernist lampstand.[16]

The black knobby eyes and ghostly white skin, the distorted features, the figure he strikes when he stands or walks, like a piece of stamped tin or a modernistic lamp for the living room, all of this reminds one of a character in a black and white cartoon or comic strip. Popeye also demonstrates the strength of a comic strip superhero, as when he plucks Temple Drake from the ground:

> His hands closed upon the back of her neck, his fingers like steel, yet cold and light as aluminum. She could hear the vertebrae grating finely together . . . . Suddenly she felt herself lifted bodily aside, Popeye's small arms light and rigid as aluminum.[17]

Usually this sort of thing can only happen in the fantasy world of the comics, and many a time the comic strip Popeye has been known to pick up a struggling Olive Oyl in just this manner.

Any reader who has picked up *Sanctuary* since it appeared in print on February 9, 1931, has found it necessary to go through a process of disassociation as it becomes evident that Faulkner's Popeye seems to have nothing to do with the beloved Popeye of comic strip and animated film fame. The selection of that name strikes one as having been a little joke at the expense of the reader, just another amusing perversity from an author who delighted sometimes in affronting his readers. It was not until 1971 that a critic even dared to note the relation between the two figures, this in a footnote to an essay on the mythological sources of *Sanctuary* by Thomas L. McHaney, where he noted "Elzie C. Segar's popular comic strip, 'Thimble Theatre,' had introduced the now-famous Popeye on January 17, 1929, and within a few weeks he had attained great popularity. The sailor replaced Ham Gravy as Olive Oyl's perpetual suitor. . . . The comic dialogue between Popeye's grandmother and the chauffeur [in chapter 31] clearly resembles the humor of Segar's strip."[18]

Then in 1973 in a brief article, the first to address the matter of Faulkner's use of the comic strips, Pat M. Esslinger expanded on the connection McHaney had made:

> Popeye may be the symbol of evil and the Pluto figure who sweeps Judge Drake's teasing daughter into the recessed Hades of Miss Reba's place, but he might also be the Popeye of E. C. Segar's comic strip. In the much disputed last chapter of *Sanctuary*, which was inserted only in the revised version of the novel, Faulkner carefully includes his clue to the joke. He prepares a long, elaborate, and seemingly irrelevant passage on how the child Popeye, who can't walk or talk and who had a great similarity to the crawling baby Swee'-pea of the comic strip, was raised on olive oil. The baby's eggs had to be cooked in it, and the incident of the broken bottle of olive oil led to the house burning which left Popeye impotent. It is this association of Faulkner's Popeye with olive oil that leads the reader to Segar's "Thimble Theatre" and the parallels between the comic strip and the *Sanctuary* Popeye. The obvious parallels occur in both characters' diminutive stature, the ubiquitous dangling cigarette that replaces the corncob pipe, the one knobby eye of each closed against the cigarette smoke, and the impotency, or in the comic strip counterpart, the weakness, which can be overcome only by an outside force such as a corncob or a magical dose of spinach. *Sanctuary's* Popeye is seen in an omnipresent, black, skin-tight suit, black rather than the white the comic strip characters wore, but its sailor overtones are established when Temple asks, "What river did you fall in and with that suit on?" The black suit and the constant reference to Popeye as "that black man" also merge the little gangster with the black man of the comic strip, Bluto, the black evil or

Elzie Crisler Segar, *Thimble Theater*, July 28, 1933.
© King Features Syndicate, Inc.

Pluto force who always carries off the fair maiden Persephone figure, Olive Oyl. And the short little Memphis bootlegger may have, as the opening page of the novel indicates, "that vicious depthless quality of stamped tin," but he also has that pale flatness of a cartoon snipped from the Sunday funnies.[19]

Two corrections are in order here. Faulkner could not have intended any association between his infant Popeye and Swee'pea since that infant character did not appear in Segar's comic strip until July 28, 1933, nor could he have intended any reference to Popeye's nemesis Bluto, later known as Brutus, since he appeared in a comic strip sequence beginning in June of 1933 and

thereafter appeared primarily in the animated films first distributed that same year. Both Swee'pea and Bluto, then, came into being over two years after the publication of *Sanctuary*. It should also be noted that the Popeye Faulkner may have seen in the funny papers did not yet derive his strength from spinach but rather from having stroked the three hairs on the head of the magical Whiffle Hen. His corncob pipe was never a source of his superhero strength, and only for the first four weeks of his existence did he wear an all-white sailor suit, to be replaced by the blue pants and black jersey with red collar, an outfit he has worn for over fifty-five years. It is interesting to note that in a 1933

"BLUTO" THE TERRIBLE!!
LOWER THAN BILGE SCUM-MEANER THAN SATAN- AND STRONG AS AN OX

CHAPTER FOUR "GOLD CRAZY"

PEJOZEES
$
GOLD
GOLD
GOLD
HAH! HAH! HAH!
I WANT GOLD

THE ONLY MAN LIVING WHO MIGHT LICK POPEYE—

The original caption reads: Real competition for POPEYE at last! How can the Right loving sailor compete against a mad brute like Bluto? Inspired to his worst mood by the lust for gold of the Sunken City, you can bet he'll make life exciting for POPEYE as long as he lasts. Watch what happens when this pair meet in the thrilling new episode pictured by E. C. Segar in THIMBLE THEATRE, STARRING POPEYE! Turn to the comic page of the Oregon Statesman every day for the latest developments!
© King Features Syndicate.

promotional piece in which Segar traced the early years of Popeye, he is shown as a young man in one drawing, "The Sailor as a Young Rake," dressed in just the sort of tight black suit Faulkner's Popeye wore.

I do not mean to question the possibility that Faulkner may have recalled Segar's comic strip

sailor when he named his character, only these inaccurate details. Popeye became famous immediately after his creation, and *Thimble Theatre* soon became the most widely circulated comic strip in the United States, so some knowledge on Faulkner's part was almost unavoidable. What the errors do suggest is the cavalier attitude scholars take when they choose to discuss comic art. They tend to bank on vague memories; assume that comic strips do not develop, change, and add characters during the course of their histories; and avoid the truly hard labor of going through newspaper collections on microfilm or locating reprints to check the accuracy of their impressions and assumptions.

Faulkner's mention of olive oil does remain a strong clue that he had Segar's character partly in mind, but there are other ways in which the worlds of *Thimble Theatre* and *Sanctuary* are alike—through the presence of violence, an atmosphere of terror, and graveyard humor. These are elements lost to the contemporary reader because the Popeye comic strip produced since Segar's death on October 13, 1938 by other hands moved into more innocent story lines and the character was reshaped into a less complex figure more compatible with the interests of younger readers. Segar's *Thimble Theatre* was a comic strip largely adult in content and orientation.

Thimble Theatre had been in progress for almost a decade before Popeye came on the scene. Designed partly as competition for Ed Whelan's popular feature satirizing the film world, *Midget Movies* and later *Minute Movies*, *Thimble Theatre* intentionally had a changing cast of characters but primarily featured a nondescript comic hero named Ham Gravy, his

Elzie Crisler Segar, newspaper promotion piece for *Thimble Theater*, 1933. The original captions reads, in order: The Infink Popeye; The Childhood Slugger in Action; The Sailor as a Young Rake; The Adulk Mariner in a Characteristic Pose.
© King Features Syndicate, Inc.

Elzie Crisler Segar, *Thimble Theater*, October 3, 1928.
© King Features Syndicate, Inc.

Elzie Crisler Segar, *Thimble Theater*, November 16, 1928.
© King Features Syndicate, Inc.

gangly but ultrafeminine girlfriend Olive Oyl, her contentious and bad-tempered brother Castor Oyl, and their parents Cole and Nanna Oyl. Beginning as a very simply drawn gag-a-day feature satirizing stage melodrama, Segar began to develop continuity and interplay among his characters and moved the feature in the direction of fantasy and adventure. Through imaginative and narrative skill, and an adept hand at creating mystery and suspense, Segar was taking the comic strip in new directions of story-telling power and adult interest.

The tone and tenor of Segar's distinctive approach to comic strip narrative is evident in the preceding eighteen weeks of the story in which Popeye was to make his first appearance.[20] On September 10, 1928, Castor and Olive's Uncle Lubry Kent Oyl returns from Africa for a visit with a rare and magical creature called the Whiffle Hen which he has named Bernice. When challenged by Uncle Lubry to kill Bernice for a $1,000 prize, Castor engages in 26 straight days of unsuccessful efforts to murder the fowl by every conceivable

Elzie Crisler Segar, *Thimble Theater*, December 11, 1928.
© King Features Syndicate, Inc.

Elzie Crisler Segar, *Thimble Theater*, December 27, 1928.
© King Features Syndicate, Inc.

method of mayhem—guns, axes, poison, cannons, drowning, hanging, starvation, dynamite, electricity, gas, feeding it to a shark, and sending after her a murderous bird called the arrow hawk intent on impaling her brain. Despite this violence, Bernice becomes fond of Castor and becomes his constant but annoying companion.

Unaware that rubbing the three hairs on the head of the Whiffle Hen brings consistent good luck, Castor is soon beset by enormous offers of money to purchase the hen from strange men,

as well as a woman fully draped in black sent by the criminal kingpen Mr. Fadewell. The competition for possession becomes so keen that Castor is subjected to several murderous threats, is finally knocked out, and is buried alive in a state of delirium. He survives, however, to witness the probable deaths of his would-be assassins. This is very unusual and strong fare for comic strips but representative of the kind of intriguing and powerful narratives created by Segar. It is the comic distance, the dark humor, and the obvious fantasy which

Elzie Crisler Segar, *Thimble Theater*, April 3, 1929.
© King Features Syndicate, Inc.

Elzie Crisler Segar, *Thimble Theater*, May 7, 1929.
© King Features Syndicate, Inc.

keeps the horror in perspective and allows the reader to view the story as one would a gothic tale or detective yarn, specifically designed to play upon our delight in being playfully frightened.

Castor decides to sail for Dice Island, the largest gambling resort in the world and owned by Fadewell, to break the bank with the luck the Whiffle Hen will bring. When he, with Olive and Ham Gravy, go to buy a boat, it is at this point that they go in search of a sailor to manage the vessel and find Popeye, as ugly and

unlikely a figure to become an internationally admired hero as one can imagine. He is completely aloof and independent, speaks his own mind (although in a bizarre and ungrammatical dialect), and has a temper that cannot be controlled. It was probably his incorrigibility that made him so attractive to funny paper readers at a time when most comic pages were still dominated by naughty children, whimsical animals, domestic comedy, and melodrama.

Popeye's penchant for extreme violence was demonstrated ten weeks after his appearance

Elzie Crisler Segar, *Thimble Theater*, May 31, 1929
(detail) and June 4, 1929 (detail).
© King Features Syndicate, Inc.

when he socks a deceitful character named
Snork simply because he doesn't like his looks.
His special powers for survival, which antedate
those of Superman by nine years, are demonstrated when the unarmed Popeye is attacked
by Snork with a gun. Although riddled with
bullets, Popeye still stands, and the incredulous
Snork exclaims, "Why don't you drop? I've shot
you a dozen times—are you a demon?!!"[21] He
finally collapses and crawls off into the dark of
the ship's hold where he survives apparently by
rubbing the head of the Whiffle Hen. After a
long night of recuperation, he finally emerges
from hiding for one more crack at Snork's jaw to
find the criminal brutalizing Olive Oyl. When
Popeye downs Snork for the final time, his
bravery elicits Olive's admiration who muses,
"He's a man all right! If he wasn't such a funny
lookin' thing, I'd give him a kiss."[22] This is the
first sign of a romance which will push Ham

Elzie Crisler Segar, *Thimble Theater*, June 15, 1929.
© King Features Syndicate, Inc.

Elzie Crisler Segar, *Thimble Theater*, November 5, 1929 (detail) and November 6, 1929 (detail).
© King Features Syndicate, Inc.

Faulkner Reads the Funny Papers   93

Gravy out of Olive's life and *Thimble Theatre* altogether. Five months later, on November 11, 1929, to be exact, Segar would come across the phrase which would best epitomize his creation's integrity, self- knowledge, and independence of mind. When an exasperated Castor Oyl asks, "Fighting! Always fighting! What kind of an egg are you anyway?", Popeye replies, "I yam what I yam and that's what I yam."[23] This would remain Popeye's sole creed (later modified to read "I yam what I yam, an' tha's all I yam"), an aid in times of distress as Temple Drake would discover when cringing in fear in the corn crib as she later reported it to Horace Benbow: "So I'd hold my eyes tight shut and say Now I am. I am now."[24]

As comic art scholar Bill Blackbeard has summarized his nature,

> Segar's Popeye is a character compounded of vulgarity and compassion, raw aggression, and protective gentleness, violent waterfront humor and genuine "senskibiliky," thickheaded stubbornness and imaginative leadership, brutal enmity and warm friendship, who can knock out a "horsk" in rage and nurse a baby carefully while it is suffering a fever that makes thermometers pop. He is no paranoid daydream, but a realistic, complex, often wrong but determined man of action who suffers continual agonies of decision, who pursues what he believes to be right far beyond the bounds of cop-interpreted law and order, who has to fight his very way to comprehensibility through the warp and woof of an English language that is often almost too much for him . . . .
>
> Popeye—human, smelly, capable of disastrous mistakes, able to slug a woman, pursue likely looking chicks with lusty interest, swear a blue streak when "irrikated," able to be cheerfully cynical about almost everything dear to the proper, from patriotism to making money, and with a capacity to look as sloppy as he behaved—was certainly more of an *anti*-superhero than anything else. Yet it was his jaunty character and behavior that wowed the public and made them turn to *Thimble Theatre* first among the comics for a full decade.[25]

These comments, of course, simply go to show that the Popeye of the funny papers was a complex, multifaceted character with more of the bizarre and anti-social in his nature than most people today are likely to know about. It is in this context, therefore, that Faulkner's use of the name becomes most appropriate. His mean-spirited, pugnacious, violence-prone, independent, and aggressive Popeye has none of his namesake's redeeming qualities but all of his

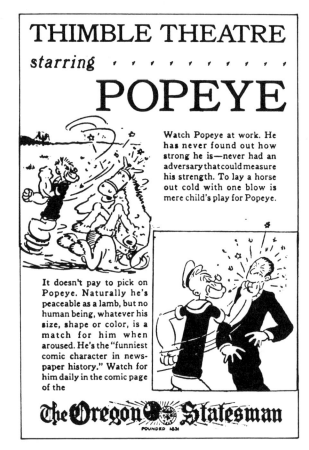

Elzie Crisler Segar, newspaper promotion piece for *Thimble Theater.*
© King Features Syndicate, Inc.

terrifying features turned to purely criminal purposes. Women find both attractive, perhaps because they are rebels and outsiders, and both live life on their own terms. Popeye Vitelli, however, places himself beyond any human sympathy by a cold and immoral cruelty. But the associations that Segar's comic strip world of violent humor would have for the reader of 1931 would serve as effective preparation for entering the evil world of *Sanctuary*. It might also be noted that both Faulkner and Segar created complete fictional communities populated by recurring and often family-related characters, took liberties with the English language in the name of stretching its creative potential, and successfully combined the tragic and the comic in revealing parables of life that reflect on the complexities of human conflict and existence.

The other major character in Faulkner's fiction besides Popeye who bears a name famous in comic strip history is Jiggs, the mechanic who is

Elzie Crisler Segar, portrait, and Popeye.
© King Features Syndicate, Inc.

George McManus, *Bringing
Up Father.*
© King Features Syndicate,
Inc.

a part of the Shumann expanded family in *Pylon*. In appearance he bears a strong resemblance to the Jiggs of George McManus's *Bringing Up Father*.[26] We are told that he has a "hard tough shortchinned face" with a "bald spot neat as a tonsure" on top of his head, has a "short thick musclebound body," wears skin-tight pants "enclosing a pair of short stocky thick legs," and walks fast with a "short bouncing curiously stiffkneed gait."[27] Also like the browbeaten Jiggs, dominated by his wife Maggie, so too does Faulkner's Jiggs have a henpecked background. He tells the bus driver in chapter one how he ran out on his wife in Kansas because she would grab the money he earned before he had a chance to tell his employer the job was finished.[28]

Here the similarities end, but as the narrative develops, Faulkner surrounds Jiggs with other types of comic references, particularly to animated films and vaudeville or stage comedy. When he puts his hand into his pocket for the money with which to make a down payment on the boots he wishes to purchase, the clerks "could follow it, fingernail and knuckle, the entire length of the pocket like watching the ostrich in the movie cartoon swallow the alarm clock," and Jiggs is also described as a "cartoon comedy centaur."[29] When he boards the bus in the beginning, he soon finds himself involved in a scene resembling "that comic stage one where the entire army enters one taxicab and drives away."[30] When Jiggs meets with the unnamed reporter, Faulkner says,

> As they stood side by side and looked at one another they resembled the tall and the short man of the unfailing comic team—the one looking like a cadaver out of a medical school vat and dressed for the moment in garments out of a floodrefugee warehouse, the other filling his clothing without any fraction of surplus cloth which might be pinched between two fingers, with that trim vicious economy of wrestlers' tights.[31]

Another apt comparison, of course, would have been the classic tall and short team of the comics, Mutt and Jeff, themselves based on the duos of stage tradition to which Faulkner refers.

The word most frequently associated with Jiggs, aside from the comic strip practice of reducing the affirmative "yes" to an irritatingly repetitive corruption "yair," is the verb to "bounce." Everything he does and everywhere he goes is with a bounce. Possessed by the boots on which he bounces, Jiggs becomes the comically singular character whose devotion to

an object or action warps him into an exaggerated stereotype. This is a standard source of humor in the comic strip and stage comedy.

What Faulkner seems to be about here in using various references from comic strips, animated films, and vaudeville or the stage, is to invest Jiggs with his dramatic role as a comic chorus or witness to the tragic events of the novel. Finally the reporter begins to laugh at the absurd actions of the characters, including his own, and tells Jiggs that what started out to be a "good orthodox Italian tragedy" has now "turned into a comedy."[32] The reporter has achieved a cynical distance on the extreme behavior and exaggerated actions of the characters, a perspective they all lack, but like them he proves unable to resist following out the fated impulses that possess them even into the jaws of death. Defiant laughter is the answer to the meaninglessness of life and death. The forlorn central figures of the novel at one point are described as forming "a tableau reminiscent . . . of the cartoon pictures of city anarchists."[33]

Given that one of the major settings of the novel is the world of journalism and the newspaper, references to comic strips are not surprising, but one wonders whether or not the thoughts of the reporter were shared by Faulkner when he describes the newspaper as a "fragile web of ink and paper, assertive, proclamative; profound and irrevocable if only in the sense of being profoundly and irrevocably unimportant . . . the dead instant's fruit of forty tons of machinery and an entire nation's antic delusion."[34] Of his work, the reporter says, "We got to eat, and the rest of them have got to read. And if they ever abolish fornication and blood, where in the hell will we all be?"[35] These are not positive views of what was then the most influential of the nation's mass media.

Given the other major physical setting, the airport where the airmeet takes place, it is surprising not to find any references to the several popular aviation comic strips of the period: *Tailspin Tommy* by Hal Forrest and Glen Chaffin (beginning in 1928), so popular that it became the first adventure comic strip to be adapted as a weekly movie serial released in 1934; Lyman Young's *Tim Tyler's Luck* (1928); *Scorchy Smith* by John Terry (1930), but rendered brilliantly after 1933 by Noel Sickles; Roy Crane's *Captain Easy* (1933), which grew out of the earlier *Wash Tubbs* (1924); and Zack Mosely's *Smilin' Jack* (1933). All of these adventure strips dwelt lovingly on the romance of

Frederick Burr Opper, *Alphonse and Gaston.*

flying and the minute details of aircraft construction, realistic detail being the standard for the latter. They dealt with airmeets, barnstorming, and death-defying feats of the sort depicted in *Pylon*. But Faulkner chose not to draw on any of these popular figures or their images, unless we are to find in Laverne and her erotic stunt in the airplane with Shumann, with her skirts flapping in the breeze, some suggestion of the curvaceously rendered women of *Smilin' Jack* called by the artist "de-icers."

As best I have been able to determine, only two comic strips are specifically mentioned in Faulkner's fiction, one by name and the other by description, both in *Light in August*. Mrs. Hines' appearance in the courthouse in Mottstown is reminiscent, we are told, of a scene out of "the Katzenjammer kids in the funny paper," and at the conclusion, when Byron Bunch and the traveling furniture repairer who tells the story to his wife compete for the position of who will sleep on the ground, "It was like those two fellows that used to be in the funny papers, those two Frenchmen that were always bowing and scraping at the other one to go first . . . . "[36] The last reference is to *Alphonse and Gaston*, a short-lived Sunday newspaper feature of 1902-1904 by Frederick Burr Opper who

dropped them to devote more attention to his better known strips *Happy Hooligan* and *Maude the Mule*. The two are extremely polite Frenchmen who have carried good manners to such an extreme that they are both immobilized and unable to act as disaster occurs around them: "You first, my dear Alphonse!" "No, no— *you* first, my dear Gaston!"[37] They reside more in the popular consciousness and language as representatives of excessive politeness rather than as comic strip characters. In both cases in *Light in August*, Faulkner seems merely to be using the two comic strips as idiomatic references since they have no integral relationship to the plot or action.

Of course, some of the children in Faulkner's fiction conduct themselves after the fashion of the eternally troublesome pranksters Hans and Fritz in the Rudolph Dirks comic strip which began in 1897. For example, the activities of young Malcolm and James Faulkner in setting the pasture afire in the 1937 comic sketch, "Afternoon of a Cow," are not unlike the typical mischief of the *Katzenjammer Kids*, except for the addition of the cook's son Grover who is equally culpable. The comic strip was based on the German verse tales of Wilhelm Busch, *Max und Moritz* (1865), and interestingly enough in the original tales, the young hell-raisers burn the schoolmaster by putting gunpowder in his pipe and are themselves burned when they fall into dough and are cooked in the baker's oven.[38] There is no evidence, however, that Faulkner knew the work of Wilhelm Busch, although translations of the grim moral fables were available.

There are several characters whose names could conceivably have been inspired by comic strips of the time, besides Popeye and Jiggs: Hawkshaw the barber of the stories "Hair" and "Dry September" after Gus Mager's *Hawkshaw the Detective* (beginning in 1913); the reporter Smitty in *Pylon* after Walter Brandt's office boy strip *Smitty* (1922); the squatter Wash Jones of *Absalom, Absalom!* and the Jefferson jailer Euphus Tubbs of several novels after Roy Crane's comic adventurer *Wash Tubbs* (1924); the treacherous horse trader and father of Flem, Abner Snopes, after Al Capp's hillbilly strip *Li'l Abner* (1934); and the mentally deficient criminal known as Monk in the story of that name in *Knight's Gambit* after Gus Mager's *Monk* series of comic strips (1904) featuring ape-like humans performing wacky deeds (such as *Knocko the Monk, Groucho the Monk,* or

Rudolph Dirks, *The Katzenjammer Kids*.
© King Features Syndicate, Inc.

Sherlocko the Monk—which served to inspire the names of the Marx Brothers in 1918). But these are mere borrowings or simply incidental uses of the same names. Occasionally Faulkner picks up a word originated in the comics, such as "twenty-three skidoo," repeated several times in *The Reivers* by Carrie's nephew Otis and the deputy Butch Lovemaiden, a coinage by political cartoonist Tad Dorgan who was popular in the first two decades of the century.[39]

This examination of Faulkner's fiction for comic strip references suggests that he looked to the funnies as a source of names for some of his characters, but rather than appropriate them in any direct way, he used the contexts of their associations in indirect ways to reflect on the situations and natures of the figures to whom they are applied. Faulkner read the funny papers, but perhaps a little more deeply and seriously than most people would suspect. But then this was the man who wanted, when he first went to Hollywood in 1932, to write film scripts for Mickey Mouse cartoons.[40] My guess is that he was not thinking about the mild-mannered Mickey of the Disney animated films

but rather the courageous, hell-raising adventures of Mickey as depicted in the breath-taking adventure comic strip version of master artist-writer Floyd Gottfredson which he produced from 1930 to 1932. When Faulkner read the funny papers, he laughed, but more wisely and appreciatively than most critics might imagine.

1. Joseph Blotner, *Faulkner: A Biography* (New York: Random House, 1974), pp. 92-93. John Faulkner tells a different story in *My Brother Bill* (New York: Trident Press, 1963), pp. 34-36, where he recalls their father reading the funny papers to the gathered children every Sunday in the Faulkner household and their disappointment when Bill returned home after his first day at school unable to read the funnies on his own.

2. Ibid., pp. 94-95.

3. Carvel Collins, "Introduction," *Mayday* by William Faulkner (Notre Dame: Univ. of Notre Dame

Press, 1978), pp. 9-10.

4. Ibid., pp. 5, 10-11; Blotner, pp. 165, 315-16, 345-46, 941.

5. Addison C. Bross, "*Soldiers' Pay* and the Art of Aubrey Beardsley," *American Quarterly*, 19 (Spring 1967), 5.

6. Ibid., pp. 3-23. Bross focuses primarily on *Soldiers' Pay*. In "Beardsley and Faulkner," *Journal of Modern Literature*, 9 (September 1976), 339-56, Timothy K. Conley summarizes Bross and expands the discussion of Beardsley's influence to include later novels. An excellent comprehensive study of Faulkner and illustration is Lothar Hönnighausen's *William Faulkner: The Art of Stylization in His Early Graphic and Literary Work* (Cambridge: Cambridge Univ. Press, 1987).

7. William Faulkner, *Mosquitoes* (New York: Boni & Liveright, 1927), p. 230.

8. For a selection of Held's characteristic work, see *The Most of John Held* (Brattleboro, Vermont: The Stephen Greene Press, 1972).

9. See John Held, Jr., *The Saga of Frankie & Johnny* (New York: Clarkson N. Potter, 1972), which reprints the 1930 edition, and Shelley Armitage's superb study *John Held, Jr.: Illustrator of the Jazz Age* (Syracuse, N.Y.: Syracuse University Press, 1987).

10. *Uncollected Stories of William Faulkner*, edited by Joseph Blotner (New York: Random House, 1979), p. 345.

11. Ibid., p. 339.

12. Blotner, pp. 492-93, 607-8.

13. Faulkner, *Mosquitoes*, pp. 178, 282.

14. *Uncollected Stories*, p. 504.

15. Ibid., p. 506.

16. William Faulkner, *Sanctuary* (New York: Jonathan Cape & Harrison Smith, 1931), pp. 3-6.

17. Ibid., pp. 227-28.

18. Thomas L. McHaney, "Sanctuary and Frazer's Slain Kings," *Mississippi Quarterly*, 24 (Summer 1971), 237, note 25.

19. Pat M. Esslinger, "No Spinach in *Sanctuary*," *Modern Fiction Studies*, 18 (Winter 1973), 556-57. Esslinger also draws some parallels between Temple/Popeye and Little Orphan Annie/Daddy Warbucks, but they are too strained to be meaningful. There are far too many differences between the independent, feisty, self-sufficient Annie and the dependent, passive, easily dominated Temple for any connections to be significant, in spite of Temple's frequently blank eyes.

20. An almost complete run of the daily comic strip from September 10, 1928 to May 12, 1930 is reprinted in Bill Blackbeard's edition of *Thimble Theatre Introducing Popeye* by Elzie C. Segar (Westport, Conn.: Hyperion Press, 1977).

21. Ibid., p. 70.

22. Ibid., p. 80.

23. Ibid., p. 120.

24. *Sanctuary*, p. 210.

25. Bill Blackbeard, "The First (arf, arf) Superhero of Them All," *All in Color for a Dime*, edited by Dick Lupoff and Don Thompson (New Rochelle, N.Y.: Arlington House, 1970), pp. 98, 117-18. This is the best appreciation of Segar's achievement which Blackbeard views as one of the masterpieces of comic strip art. See also Blackbeard's introductions to *Thimble Theatre Starring Popeye the Sailor* by E. C. Segar (Franklin Square, N.Y.: Nostalgia Press, 1971) and *Thimble Theatre Introducing Popeye* by Elzie C. Segar (Westport, Conn.: Hyperion Press, 1977). For other interpretations see Bud Sagendorf, *Popeye: The First Fifty Years* (New York: Workman Publishing, 1979), and Alan Gowans, *Prophetic Allegory: Popeye and the American Dream* (Watkins Glen, N.Y.: American Life Books, 1983).

26. For a selection of this comic strip spanning its 42 years under McManus's hand, see George McManus, *Bringing Up Father Starring Maggie and Jiggs* (New York: Charles Scribner's Sons, 1973).

27. William Faulkner, *Pylon* (New York: Harrison Smith and Robert Haas, 1935), pp. 8, 11, 56.

28. Ibid., p. 16.

29. Ibid., pp. 10, 270.

30. Ibid., p. 15.

31. Ibid., p. 56.

32. Ibid., p. 279.

33. Ibid., p. 81.

34. Ibid., p. 111.

35. Ibid., p. 239.

36. William Faulkner, *Light in August* (New York: Harrison Smith and Robert Haas, 1932), pp. 375, 473.

37. Richard A. Milum, in "Faulkner and the Comic Perspective of Frederick Burr Opper," *Journal of Popular Culture*, 16 (Winter 1982), 139-50, finds in *Alphonse and Gaston* "an exasperating and unrelenting dedication to chivalry" which he applies to numerous characters in Faulkner's fiction, but the relationship is too tenuous to bear such broad interpretation. His entire essay, which is intended to demonstrate the influence of the comics on Faulkner, never establishes a specific connection between the two beyond this reference.

38. See *The Genius of Wilhelm Busch*, edited and translated by Walter Arndt (Berkeley: Univ. of California Press, 1982), pp. 29-34.

39. See "Comics and American Language," in this volume.

40. Blotner, p. 772. For an exploration of similarities between Faulkner's comic literary techniques and those found in animated films, see D. M. Murray, "Faulkner, the Silent Comedies, and the Animated Cartoon," *Southern Humanities Review*, 9 (Summer 1975), 241-57.

Charles Schulz, *Peanuts*, February 15, 1981.
© United Feature Syndicate, Inc.

Peanuts and American Culture

I am reluctant to begin an essay in appreciation of the achievement of Charles Schulz by disagreeing with him, but the occasion seems to require it. More than once he has acceded to the idea that the comic strip does not occupy a position of consequence in the world of American culture. He put it this way in *Peanuts Jubilee*:

> It is important to me, when I am discussing comic strips, to make certain that everyone knows that I do not regard what I am doing as Great Art. I certainly am not ashamed of the work I do, nor do I apologize for being involved in a field that is generally regarded as occupying a very low rung on the entertainment ladder.[1]

Partly this has to do with what seems to be a personal humility characteristic of Charles Schulz, but it is also a fairly traditional stance on the part of several of America's most talented comic strip artists. From the master of whimsical fantasy George Herriman (*Krazy Kat*) to the brilliant originator of realistic adventure in comics Roy Crane (*Captain Easy* and *Buz Sawyer*), cartoonists have not been among the first to recognize the quality of the art they have practiced so well. Finally, however, it is an attitude that must be questioned, since Schulz's own work serves to prove it faulty.

A truly significant piece of art, be it visual, plastic, verbal, or musical, is one that draws from the cumulative traditions that have preceded it, at the same time that it reshapes the traditional form in such a way that it gains new life and relevance for the future. *Peanuts* perfectly fits this definition. Schulz's comic strip draws on a rich tradition of creative accomplishments in graphic humor, reflects a whole range of high points in popular culture, and ultimately revives the comic strip form for the remainder of the century by demonstrating its versatility in dealing with the social, psychological, and philosophical tensions of the modern world. If we were allowed to select only one artifact for deposit in a time capsule, something which would tell future historians what life in twentieth-century America was all about, we could do not better than to select a complete run of *Peanuts*. It would be considerably more revealing than the Rosetta stone.

Schulz has acknowledged the influence on his work of several of the classic practitioners of comic art—among them Roy Crane, Milton Caniff, Clare Briggs, J. R. Williams, Percy Crosby, Elzie C. Segar, and George Herriman.[2] Roy Crane brought to the comic strip a bent for exciting narratives and realistic settings in what Schulz has characterized as a "rollicking style" first in *Captain Easy and Wash Tubbs* and later in *Buz Sawyer*.[3] Crane's splendid tales of adventure would inspire a host of followers, the most talented of whom was Milton Caniff who like Crane would create two enduring narratives about soldiers of fortune in *Terry and the Pirates* and *Steve Canyon*. The Crane and Caniff inspiration shows through in *Peanuts* whenever Snoopy's over-active imagination takes him on flights behind enemy lines in pursuit of the Red Baron. Yet Schulz does them one better by creating a sense of excitement and suspense entirely through Snoopy's thoughts rather than graphic realism.

Roy Crane, self portrait, 1925.

Clare Briggs, J. R. Williams, and Percy Crosby were, before Schulz, our most popular delineators of the American family and child life. Briggs, through a variety of comic features like *When a Feller Needs a Friend* and *Mr. and Mrs.*, chronicled the unglamorous, simple emotions of ordinary people, sometimes with a heavily sentimental hand but usually with a counterbalance towards reality. Also effectively balanced in its realism and sentimentality was *Out Our Way* by J. R. Williams, whose scenes alternated between urban family life, the world of the cowboy, and workers in a machine shop, but in all cases, as Schulz has said, with a style that was "warmhearted." Percy Crosby's *Skippy* paved the way for *Peanuts* by proving that the world of the child, if handled with insight and sensitivity, offered a varied fare that would sustain the interests of comic strip readers. Skippy was a curbside philosopher with a pessimistic attitude towards his playmates and the adult world, and his concern with alienation and failure partly anticipates the world of Charlie Brown.[4] These artists all served as examples of how ordinary people and homely problems could be used as an inexhaustible source of high comedy and how the child's world serves as a reflection of the common concerns of people of all ages and classes.

In expressing his admiration for *Popeye* and *Krazy Kat*, Schulz has allied himself with two of

Elzie Crisler Segar, *Thimble Theater*, 1938 (detail).
© King Features Syndicate, Inc.

the comic strip's most powerful creative minds—Elzie Crisler Segar and George Herriman. Segar began in 1919 a comic strip called *Thimble Theater* which would become world famous in 1929 when he introduced a cantankerous, ugly, and independent, but enduring sailor named Popeye. Until his death in 1938, Segar created a brilliant sequential narrative in which violence, suspense, and graveyard humor compelled the nation to pay attention and take delight in his gothic imagination. The incorrigible Popeye of the original Segar sequences had little in common with the sweet, naive Popeye we know today who has survived in name only under the hands of artists lacking Segar's special touch (although the current daily strip by Bobby London has its own gothic power). Schulz has said, "Although there seems to be no comparison on the surface, in many ways my comic strip is like *Popeye* . . . if you are able to break through the surface to see it. Many of the things that happen to Charlie Brown are outrageous, and likewise many outrageous things happened in *Popeye*. I think *Popeye* was a perfect comic strip."[5]

Krazy Kat had violence of another outrageous kind—bricks tossed against the head of a loving cat by the object of affection, a mouse named Ignatz. This crazy love affair was enacted against a changing abstract landscape drawn in the free-association style of dada and surrealist art. Herriman's self-contained world of Krazy, Ignatz, the benevolent Offisa Pup, and the other inhabitants of Cocinino County, was one of the most poetic, whimsical, and fanciful creations of the modern artistic sensibility. Schulz encountered *Krazy Kat* by way of the 1946 anthology, graced with an appreciative introduction by poet E. E. Cummings, issued two years after the death of Herriman. *Krazy Kat*, says Schulz, "did much to inspire me to create a feature that went beyond the mere actions of ordinary children."[6] The effect of Segar and Herriman

was to open the floodgates of Schulz's imagination by demonstrating the full potential of the comic strip for unbridled fantasy. He felt free to allow the outrageous, the unexpected, and the fanciful to enter his world of diminutive characters who are wiser than their years and who stave off the encroachment of reality by rejecting a false rationalism in favor of a healthy appreciation for the absurd and the uncertain. In the work of all three—Segar, Herriman, and Schulz—the violence of life has been softened by the transfiguring power of comedy and love.

The comics were not the only source of inspiration to the cartoonist as a young man. There were motion pictures, for example, such as Victor McLaglen in *The Lost Patrol* or the Walt Disney animated cartoons, which Schulz saw in Minnesota: "I have drawn many cartoons showing the children standing in line to buy tickets to a movie, because my memories of Saturday afternoons at the Park Theater in St. Paul are so vivid. Almost nothing could prevent us from seeing the latest episode of the Saturday afternoon serial and the movie that followed."[7] Also, reports Schulz, "In my childhood, sports played a reasonably strong role, although they were strictly the sandlot variety." These included baseball, football, skating, hockey, golf, and marbles, most of which have figured in *Peanuts* from time to time, especially baseball which provides a useful situation in which children naturally stand around expressing their opinions. "The challenges to be faced in sports work marvelously as a caricature of the challenges we face in the more serious aspects of our lives," Schulz notes. "And when Charlie Brown has tried to analyze his own difficulties in life, he has always been able to express them best in sports terms."[8]

A surprising source of inspiration is the world of country music. Schulz has a particular fondness for the music of Faron Young, after whom he named a cat that appeared briefly in

Charles Schulz, *Peanuts*, October 11, 1968.
© United Feature Syndicate, Inc.

Charles Schulz, *Peanuts*, February 13, 1979.
© United Feature Syndicate, Inc.

the strip. Another favorite was Hank Williams, who had, Schulz says, a direct influence:

> . . . I had an album of Hank Williams songs to which I used to listen over and over. One night, saddened by the plaintive lyrics of a lost love, I created the first of a long series where Charlie Brown tried so desperately to get up the courage to speak to the little red-haired girl. It would be difficult to explain to someone how a Hank Williams song had prompted such thoughts, but this was the way it happened.[9]

Is it not fitting and proper, however, that America's greatest singer and song writer on behalf of lost and betrayed love should have inspired another of our best loved losers? At any rate, drawing as it does on comics, film, sports, and country music—all areas of popular culture which Americans have either created or in which they have excelled—*Peanuts* is as distinctively American as Mom and Apple Pie.

Just as *Peanuts* seems to have absorbed so much of the popular culture which preceded it, the comic strip has had a profound influence on the society and culture of its own time. *Peanuts* affects and inspires our daily lives, and not simply because we can open our daily newspapers and find it there without fail (for over 14,000 days now without interruption—one of the few certainties in a world beset by unset-

Charles Schulz, *Peanuts*, August 16, 1953 (detail).
© United Feature Syndicate, Inc.

tling changes). *Peanuts* has become an integral part of the history of American culture through its influence in so many areas of our life and society.

For example, what may be Schultz's most important contribution to American English is his extremely useful phrase for any object or person that has the effect of reducing anxiety, "security blanket," inspired by Linus's clutched weapon against the world. The phrase is already so familiar that one can't easily recall a time when it wasn't used. The phrase is in many dictionaries, though none yet seem to give Schulz the credit. Also, in the area of language, while Schulz did not invent either of the

Charles Schulz, *Peanuts*, October 20, 1960.
© United Feature Syndicate, Inc.

Charles Schulz, *Peanuts*, March 11, 1980.
© United Feature Syndicate, Inc.

exclamations "Good grief!" or "Rats!" he gave them new life and an entirely new set of associations by putting them into the mouths of his characters.

Americans are great lovers of ritual and tradition, and so powerful is the influence of Schulz that some of the rituals created in sequences of *Peanuts* threaten to become national holidays and folk traditions. The Easter Beagle may not replace the Easter Bunny, but the wait for the Great Pumpkin has taken on the power and charm of an annual observance which seems like a holiday even if it isn't on the books yet. Other equally intriguing rituals, without which our lives would be less rich, are Charlie Brown's inevitable effort in the fall to kick the football temptingly held by Lucy (such blind faith in the face of tragic experience is one of his endearing qualities), Charlie's doomed struggle in the spring with kite-eating trees, and Snoopy's courageous efforts to bring down that figure of world mythology, the Red Baron.

There is also a heroic folk tradition to which Charlie Brown belongs—the figure of the little man, the lost soul, or what Charlie Chaplin called the Little Fellow. This seemingly inadequate hero has come about in response to the overwhelming anxieties and insecurities of the technological society caused by the Industrial Revolution. This tradition includes such figures as the heroes of James Thurber's fables and cartoons, Chaplin's Tramp, Herriman's Krazy Kat, Chic Young's Dagwood Bumstead, Buster Keaton's screen persona, and characters in the writings of Robert Benchley, S. J. Perelman, E. B. White, Ring Lardner, Langston Hughes, and Art Buchwald, and speaking for the feminine side Dorothy Parker and Judith Viorst. Like Woody Allen, who belongs as well, Charlie Brown is a particularly appropriate little soul for the past three decades because of his preoccupations with what has possessed all of us—anxiety over our neurotic behavior, the need to establish our identities, the relationship of the self to society, and the overwhelming need to gain control of our destinies. The power of Charlie, and the timid souls who preceded him, lies in his resilience, his ability to accept and humanize the dehumanizing forces around him, and his eternal hope for improving himself and his options in life. In his insecurities and defeats, Charlie is someone with whom we can identify, and through his comic grace we experience a revival of spirit and a healing of the psyche. I'm O.K. if you're O.K., Charlie Brown.

Charles Schulz, *Peanuts*, May 24, 1979.
© United Features Syndicate, Inc.

A more evident area of influence in the larger culture has been the multitude of spinoffs fostered by Schulz—the hardcover and paperback anthologies and original books based on *Peanuts* which have sold in untold millions of copies, two volumes of theological commentary illustrated by selected comic strips which have sold over 2 million copies, a large number of animated feature film and television specials, two stage musicals based on *Peanuts* characters one of which (*You're a Good Man, Charlie Brown*) has been one of the most widely performed shows in American theatrical history, not to mention the thousands of toy and gift items bearing the likenesses of well-known figures from Schulz's cast of characters. One evening in December of 1969, Charlie Brown was performing before a sellout stage show audience in New York, another sellout audience at Radio City Music Hall for a feature film, a repeat television special viewed by fifty-five million Americans throughout the country, as well as more than 100 million newspaper readers here and abroad in a multiplicity of languages. No other American artist or writer in any other field of creative endeavor has ever been known to reach and earn the admiration of so many people simultaneously as Charles Schulz has done at such magic moments in his career. And when one recalls that Apollo 10 carried *Peanuts* into outer space, it becomes necessary to recognize Charles Schulz as truly a universal man of the arts.

Schulz has said that "I subscribe to the theory that only a creation that speaks to succeeding generations can truly be labeled art."[10] That is a definition we can agree with, and under that definition *Peanuts* certainly qualifies as art. Charlie Brown and friends have been speaking to several generations now for almost forty years, and they have never been stronger. In 1984, for the first time in the history of the newspaper, a single comic strip reached over two thousand subscribing papers—*Peanuts* of course. Schulz has been the major pop philosopher, theologian, and psychologist for the second half of the twentieth century in America, but more importantly he has combined these concerns in an eloquent and enduring art form, the comic strip. When *Peanuts* is fifty years old, on October 2, 2000, we will see even more clearly in retrospect the genuine power and brilliance of his artistry.

1. Charles Schulz, *Peanuts Jubilee: My Life and Art with Charlie Brown and Others* (New York: Holt, Rinehart and Winston, 1975), p. 9.

2. Schulz, pp. 11-12, 98. Lee Mendelson, *Charlie Brown and Charlie Schulz* (New York: New American Library, 1971), p. 54.

3. Schulz has said, "I think the fellow who influenced me the most was Roy Crane. . . . I really liked the things that he did, and I wanted to do something of that kind myself for a long time." Quoted in Mendelson, pp. 51 and 54.

4. Schulz has reported on the influence of *Skippy* in his early backgrounds for the characters in *Peanuts*: "When I began to draw the kids in the strip talking to each other, the obvious pose was to draw them sitting on the curb, reminiscent of the early 'Skippy' strips, drawn by Percy Crosby. The characters in *Peanuts*, however, were much younger than Skippy and his friends, and I was always sensitive about showing them sitting on a street curb, where they would easily get run over. Therefore, I always drew them sitting at the end of the front walk that ran down from the steps out to the main sidewalk." Schulz, p. 98.

5. Quoted in Mendelson, p. 54.

6. Schulz, p. 12.

7. Schulz, pp. 11 and 86.

8. Schulz, pp. 18-21.

9. Schulz, p. 97.

10. Schulz, p. 10.

Charles Schulz, *Peanuts*.
© United Feature's Syndicate, Inc.

"All right, have it your way—you heard a seal bark!"

James Thurber, cartoon, *The New Yorker*.
© 1945 James Thurber.
© 1973 Helen and Rosemary Thurber.

9

The *New Yorker* Cartoon and Graphic Humor

When Harold Ross issued his often quoted prospectus for his new magazine in 1925, he noted in the first sentence, "The *New Yorker* will be a reflection in word and picture of metropolitan life."[1] Thus the graphics were to share equal importance with the text. And if *The New Yorker* has, as one historian of modern magazines claims, "changed the character of American humor, introduced a new approach to magazine biography, set high standards of reporting, and thereby influenced the course of American journalism,"[2] it has also profoundly influenced the development of the American gag cartoon and established the standards against which the works of all modern practicing cartoonists are measured.

When American readers picked up the premier issue of February 21, 1925 from their newsstands, the first thing they saw was a cartoon on the cover. This was a drawing in watercolor of a Regency figure of aristocratic bearing dressed in top hat and a riding habit with a monocle in his gloved hand. (A similar figure had appeared in 1894 on the cover of the first issue of the Chicago literary magazine *The Chap-Book*, whose high literary standards served to inspire many American magazines who sought a sophisticated audience.[3]) There is some suggestion of a pastoral setting by way of an abstract butterfly and a cloud. The figure, as rendered by artist Rea Irvin, eventually was given a name by writer Corey Ford—Eustace Tilley—and it came to symbolize *The New Yorker* itself and its reputation for urbane wit

Cover, *The Chap-Book*, May 15, 1894.

"You might ask your mistress if she is at home."
"It's no use, sir. She saw you coming."

Charles Dana Gibson, cartoon, *Life*, 1904.

and commentary. The cover is reprinted each anniversary issue. From the beginning, then, graphic and verbal humor went hand in hand.

It was under Ross's eccentric but superb editorship from the beginning until his death in 1951 that the *New Yorker* cartoon was formulated and achieved its definitive and influential form. As was true with the entire premise for the magazine, what was wanted was vaguely somewhere in Ross's mind, so discovering the right artists and styles was a hit or miss proposition and usually frustrating for those around him. At the beginning Ross saw a possible model in the durable British humor magazine *Punch*, and he would leaf through recent issues with Rea Irvin, his first art editor, and point out examples of the kind of thing he thought suitable. While the *Punch* artists satirized contemporary fads, fashions, and social mores, they did so with all the stilted style of magazine illustrators more interested in gracing the page with an attractive drawing than in creating a comic image. While a few *Punch* cartoons inspired direct imitations in the early

issues of *The New Yorker*, it was soon clear to everyone that a more original approach had to be found, some distinctive concept that would establish a modern comic art for the modern sophisticated reader.

In the first place, Ross asked of the cartoon the question literary critics were asking of a modern piece of fiction, which by then was distinguished by its consistent use of point of view. As the reader, he wanted to know "Where am *I* in this picture?" That is, he felt that the reader's vantage point should be one that reasonably would allow him or her to eavesdrop, observe the action, or even be a part of the proceedings being humorously treated. This was a question seldom considered by most cartoonists of the time. His second question was more subtle than it sounded: "Who's talking?" Ross believed there should be no confusion in the reader's mind about who is talking to whom, as was often the case in contemporary cartoons which required captions identifying the speakers, as in the style of a play script.[4]

These concerns over point of view and dialogue not only made contributing artists more conscious craftsmen, but they led gradually to a major innovation in comic art and made *The New Yorker* the most influential force in the evolution of the single panel gag cartoon of this century. Cartoons in other humorous publications of the time, such as *Punch* or the American *Life*, where Rea had worked as an art editor before joining the staff of *The New Yorker*, had at least two lines of dialogue, usually introduced by the names of the speakers, more often than not simply identified by *he* and *she*. In a 1904 *Life* cartoon by Charles Dana Gibson, for example, a gentleman caller inquires, "You might ask your mistress if she is at home." The maid responds, "It's no use, sir. She saw you coming."

Sometimes the captions are lengthy and insufferably tedious, as in the following for a drawing by a *Life* artist named Foster:

> *Mrs. Pileitton (To her coachman):* "James, I trust that you are an attendant at religious exercises?"
>
> "Oh, yes, mem. I goes as often as I has the chance, mem."
>
> "And I trust that you feel it your duty to lead such a life here as will assure you a place among the good in the next world?"
>
> "Oh, yes, mem, I tries to. Thank you kindly, mem."

"I am glad of it James. I have been so much pleased with your services that it is a real comfort to me to know that if we are permitted to have coachmen in Heaven, I may continue to employ you there."[5]

Whatever humor resides in these two examples is hopelessly lost in a social decorum and a class structure that no longer exist, but what is useful for my purposes is to note that in neither case does the drawing add anything to the effect. Basically magazine cartoons before Ross were merely illustrated dialogues with punchlines that carried the full freight of the comedy. The single line caption was the exception rather than the rule. Ross was personally irritated by the classic two-line joke to the extent that he published one he particularly detested in each anniversary issue of *The New Yorker* but with its lines transposed:

Pop: A man who thinks he can make it in par.
Johnny: What is an optimist, pop?[6]

In his drive for originality and distinction, Ross initiated a trend towards simplicity in dialogue, clarity in the identity of the speaker, and integrity in the relationship between picture and text. This resulted in the development of the successful *New Yorker* style one-line cartoon. All of the earlier humor magazines, European and American, had used the one-line cartoon from time to time, but not with a systematic eye towards developing its full comic potential. If the one-liner was to work best, there had to be no doubt about who was speaking because it was the picture that came first in the eye of the viewer and the speaker afterwards. Either a clear verbal gesture had to be evident in the drawing or the caption had to infer the speaker unmistakably, principles which in the application would immediately distinguish the poorly thought out and carelessly executed cartoons from the thoughtful ones. Finally, both picture and caption had to work together simultaneously to achieve a total effect which neither would have alone. This last single transition rendered most of the contemporary humor magazines old-fashioned and quaintly irrelevant. In sum, Ross's standards marked a singular new development in the history of graphic humor here and abroad. The practice of effective cartooning would never be the same.

The change Ross had accomplished was viewed by some as a natural kind of evolutionary process, at least according to one report of a luncheon conversation between *New Yorker* staff writer James Kevin McGuinness, British cartoonist and writer Oliver Herford, and famed artist and then publisher of *Life* Charles Dana Gibson:

Gibson remarked to Herford and McGuinness that he did not think the *New Yorker* would last. Herford disagreed. *Punch*, he said, had succeeded with the long narrative joke below the cartoons. *Life* had succeeded by condensing the joke to the he-she formula. *The New Yorker* had condensed it further to the one-line joke and so, he thought, could not fail.[7]

Ross's interest in simplicity and direct impact on the reader was so intense, in fact, that he would have been happy to abandon the caption altogether, had that been possible. A cartoon which told its own story without recourse to a punchline seemed to him the ultimate form of graphic humor. But cartoonists who could achieve pure pantomime and yet maintain humor of a complex or sophisticated nature were very rare. The closest Ross could come was a cartoonist named Otto Soglow who specialized in very simple line drawings without benefit of shading or complicating detail. One of his creations for *The New Yorker*, a mute ruler of a fantasy kingdom simply called *The Little King*, made the transition to the pages of the color Sunday funny papers as a popular character, but most of Soglow's work, while it seemed to delight Ross, was oddly naive and unsophisticated for the pages of the magazine, particularly when compared with the highly talented work that was emerging under Ross's tutelage.

One by one Ross discovered and brought into his fold of regular contributors some of America's finest cartooning talents. In the first year of publication Ross used a drawing submitted by a fashion illustrator named Helen Hokinson. It featured a plump woman hanging over a rail to wave bon voyage to a departing ship at the pier. She was the first of the soon to be famous Hokinson Girls, a collection of chubby, ample-bossomed, society women who carried out their responsibilities as clubwomen in a befuddled, vague, but amiable way. Although her cartoons constituted one of *The New Yorker*'s most popular features until her death in an air accident in 1949, and she had no more avid a set of followers than the actual matrons she satirized, her humor today would be considered antifeminist and demeaning.

One day a carelessly dressed but handsome

young man of aristocratic appearance dropped off at the office some drawings for consideration. The son of a prominent New York family, Curtis Arnoux Peters was then living the bohemian life of a musician in jazz age speakeasies until Ross signed him up under the name of Peter Arno. His early cartoons featured two tipsy slap-stick women called the Whoops Sisters, but he abandoned them despite their popularity for a more wordly-wise series featuring chorus girls, kept women, and businessmen in pursuit of hedonistic pleasures. His lecherous gentlemen and young women established a genre which such publications as *Esquire* and *Playboy* would later imitate with endless variation.

Also among these early contributors were George Price, distinguished by a clean but expressive line used to portray the eccentricities of mean-tempered old men and working-class couples (the only member of that original group who drew into his eighties with over 3,000 cartoons published); Gluyas Williams, who specialized in neatly outlined and stylized depictions of the life and times of the American businessman and suburbanite (well-known also for his splendid illustrations for the books and essays of Robert Benchley); Alan Dunn, who mastered the use of charcoal and grease pencil in his broad satires of urban living and was one of the most prolific of the *New Yorker* cartoonists (over 1,900 cartoons and 9 covers published between 1926 and 1974); Gardner Rea, whose strong sense of design and balance resulted in pleasing patterns; and last but not least James Thurber, a very special case.

Through his friendship with E. B. White, with whom he would collaborate on a book, *Is Sex Necessary?*, in 1929, Thurber was hired as a member of the editorial staff (even though his writings had been rejected 20 times before a submission was accepted). White and Thurber established, through their "Talk of the Town" columns, the *New Yorker* style of humorous comment, but Thurber also wanted to do cartoons. His drawing style was so naive and undisciplined, his ideas were so absurd and whimsical, and the end products so eccentric and individual, however, that Ross resisted using them. When he yielded, it was these very idiosyncracies that won over the readers, and Thurber's irresistible sketches of the seal in the bedroom, the battle between the sexes (including the seventeen-part series "The War Between Men and Women"), implausible dogs

"*It's broccoli, dear.*"
"*I say it's spinach, and I say the hell with it.*"

Carl Rose, cartoon, *The New Yorker*, 1928.
© *The New Yorker*.

and other creatures, and bewildered little men overcome by the complexities of existence—these became inextricably associated with the entire *New Yorker* school of humor. When critics complained to Ross that Thurber was a "fifth-rate" artist, Ross whimsically defended him by asserting that he was at least "third-rate."[8] The truth is that Thurber as a cartoonist was delightfully *sui generis* and without equal in American humor.

In addition to Al Frueh, Mary Petty, and Carl Rose, who were on the list of regular contributors at the start, the 1930s witnessed the addition of a number of brilliant wielders of pen and ink, including Charles Addams, Perry Barlow, Whitney Darrow, Jr., Robert Day, Richard Decker, Syd Hoff, C. E. Martin, Garrett Price, Barbara Shermund, William Steig, and Richard Taylor. In the 1940s, these would be joined by another talented generation, including Sam Cobean, Joseph Farris, Dana Fradon, Frank Modell, Mischa Richter, Saul Steinberg, and Barney Tobey.

Perhaps one of the things that accounted for the success of *The New Yorker* in its golden years from 1925 to Ross's death in 1951 was the fact that it had steady unbroken editorial leadership, and the same has largely been true in the cartoon department with Rea Irvin serving as art director from 1925 to 1939 and James Geraghty succeeding him until 1973. While Ross always made the final decision, he liked for the weeding out to be a group process, with selected members of the staff sitting in on the selection of finalists after an initial selection by the art director. Thus a group sensibility was brought to bear in achieving the *New Yorker* style of comic art.

Also, the cartoons themselves were often the products of a staff effort rather than the works of individual artists. Sometimes the artist was supplied with an idea for a cartoon, other times the caption would be changed after the cartoon was submitted, or even the cartoon alone might be purchased with the staff providing the punchline. One of the best known cartoons to appear in the magazine was the result of such collaborative effort in 1928. Carl Rose had submitted a cartoon featuring a young mother at the dinner table with her daughter, but no one found his caption, now forgotten, suitable. E. B. White saw the drawing and suggested a caption which would become famous: "It's broccoli, dear," says the mother, and the daughter replies, "I say it's spinach, and I say the hell with it." The shocking sophistication of the child is the incongruity at the heart of the comedy here, but so appropriate was the cartoon's depiction of a response to a common situation that "spinach" entered the language as a term of disparagement and the girl's retort came to signify "Don't confuse me with the facts when I want to indulge my prejudices."[9] Ironically, this sort of two-line caption was the very thing Ross was working away from in his insistence on the single-line caption.

Other *New Yorker* cartoons have made lasting contributions to the American language. In 1941 a cartoon by Peter Arno appeared which featured an aircraft designer with plans under his arm walking away from a plane crash to which the military, ground crew, and ambulance are racing (the pilot, fortunately, we see at a distance has bailed out with a parachute). The caption, "Well, back to the old drawing board," has become a standard response to a situation which has failed to develop as planned. A 1950 cartoon by Alex Graham, in which a flying saucer has landed in a field and its two extraterrestrial occupants are talking to a horse, has the punchline "Take me to your president." Slightly transposed to "Take me to your leader," this phrase was repeated to humorous effect in thousands of other cartoons, films, and visual media.

Three of what are probably the best known cartoons in the world appeared in *The New Yorker*, two of them by James Thurber from the early 1930s. In one, a seal is leaning over the headboard of a bed while the wife complains to the husband: "All right, have it your way—you heard a seal bark!" In the second, a fencer has

"*Well, back to the old drawing board.*"

Peter Arno, cartoon, *The New Yorker*, 1941.
© *The New Yorker*.

"*Touché!*"

James Thurber, cartoon, *The New Yorker*.
© 1945 James Thurber.
© 1973 Helen and Rosemary Thurber.

Charles Addams, cartoon, *The New Yorker*, 1940.
© *The New Yorker*.

neatly decapitated his opponent with the ex-
clamation "Touché!" The third by Charles
Addams, a specialist in macabre humor, is from
1940 and has no caption. It features a myste-
rious skier who has somehow maneuvered a tree
so that one ski track appears on each side. In all
three it is the inexplicable, the surprise, and the
mystery of the event which intrigue the reader.

Just as there is really no such thing as a *New
Yorker* short story, general belief to the contrary, there is no such thing as a *New Yorker*
cartoon. As British cartoonist William Hewison
facetiously put the argument, the *New Yorker*
artists "produced four drawings: a sugar daddy
and a dewey blonde; two hoboes sitting on a
park bench in Central Park; a drunk tête-à-tête
with a barman; a man and wife getting into a
car after a dinner party."[10] Such a summary
points up the problem of attempting to identify
a typical cartoon from the magazine. Each of
these scenes serves to remind us of individual
cartoonists, and the truth is that *The New
Yorker* has served primarily as a vehicle for

major comic talents to develop their individual
styles and distinctive visions.

If there is any single thread that connects the
thousands of cartoons to appear in *The New
Yorker*, it is the demands they place on the
reader. One must be well-read, in touch with
culture of the past and present, sensitive to the
eccentricities of human nature, and familiar
with the latest trends in society, politics, and
the mass media, to understand and appreciate
them. Along with other developments in film,
television, and the graphic arts, the *New Yorker*
cartoon has served to create a visually literate
society, but one which must also be literate in
traditional ways to respond to the sophisticated
humor of the subject or situation.

Under the editorial direction of William
Shawn, who succeeded Harold Ross in 1951, and
art director James Geraghty, *The New Yorker*
continued to seek out and use the work of each
decade's best cartoonists in the 1950s and 1960s.
Eldon Dedini, Lee Lorenz, Henry Martin,
Charles Saxon, and James Stevenson became

contributors in the 1950s, and in the 1960s were added George Booth, Mort Gerberg, William Hamilton, Bernard Handelsman, Edward Koren, Warren Miller, Ronald Searle, and Robert Weber. Lee Lorenz succeeded Geraghty as art director in 1973 and has added to this stellar list such artists as Sam Gross, Arnie Levin, Robert Mankoff, Lou Myers, Bill Woodman, and Jack Ziegler. Clearly there has been no letdown in effort to maintain the quality of the *New Yorker* tradition in comic art.

Some, however, feel that the first 25 years were the best and that now the magazine has settled into a comfortable routine that is all too predictable and only smugly humorous. William Hewison, one of the best commentators on the art of the cartoon, has put it this way:

> Ross's boys shook the old cartoon formula to pieces and kicked most of the bits away—where formerly it was static, congested and ponderously naturalistic they went after simplicity, directness and movement. They were after a humour that was essentially quick and visual. I would guess that every cartoon produced today—in Britain or Europe or anywhere else—is in direct descent from *The New Yorker* humorous drawings of that period.[11]

One would not argue with this conclusion, yet *The New Yorker* is the one publication to which readers still turn for America's best graphic comedy. The editors receive today over 2,500 submissions a week from which approximately 20 are selected for publication, and most of these come from the 40 to 50 artists on whose work they have first option. *The New Yorker* remains for cartoonists the most prestigious place to publish and for readers the most consistently entertaining source of that form of humor it has itself revitalized and transformed for the twentieth century—the cartoon.

1. Cited in Theodore Peterson, *Magazines in the Twentieth Century* (Urbana: Univ. of Illinois Press, 1964), p. 247.

2. Peterson, p. 244.

3. The first to point out the similarity were Walter Blair and Hamlin Hill in *America's Humor: From Poor Richard to Doonesbury* (New York: Oxford University Press, 1978), pp. 380-81, where the first covers of *The Chap-Book* and *The New Yorker* are reprinted opposite each other without additional comment.

4. Dale Kramer, *Ross and The New Yorker* (Garden City, N.Y.: Doubleday & Co., 1951), pp. 125-28.

5. This and the previously mentioned cartoon are found in *The Comedy of Life* (New York: Life Publishing Co., 1907), unpaged.

6. Cited in Peterson, p. 254.

7. Kramer, p. 130.

8. Maurice Horn, ed., *The World Encyclopedia of Cartoons* (New York: Chelsea House, 1981), p. 550.

9. William Safire, "Punch-Line English," *New York Times Magazine*, March 11, 1984, p. 28.

10. William Hewison, *The Cartoon Connection* (London: Elm Tree Books / Hamish Hamilton, 1977), pp. 111-12.

11. Hewison, p. 112. A useful selection of cartoons from the first 25 years, arranged in chronological units, is *The New Yorker Twenty-Fifth Anniversary Album, 1925-1950* (New York: Harper & Brothers, 1951). Less useful, since it lacks dates and chronological arrangement, is *The New Yorker Album of Drawings, 1925-1975* (New York: Viking Press, 1975).

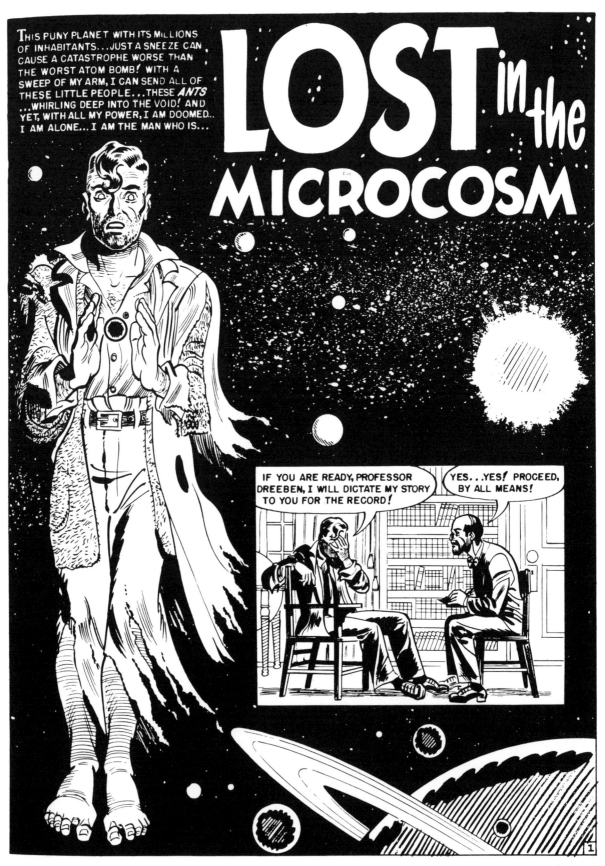

Harvey Kurtzman, "Lost in the Microcosm," *Weird Science*, May, 1950 (splash page).
© William M. Gaines.

10

The EC Comic Books and Science Fiction

Beginning in April of 1950 with the appearance of two new comic book titles, *Crypt of Terror* and *The Vault of Horror*, to be followed in May by *The Haunt of Fear, Weird Science*, and *Weird Fantasy*, the publishing firm of Educational Comics (later Entertaining Comics, or simply EC) began a five-year period of production which would see into print what many consider the supreme works of the Golden Age of comic books. Close on the heels of these five winning titles came even more stunning books, such as *Crime SuspenStories* in October, *Two-Fisted Tales* in November, *Frontline Combat* in July of 1951, *Shock SuspenStories* in February of 1952, and finally in October of 1952, an important event in the history of American humor, *Mad*.

The whole thing began when William Gaines inherited a faltering comic book business from his father, Max Gaines, a pioneer in the field and one of the creators of the comic book. A young artist and writer named Al Feldstein wandered into William Gaines' office one day shortly after he took over the firm and struck up a friendship which would develop into a creative collaboration of incredible productivity. After dreaming up some new concepts for comic book series and plot lines for stories within the series, and hiring some of the best comic book artists available (although that may have been as much happenstance as intent), Gaines and Feldstein oversaw the creation of a striking array of titles. Drawing on the popular culture of their time and place—motion pictures, radio, pulp fiction, detective novels, and science fiction—and giving the artists unprecedented freedom in their work with more editorial

encouragement than control, the talented staff proceeded to carry the comic book into new frontiers of artistic accomplishment. Among innovations the EC staff brought into comic book art were the use of highly literate and stylistically effective narrative captions, realistic dialogue which permitted characters to use blasphemy (though without obscenity or cursing), an engaging plot line which always concluded with an ironic twist or a surprise ending, and some of the most distinctive visual effects ever produced for the pages of comic books. Here was creativity of the first order, an inspired blending of the visual and literary media possible only when artists and writers are free to pursue their own standards of excellence.

What happened to this inspired community and how they fell prey to the hysteric censorship of the 1950s is a sorry chapter in American cultural history. Nineteen Fifty-four was a frantic year of Communist witch hunts and blacklists, of frenzied name-calling and paranoia. While the U.S. attempted to curb Communist expansion abroad, the nation entered a period of self-purgation as Congressional committees sought to ferret out Communist infiltration in the government, labor unions, and the motion picture industry. Senator Joseph McCarthy led the charge against alleged traitors in the State Department, while Senator Estes Kefauver investigated what some considered the worse form of subversion—the seduction of the innocent minds by the comic book industry. The spiritual leader of this crusade, the "Joe McCarthy" of the comic book

FOR MY WORLD IS THE WORLD OF SCIENCE-FICTION...
CONCEIVED IN MY MIND AND PLACED UPON PAPER WITH
PENCIL AND INK AND BRUSH AND SWEAT AND A GREAT
DEAL OF LOVE FOR MY WORLD. FOR I AM A SCIENCE-
FICTION ARTIST. MY NAME IS WOOD.

THE END

Wallace Wood, "My World," *Weird Science*, November-December, 1953 (detail). © William M. Gaines.

purge, was Dr. Fredric Wertham, psychiatrist and author of *Seduction of the Innocent* (1954), a single-minded and scientifically unsound piece of research linking juvenile delinquency with the practice of reading comic books. In an effort to survive, the industry created its own self-censoring board, the Comics Code Authority, with the most stringent set of prohibitions applied to any mass media. Under such restrictive guidelines, the EC line could not continue, so after a few efforts to move in a new direction (with such titles as *Impact, Valor, Aces High, Extra, M.D.,* and even *Psychoanalysis*), William Gaines left comic book publishing and converted the *Mad* comic book into this century's most influential humor magazine.

In the early years, circulation was never a problem for the horror and crime books published by EC, but the two science fiction titles were always in the red. Even so, William Gaines recalled in 1969, "EC was proudest of its science fiction comics. . . . It was just that the s-f comics were kind of special. . . . Al [Feldstein] and I enjoyed writing the s-f most. I guess we felt more intellectually stimulated, and we believed we were reaching an older and more intelligent group of readers with them."[1] Be-

cause they were special to the staff, both *Weird Science* and *Weird Fantasy* were permitted to operate at a financial loss. Both ran for 22 issues between May, 1950, and November, 1953. In order to decrease the deficit, they were then merged into one title, *Weird Science-Fantasy,* for a run of another seven issues to May, 1955. Because the Comics Code Authority prohibited the use of the word "weird" in a title, it was finally changed to *Incredible Science Fiction,* only to expire after four issues in January, 1956.

The principal editor and writer for the series of 55 issues (containing more than 200 individual stories) was Al Feldstein, who had a stiff and rigid cartooning style which relied on heavy outlines and frozen tableaus. The artists used more frequently were Wallace Wood, Joe Orlando, Al Williamson, and Jack Kamen. Wood had a predilection for handsomely built males and buxom females, both delineated with sharp attention to anatomical detail and against realistic backgrounds. His pages were nicely balanced and offered case studies in effective use of perspective and depth illusion. Al Williamson, Wood's nearest disciple, also relied upon perfect specimens of masculinity and femininity (although his men were often distractingly reminiscent of such actors as Farley Granger or Buster Crabbe) and upon realistic detail. But he had a more open and free-flowing style than Wood, a kind of lyric grace that partly derived from Alex Raymond's early work on *Flash Gordon*. Although Joe Orlando was influenced by Wood as well, his work was usually unmistakable because of its sense of humor, its reliance on caricature and exaggeration, and its satiric thrust. Orlando would later prove to be a supreme comic satirist in his work for *Panic* and the *Mad* magazine. When required, however, he could also turn out a sober piece of work. The least interesting of the group was Jack Kamen, whose wooden figures and poor use of perspective left much to be desired. But what a stellar group of artists otherwise! From time to time, other EC staff artists would contribute, especially Harvey Kurtzman, Bill Elder, Bernard Krigstein, Jack Davis, and even a young Frank Frazetta for one story and a cover and several collaborative efforts with Al Williamson.

The writing was done at a breakneck speed, according to Gaines. "We turned out our stories at a fantastic rate in those days," he has recalled. "Al Feldstein and I plotted, and Al wrote, four stories a week. The fifth day was for the letters page and odds and ends."[2] Working at such speed it is little wonder then that they often freely borrowed and adapted stories from a wide variety of sources, such as the science fiction pulp magazine *Amazing Stories*, or the works of such writers as Edgar Allan Poe, John Collier, Nelson Bond, Anthony Boucher, Fredric Brown, and others. In the very first story in the first issue of *Weird Science*, in fact, "Lost in the Microcosm," beautifully illustrated by Harvey Kurtzman, they probably borrowed from Henry Hasse's novelette, "He Who Shrank," first published in the August, 1936 issue of *Amazing Stories*. Hasse had been one of the early writers to use in his fiction the concept that our universe may be nothing more than a minute particle or atom within a larger universe, which in turn may be but an atom within another larger universe, and *ad infinitum*. A shrinking person then would move downward through each universe progressively, becoming first a giant and finally a small particle again in his journey towards the infinite center of all things, a process repeated over and over forever.

"Lost in the Microcosm" begins with a startling splash page by Kurtzman, itself a symbolic summation of the entire story, a man floating in space and warming himself by a small heat-generating planet. Thus the macrocosmic and the microcosmic existence of the hero, Karl, are suggested simultaneously. In the first panel, boxed within the splash page, Karl begins to tell his story to a listening professor (the EC books were given to using the first person narrative, a sophisticated technique for comic books at that time). Working as a biochemistry fellow with a Professor Einstadt, Karl assists in the discovery of a solution which will shrink and compress matter to an infinitely small size. Einstadt rushes out to announce his discovery leaving Karl to disconnect the equipment. In the classic laboratory fumble, Karl exposes himself to the solution accidentally and begins his journey into the interior of the physical universe. Traveling first through Professor Einstadt's body and sweat glands and fighting off a hungry white blood corpuscle, he floats among molecules and atoms. He discovers that each atom itself is actually a minute solar system composed of a star and surrounding planets, the heart of the theory in Henry Hasse's original novelette. Onward he travels through one planet and solar system after another finding life at all levels, sometimes primitive and sometimes civilized. In the final page, we find Karl seeking help on a planet he hopes is civilized technologically enough to stop his shrinking, but he discovers it to be too crude and backwards. That planet, we are told in the conclusion, is earth.

Like so many of the coming science fiction stories in the EC series, this first one accomplished several things. It exposed the reader to a brief lesson in the nature of the physical universe, it offered an unexplored possibility about the known universe, it caused the reader to reflect on the actual limitations of scientific inquiry on our planet, and it made a statement about the human condition—that is, no matter what his size, man is no more than a finite, helpless creature in the face of the infinite universe.

The first issue of *Weird Fantasy* also led off with an adaptation. "Am I Man or Machine?" illustrated by Al Feldstein, was presumably based on M. H. Hasta's "The Talking Brain" published in the August 1926 issue of *Amazing Stories*. The "Adam Link" stories written by Otto Binder for *Amazing Stories* in the 1940s, as well as other Binder pieces, also found their way into the pages of EC titles. Except for the

"Adam Link" series, these sources were never credited, with one notable exception when they were caught redhanded. The 13th issue of *Weird Fantasy* (May-June, 1952) included a Wally Wood story called "Home to Stay!" about a boy and his mother awaiting the return of the astronaut father. What Feldstein failed to note was that the story was based on two short stories called "Kaleidoscope" and "Rocket Man" from Ray Bradbury's book *The Illustrated Man* (1951). Several readers—among them, Bradbury himself—promptly wrote to point this out. But Bradbury, a longtime fan of the EC comic books as well as comic strip art in general, was pleased and made a happy settlement by granting permission for the adaptation of any of his works, as long as credit was given. Soon the covers of the EC titles were boasting the inclusion of authorized Bradbury adaptations, and over the next few years a total of 14 additional adaptations appeared in the science fiction books and another ten appeared in the horror and crime titles. Two selections from these stories were collected in 1965 and 1966 in two Ballantine paperback editions, *The Autumn People* and *Tomorrow Midnight*, now considered rare items among Bradbury collectors.

For impressionable young readers in the 1950s, these books were opening up new vistas of scientific knowledge and speculation about the universe and man's place in it (although the avid science fiction novel readers were already way ahead on these matters, of course). Specific experiences in reading these stories contributed to the readers' education and provided philosophic epiphanies of a sort, after which they probably never thought the same about a particular subject again. One example was "He Walked Among Us," a story startling in its theme and controversial in its treatment of sensitive material—the roots of religion. It was illustrated by Wally Wood, and published in *Weird Science* for May-June, 1952. Nine years later, Robert Heinlein would use a similar concept in his classic novel *Stranger in a Strange Land* (1961).

The hero of the story, Jerome Kraft, is landed on an unexplored planet in a solar system located at the edge of the galaxy. The year is 2963 and the Galactic Exploration Authority on the planet Earth has sent Kraft to classify the animal life and vegetation and report on the mineral deposits. As Kraft explores the planet, he discovers an alien settlement inhabited by humanoids in a stage of civilization roughly equivalent to that of earth three thousand years earlier. He moves into the settlement and encounters a series of local problems to which he can apply the advanced technology he has brought with him. He cures a feverish child with a hypodermic shot of anti-bacillum. He feeds the poor and starving by dropping dehydrated food pills into bowls of water, thus turning water into milk, soup, bread, and meat. He is acclaimed a savior and deliverer by the enslaved and dispossessed, and his explanation of having come from another and better world only enhances his prestige. When the High Priest orders him to cease because of the threat to his authority, Kraft refuses and is executed. Another two thousand years pass before another mission arrives from Earth (Kraft's mother ship had been destroyed on its journey home). What the visitors find is a more advanced society in which a stretch-rack is a primary symbol on buildings and jewelry. They find that it is a religious symbol, the aliens call themselves Kraftians, and they worship a wise man who once performed many miracles but was put to death by torture on the stretch-rack by the authorities because of his challenge to their dictatorial power.

In certain ways, this is merely a retelling of the Christ story in science fiction terms (with a nod to Mark Twain's *A Connecticut Yankee in King Arthur's Court*), but it also suggests the intriguing possibility that perhaps Christ could be explained best as a visitor from another planet, whose miracles were simple applications of his advanced technology. This is a premise used most recently in the John Carpenter and Steven Spielberg film *Starman*. (Both are admirers of comic book art.)

"The Reformers," written by Al Feldstein, drawn by Joe Orlando, and published in *Weird Science* No. 21 (July-August 1953), is a typical EC story in its use of fantasy to deal with a matter of philosophical and theological import and its surprise ending that totally reverses what the reader's expectations have been throughout the story (even though the careful reader was given clues to suggest the outcome). It is also an incisive satire of many of the elements in society who were out to censor and control the content of comic books and other mass media at the time.

Three self-styled "reformers" arrive in a space ship at an unidentified planet, after having visited earth, and begin a program to improve the inhabitants by rooting out laxity,

IT TOOK JERRY SEVERAL DAYS TO ANALYZE THE GUTTERAL TONGUE...DURING WHICH TIME HE MOVED ABOUT AMONG THEM, STUDYING THEIR HABITS... THEIR LIVING-CONDITIONS...

THIS SOCIETY SEEMS DIVIDED UP INTO TWO *CASTES!* THE MEMBERS OF THE LOWER CASTE ARE *POOR* AND *UNDER-NOURISHED!* THAT OLD ONE OVER THERE LOOKS LIKE HE'S *STARVING* TO DEATH!

KRAFT APPROACHED THE AGED ALIEN AND SPOKE TO HIM IN THE ALIEN TONGUE HE'D MASTERED...

I HAVE NOT EATEN IN THREE DAYS, STRANGER!

FILL YOUR BOWL WITH WATER FROM THE FOUNTAIN THERE AND BRING IT BACK TO ME, OLD ONE!

THE RAGGED OLD BEGGAR STAGGERED TO THE PUBLIC FOUNTAIN AND FILLED HIS BOWL WITH WATER! MEANWHILE, KRAFT TOOK OUT A MILK-ANHYDRATE PILL FROM BENEATH HIS ROBE! WHEN THE OLD ONE RETURNED, JERRY PASSED HIS HAND OVER THE BOWL... DROPPING IN THE PILL...

THERE! DRINK THAT!

IT... IT'S A *MIRACLE!* MILK! YOU TURNED THE *WATER* TO MILK!

OTHER ALIENS GATHERED AROUND KRAFT, WIDE-EYED IN AMAZEMENT! MANY OF THEM WERE HUNGRY AND SICK! JERRY FELT SORRY FOR THEM! AGAIN AND AGAIN HE DROPPED INTO THEIR OUTSTRETCHED BOWLS OF WATER VARIOUS DEHYDRATED FOOD-PILLS...

THE STRANGER'S TURNED *MY* WATER TO *SOUP!*

...*BREAD!*

...*MEAT!*

HE IS THE ONE WHO *CURED MY SICK CHILD!*

Wallace Wood, "He Walked Among Us," *Weird Science*, May-June, 1952 (detail).
© William M. Gaines.

self-indulgence, promiscuity, and crime, "which must exist wherever there is an unequal distribution of basic needs." They are greeted by an official welcomer named Peter who conducts them on a tour, and to their total surprise, none of the evils they seek to reform can be found there, even though alcoholic beverages are consumed, women dress scantily, and people are allowed to read books and magazines about murder, crime, and mystery—including fantasy and horror comic books of the EC variety (two of the reformers are seen reading issues of *Vault of Horror* and *Weird Fantasy*).

The reformers are totally perplexed. Everywhere else they have traveled in the universe, they could always blame social problems like alcoholism and crime on the presence of alcohol and crime literature. "We could preach against them," says one, "because we could blame them for society's ills." But now, "How can we preach against evils that do not produce evils?" They decide that they must set about producing criminal behavior so that it can be blamed on causative factors, but when they check in with headquarters for approval of their plan, they make a horrifying discovery. The chief comes on the television screen to announce, "There's no use trying to advocate reform where you are now, you fools! That place just can't be tormented! I've checked your location! That's . . .

The REFORMERS

THE SHIP CAME DOWN FROM THE SPACE-VACUUM BELCHING FLAME AND SMOKE AND KICKING UP GREAT CLOUDS OF DUST THAT SWIRLED GOLDEN IN THE PLANET'S WARM SUNLIGHT. WITHIN THE SPOTLESS HULL, THE REFORMERS CROWDED TO THEIR SHIP'S PORT AND PEERED OUT...THROUGH THE SETTLING ROCKET EXHAUST... OUT OVER GREEN FORESTS AND GOLDEN FIELDS CUT THROUGH BY SILVER RIVER-RIBBONS. THE REFORMERS STOOD AT THEIR SHIP'S PORT WITH TIGHT GRIM LIPS AND COLD EYES AND LINES OF SOBER DISAPPROVAL ETCHED IN THEIR HUMORLESS FACES. THEY LOOKED AT EACH OTHER AND OUT ACROSS THE PLANET'S TERRAIN AND THEY SHOOK THEIR HEADS...

JUST LIKE THE *OTHER* PLANETS WE'VE BEEN TO. JUST LIKE THE *LAST ONE* AND THE ONE *BEFORE* THAT... THE ONE CALLED *EARTH*.

AND PROBABLY *JUST AS EVIL...* JUST AS *SELF-INDULGING.* WELL. *REPORT IN* THAT WE'VE *LANDED,* GIVE THE PLANET'S *POSITION,* AND THEN WE CAN *DISEMBARK* AND BEGIN OUR *WORK!*

A SWITCH CLICKED ON. SOMEWHERE, WITHIN THE CONTROL PANELS, TUBES HEATED AND TRANSFORMERS HUMMED. THE PHONO-VISOR SCREEN LIT UP AND FOCUSED AND A FACE APPEARED...

THIS IS *HEADQUARTERS.* CLERK 195. READY. GO AHEAD...

THIS IS *TEAM 7 REPORTING.* HAVE *LANDED* AND WILL PROCEED WITH *USUAL PROGRAM.* LOCATION OF LATEST OBJECTIVE: MAP 5392, 3RD QUADRANT, AZIMUTH 12°. WILL REPORT ON PROGRESS LATER. SIGNING OFF...7.

THE PHONO-VISOR SCREEN DIMMED. THE TUBES COOLED. THE REFORMERS CLIMBED FROM THEIR SHIP. OFF IN THE DISTANCE, A STRANGE-LOOKING VEHICLE APPEARED ON THE HORIZON, SWEEPING TOWARD THEM...

LOOK. AN INHABITANT OF THE PLANET APPROACHES IN A *VEHICLE.*

A SIGN OF *PHYSICAL LAXITY...* TRANSPORTATION.

YES. THERE WILL BE MUCH *WORK* FOR US *HERE.*

Above and the five following pages: Joe Orlando, "The Reformers," *Weird Science*, July-August, 1953. © Willliam M. Gaines.

THE REFORMERS CLIMBED INTO THEIR SHIP AS THE BEETLE-CAR SPED OFF. THEY SAT DOWN IN THEIR SHOCK-COUCHES AND THEY LOOKED AT EACH OTHER IN DISBELIEF...

HOW CAN IT BE *TRUE*? HOW CAN THEY *DRINK* AND *NOT* BE *DRUNKARDS*?

HOW CAN THEY HAVE *CRIME LITERATURE* AND *NOT* HAVE *CRIME*?

HOW CAN WE *PREACH AGAINST EVILS* THAT *DO NOT PRODUCE EVILS*?

WHEREVER WE'VE GONE, WE'VE *FOUND* THESE THINGS. WE COULD PREACH *AGAINST* THEM BECAUSE WE COULD *BLAME* THEM FOR THE SOCIETY'S *ILLS*.

BUT HERE, THE SOCIETY IS *PERFECT*. THERE *ARE NO ILLS*. WE CANNOT MAKE *SCAPEGOATS* OF THEM!

WHAT CAN WE *REPORT BACK*? *HOW* CAN WE *REFORM* WHEN THERE IS *NOTHING* TO *REFORM*?

PERHAPS *HEAD-QUARTERS* WILL TELL US WHAT TO DO! THIS IS A *NEW EXPERIENCE* FOR US.

WAIT! I *KNOW* WHAT TO DO! OF *COURSE!* IT'S SO *SIMPLE!*

TELL US! *WHAT* CAN WE DO?

BEAR WITH ME A MOMENT. UP TO *NOW*, WE HAVE VISITED *MANY CIVILIZATIONS* THROUGHOUT THE UNIVERSE...

WE *FOUND*, IN EACH SOCIETY THAT WE VISITED, A *GREAT MANY EVILS*: *CRIME, GAMBLING, DRUNKENNESS, SEXUAL PROMISCUITY*. AND IN *EACH SOCIETY*, WE *ALSO* FOUND CERTAIN *INDULGENCES* THAT WE COULD *BLAME* FOR THESE *END-PRODUCTS*...

WE COULD BLAME *CRIME LITERATURE* OF ALL KINDS FOR THE *RESULTANT CRIME*. WE COULD PREACH *AGAINST* THESE BOOKS AND STORIES AND MAGAZINES, CLAIMING THEY *CAUSED* THE CRIME, CLAIMING THEIR *ABOLISHMENT* WOULD *END* CRIME.

AND THE SAME WITH GAMBLING... *DRINKING!* WE PREACHED FOR THE *OUTLAWING* OF *ALCOHOL*... CLAIMING IT WOULD *END DRUNKENNESS*.

WE WERE ABLE TO ADVOCATE *SEXUAL TABOOS* AS THE ANSWER TO *SEXUAL LAXITIES*. EVERYWHERE, WE FOUND *SCAPEGOATS* TO BLAME FOR THE *SOCIETY'S EVILS*.

BUT HERE, THERE *ARE NO EVIL END-RESULTS* TO THESE *VERY SAME SELF-INDULGENCES*. HOW CAN WE *USE THEM* AS *SCAPEGOATS*?

⑤

SIMPLE! BY *PRODUCING THESE EVIL END-PRODUCTS* OURSELVES!

PRODUCING THEM? YOU MEAN *CAUSING* THEM TO HAPPEN?

EXACTLY! IF THERE *IS NO CRIME,* WE'LL *CREATE* A FEW CRIMES. LET THEM FIND A FEW *MURDERS,* A FEW *ROBBERIES,* AND YOU'LL SEE HOW QUICKLY THEY LOOK FOR A *SCAPEGOAT!*

YES, YES. IF THEY *FOUND* A FEW *DRUNKARDS...*

... IF THEY *DISCOVERED* THE PRESENCE OF *PROMISCUITY...*

OF COURSE, *OF COURSE! THAT'S* WHAT WE'LL *DO!* WE'LL *CREATE THE EVILS...* AND *THEN* PREACH FOR THE *REFORMS* WE *WANT!*

THE REFORMERS GRINNED EVIL GRINS AND SLAPPED EACH OTHER ON THEIR BACKS AND DANCED ABOUT THE SHIP, EAGER AND HAPPY WITH THEIR PLAN...

A SWITCH CLICKED ON. WITHIN THE CONTROL PANELS, TUBES HEATED AND TRANSFORMERS HUMMED AND THE PHONO-VISOR SCREEN LIT UP. A FACE APPEARED...

HURRY! REPORT IN! TELL HEADQUARTERS THE *SITUATION HERE...*

...AND *THEN* TELL THEM *OUR SOLUTION!*

THIS IS *HEADQUARTERS.* CLERK 195. READY. GO AHEAD.

THIS IS *TEAM 7* REPORTING. NOW, *HERE'S* WHAT WE'VE *FOUND...*

ON THE PHONO-VISOR SCREEN, THE CLERK'S FACE PALED...

THE FACE OF THE CLERK DISSOLVED AND ANOTHER FACE APPEARED ON THE SCREEN... A DARK FACE...

OH... *TEAM 7!* WE'VE BEEN *TRYING* TO GET IN *TOUCH* WITH YOU! *STAND BY!* THE CHIEF WANTS TO *SPEAK* TO YOU.

THE *CHIEF?!* LUCIFER *HIMSELF?*

THERE'S *NO USE* TRYING TO ADVOCATE *REFORMS* WHERE YOU ARE *NOW,* YOU *FOOLS! THAT* PLACE JUST *CAN'T BE TORMENTED!* I'VE CHECKED YOUR *LOCATION! THAT'S...* *HEAVEN...*

CHOKE...

Heaven . . . . " The chief, of course, is Satan.

In addition to achieving a clever surprise ending, the story is also a satiric defense of the kinds of books EC was publishing, and a caricature of the social reformer. It supports the belief that criminal behavior is the result of complex social and economic problems and not a result of reading imaginative literature. "After all," St. Peter says, "one cannot learn what is right without also learning what is wrong!" Feldstein is in agreement with Nathaniel Hawthorne, who believed that a virtue untested on the battlefield of error and temptation is no virtue. Morality exists only when the individual successfully withstands the temptations of life and experience.

The story also supports Hawthorne's belief that reformers, whatever their cause, are more likely to be doing the devil's work than God's. In a prophetic fantasy Hawthorne wrote in 1844, "Earth's Holocaust," he depicted a time when all of the earth's reformers are gathered together before a huge bonfire into which they are throwing all of those things thought to cause evil—royal and noble pedigrees, wealth, liquor and wine, tobacco, weapons of war and destruction, fashions, and finally all books and literature, including "yesterdays newspapers, last month's magazines . . . . " Just as they have decided to throw the Bible into the blazing conflagration, and several people have decided to hang themselves since there is nothing left for them to oppose, a Satanic figure appears to remind them of the foolishness of their efforts: "There's one thing that these wiseacres have forgotten to throw into the fire," and that is "the human heart itself." And, "unless they hit upon some method of purifying that foul cavern, forth from it will reissue all the shapes of wrong and misery—the same old shapes or worse ones—which they have taken such a vast deal of trouble to consume to ashes. I have stood by this livelong night and laughed in my sleeve at the whole business."[3] This is a sentiment in accord with "The Reformers" and many of the classic EC stories.

Such stories and many others were heady stuff for the intelligent young readers of comic books in the 1950s. There was plenty of escapism available in the *Superman* and *Captain Marvel* comic books, while the EC line was devoted to the serious treatment of social problems and the human condition. The stories were well written and memorably drawn, and they provided food for thought. The science fiction titles were particularly impressive for their combination of entertainment and ideas, and they made a contribution to understanding seldom matched by the other mass media of the 1950s. Despite Dr. Wertham's concerns that they would make us social deviants, they actually helped make us better human beings.

1. Interview by John Benson, *Squa Tront*, No. 3 (1969), 50.
2. Benson, p. 50.
3. Nathaniel Hawthorne, *Selected Tales and Sketches*, (New York: Holt, Rinehart and Winston, 1950), pp. 371-72.

Opposite page: Advertisement, *Weird Science*, September - October, 1952, inside front cover. © William M. Gaines.

E.C. FANS!
WE ARE PROUDEST OF OUR SCIENCE-FICTION MAGAZINES! LOOK FOR
AN ENTERTAINING EC COMIC
NO. 14 JULY-AUG.
WEIRD FANTASY
SCIENCE
10¢
INCREDIBLE SCIENCE-FICTION STORIES!
ON SALE NOW
AT ALL NEWSSTANDS!

Cover, *Action Comics*, June, 1938.
© DC Comics Inc.

11

American Industrial Culture and the Comic Book

Coming into existence as it did in 1933, at the end of the era of industrialization in America, the comic book was an original and powerfully attractive culmination of several mainstreams of national culture and technology. Without the successful demonstration of the popularity of illustrations for narratives and novels in the nineteenth century, publishers might not have been willing to invest in further ways to tell stories through pictures. Without the invention of the color press and its application to the comic strip in newspapers, the idea of reprinting the Sunday funnies in periodical form, which led to the publication of the first comic book, might not have occurred. Without the intense interest of Americans in folk tales and mythology of the heroic variety, the concept of the superhero might not have occurred to the two young Cleveland students who created Superman, the character that made the comic book a financial success and established the pattern for its major preoccupation. Finally, without the rapidly expanding influence of motion pictures, the telling of stories primarily through visual means might not have seized the interest of young readers the way the comic book did. In other words, the comic book brought together into one appealing form of visual literature many of the folk traditions and technological changes of late nineteenth and early twentieth-century America. It would prove to be from 1940 onwards one of our best known and internationally influential forms of popular culture, and it would also

instruct several generations of beginning readers in the themes of Western literature.

Since nearly all art is illustrative, one could argue that illustration is as old as art and even preceded literature. To the educated medieval mind, there was little distinction between picture and word in that the manuscripts of the time were invariably illuminated, often in outlandish and fantastic ways, although there was no premium placed on originality lest it verge towards heresy (a point made very well in Umberto Eco's novel *The Name of the Rose*, itself a wonderful paradigm of modern popular culture despite its medieval setting). It was the technological development of the printing press and movable type that brought about an end to the natural alliance of picture and word and established the book as a literary form in which the importance of text preceded that of illustration. At that moment, because they were impractical, illustrations became mere decorations, and they were not to become fully wedded again with the printed word until the development of comic art.

In looking to the history of book illustrations as a source of the comic book, we must remind ourselves that drawing and writing followed parallel paths of development and have a common origin—that is, the need to communicate. It was a master artist and creative genius who made the best argument for the need to use both pictures and words in communicating ideas

Jost Ammam, *The Printer*, woodblock, 1568.

H. K. Browne, "The Dombey Family," from Charles Dickens, *Dombey and Son* (1848).

most fully. This was Leonardo da Vinci who said, "And you who wish to represent by words the form of man and all the aspects of his membrification, relinquish that idea. For the more minutely you describe the more you will confine the mind of the reader, and the more you will keep him from the knowledge of the thing described. And so it is necessary to draw *and* to describe."[1] Only a few artists/authors would know this, as simple a truth it may be, such as William Blake or Edward Lear, both of whom practiced a fully integrated form of expression in which both picture and word are essentially related.

The move towards a more fully developed relationship between the text and illustration came about in England in the nineteenth century with the appearance of serialized fiction published in monthly parts. More precisely, this was April, 1836, when the first of twenty installments of Charles Dickens' *Pickwick Papers* appeared in the bookstalls. From the start, in the serial novels, illustrations were considered an important adjunct to the text. Dickens had available to him in London any number of talented practicing comic artists, such as George Cruikshank, John Leech, and George

Cattermole, all of whom he used, but especially a creative soulmate Hablot K. Browne, better known as "Phiz," who proved a perfect match for the Hogarthian humor and grotesque comedy of Dickens' fiction.

In his study of *Victorian Novelists and Their Illustrators*, J. R. Harvey has outlined the close collaboration of Dickens and Browne:

> The actual working conditions of author and artist involved constant contact, the artist drawing while the author was still writing. The artist might even prepare his illustration first, and the author simply write up his text from it, transposing into the novel a whole scene that the artist had imagined on his own initiative. . . . Between them, they developed a visual art of great communicative power, a live part of the novel with important functions entrusted to it by the novelist.[2]

Recent critics have argued that Browne's etchings must be considered an integral part of Dickens' novels and "have the status of contemporary critical commentary of an especially pertinent kind, since they were created while the novel was in progress and the illustrator in repeated communication with the author."[3]

The nearest parallel to this situation in the United States was the relationship between

Mark Twain and his illustrators, except the causative factor was not the serial novel but rather the method of selling books by subscription. Twain was already part of a comic periodical tradition that called for humorous drawings to accompany the popular sketches and tales that emerged from life on the frontier. He had discovered early too that the most effective way to make a profit from his books was to have them sold by subscription agents who roamed America's byways and backwoods with order blanks and a dummy copy of the forthcoming book in hand. Thus the publisher was assured of a profit before the book hit the presses. What the public seemed to demand, however, was a sizeable book, 500 to 600 pages minimum, in a gilt-embellished binding, *and* heavily illustrated—a volume that would handsomely grace a parlor table but also serve as a door-stop in an emergency. It would be condescending to assume that the purchasers wanted books merely to leaf through and to look at the pictures rather than read. The peddlers were simply bringing books to those who had no access to bookstores and were not catering to a special audience. The buyer simply wanted the best possible return on his hard-earned money.

One obvious way to increase the size of a book was to fill it with illustrations, which Twain learned was easier said than done. It was relatively easy to fill it with just any illustrations but more difficult to make sure that they complemented rather than detracted from the text. Beginning with *The Innocents Abroad* issued in 1869, Twain became more involved with the process of commissioning and approving the illustration of his works since all of them were composed and produced with a direct eye on their sale and marketability. Occasionally Twain's intentions misfired, as in the case of *Adventures of Tom Sawyer*. While artist True Williams had proved competent on earlier Twain projects, when he was sober, he was a disaster on capturing the spirit of what would be Twain's first classic novel. The designs were inferior, the scenes dark and lacking in lively activity, Tom portrayed as too fastidious, Huck Finn inconsistently and drearily pictured, many events and characters misinterpreted, and the craftsmanship in general shoddy. The sales were disappointing, the book was poorly promoted, and the reviews were not very encouraging.

Thus when Twain was ready to publish *Adventures of Huckleberry Finn* in 1885, he began his own publishing firm and determined

True Williams, "Huckleberry Finn," from Mark Twain, *Adventures of Tom Sawyer* (1876).

to be particularly selective and demanding about the illustration of this one. Thus he looked to one of the most popular humor magazines of the time, *Life*, where he spotted the work of a young cartoonist, a two-page spread on "Some Uses For Electricity" in the issue of 13 March 1884. The artist was Edward Windsor Kemble, only 23 years of age but already much in demand for his comic penmanship and editorial cartoons. While Twain gave him free rein in the interpretation of the manuscript, he also reviewed and commented on the drawings, requiring corrections and deletions where he thought necessary. At first, Twain was only moderately pleased, noting of the first drawing of Huck, "All right & good, & will answer; although the boy's mouth is a trifle more Irishy than necessary." As the working relationship improved and developed, however, soon Twain was commenting that the drawings were "rattling good" and "They please me exceedingly."[4]

So successful was this collaboration that the illustrations have come to be considered a necessary part of the text. Thus, when the Mark Twain Project issued its centennial edition of *Huckleberry Finn* in the Mark Twain Library series in 1985, all the Kemble drawings were

E. W. Kemble, "Some Uses for Electricity," *Life*, March 13, 1884.

E. W. Kemble, "Huckleberry Finn," from Mark Twain, *Adventures of Huckleberry Finn* (1884).

retained and reproduced from the original art. It is through Kemble that our image of Huck has been formed, and necessarily so, since the novel is a first-person narrative which does not allow for the protagonist to describe himself. Twain retained Kemble for later books, such as *Pudd'nhead Wilson* and *The Library of Humor*, but Kemble went on to continue his work as a popular cartoonist by contributing Sunday comic strips and panels to the Hearst newspapers and other periodicals. At this point in American cultural history, two brilliant talents—one in literature and the other in comic art—touched hands and demonstrated the value of stories told by picture *and* word.

Mark Twain continued to believe in the power of pictorial narrative in his later books, and on one occasion even allowed the pictures to move beyond the text itself. He had selected Daniel Carter Beard, another popular cartoonist from the comic periodicals of the day, to illustrate his satire of medieval chivalry and Arthurian romance, *A Connecticut Yankee in King Arthur's Court*, published in 1889. Beard was so inspired by the material that he started incorporating living personalities in the pictures, among them actress Sarah Bernhardt, poet Alfred Lord Tennyson, robber baron Jay Gould, King Edward, the Prince of Wales, and the Emperor of Germany. The point was to link the novel's satire with the immediate scene, and Twain was

"GO 'LONG," I SAID, "YOU AIN'T MORE THAN A PARAGRAPH."

Daniel Carter Beard, illustration from Mark Twain,
A Connecticut Yankee in King Arthur's Court (1889).
Actress Sarah Bernhardt served as a model for the
page Clarence.

Daniel Carter Beard, illustration from Mark Twain,
A Connecticut Yankee in King Arthur's Court (1884).
The Slave Driver's face was made to resemble the
Robber Baron Jay Gould.

so pleased with the drawings that he allowed
Beard to include political cartoons about things
not mentioned or only indirectly related to the
text. Thus in this case the drawings take on an
independent life and extend rather than simply
illustrate the narrative's meaning. Without the
pictures, truly a part of the book received by its
contemporary readers is lost. Mark Twain confessed that Beard had "illustrated the book
throughout without requiring or needing anybody's suggestions; & to my mind the
illustrations are better than the book—which is
a good deal for me to say, I reckon."[5]

The point here is not merely that one of
America's major writers drew on the talents of
the best cartoonists of his day to illustrate his
books, but that Twain understood the commercial appeal and power of the word in
combination with the picture, and not simply as
decoration but as an integral, inseparable part
of the text. That other authors and publishers
realized the same thing is indicated by the
number of other books whose success was
partly or largely supported by the judicious
choice of an illustrator—as in the case of A. B.
Frost's lively animal drawings for Joel Chandler

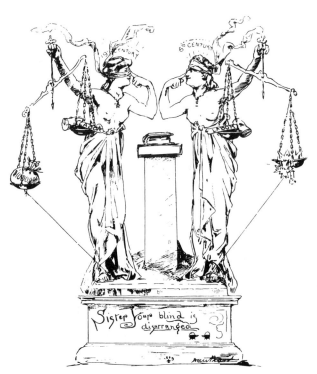

Daniel Carter Beard, illustration from Mark Twain,
A Connecticut Yankee in King Arthur's Court (1889).
A typical Beard political cartoon that extended the
meaning of Twain's text.

A. B. Frost, illustration from Joel Chandler Harris, *Nights with Uncle Remus* (1883).

W. W. Denslow, illustration from Frank L. Baum,
The Wonderful Wizard of Oz (1906).

Harris's *Uncle Remus* in 1892, W. W. Denslow's inspired renditions of Frank L. Baum's fantasy world of *The Wonderful Wizard of Oz* in 1906, or N. C. Wyeth's definitive portrait of Long John Silver in Robert Louis Stevenson's *Treasure Island* in 1911. Special mention should be made of Howard Pyle, who in 1883 both wrote and illustrated his *Merry Adventures of Robin Hood,* one of the first books to be designed and written by an American artist as an integrated whole, the kind of dual creative challenge that would face many comic book artists before the tasks of writing and drawing were separated. In discussing such artists and works, we are, of course, in the very middle of the golden age of American book illustration in the decades around the turn of the century. No wonder the books of Twain and his fellow authors were so attractive to thousands of readers.

Not only did these artists open up a market for further developments in the art of the pictorial narrative, which would eventually lead to the comic book, but they would collectively serve as a major source of inspiration to several generations of comic book artists. Many a pirate by Wyeth or a member of the merry band of Sherwood Forest by Pyle would reappear, with very slight modification or entirely swiped, on the pages of the adventure comic books. Many an artist would begin his career by first attempting to imitate the clean but fancifully fluid pen and ink style of W. W. Denslow in his Oz drawings, perhaps Walt Kelly being his best known disciple in his early comic book work before *Pogo*. (Following his success with the Oz book, Denslow drew several Sunday comic page features for the McClure syndicate, including one about the Scarecrow and the Tinman.)

If illustrations boosted the sale of books during the nineteenth century, it is likewise true that they proved to do the same thing for newspapers, perhaps the most influential product of the technological revolution in printing during the industrialization of America. It early became evident that breaking up the solid columns of black type on white paper in newspaper columns with illustrations made them more readable. The first daily paper to use political cartoons on a regular basis was James Gordon Bennett's New York *Evening Telegram* in 1867, but their popularity had been established earlier during the Civil War by Thomas Nast's bold

and effective cartoons for *Harper's Weekly*. Also, another weekly, *Frank Leslie's Illustrated Newspaper*, had created a sensation with its battlefield sketches of the Civil War and drawings of murders and disasters—often within two weeks of their occurrence, a record for the time. Working for the weeklies and the humor periodicals was the proving ground for many book illustrators and cartoonists who would come to prominence later in the century.

When Joseph Pulitzer bought the New York *World* in 1882, he doubled the circulation within four months, not only by adopting an aggressive editorial policy but by becoming a leader in newspaper illustration with cartoons, portraits, fire scenes, and diagrams of murders and crimes. In the Sunday editions, the use of pictures became outlandish with spectacular full-page spreads. The competitors soon charged the *World* with appealing to readers' infantile interests and with resorting to purely sensational journalism in the frequent use of illustrations, but one by one, with the New York *Herald* taking the lead in 1889, they too added news pictures and cartoons to their columns. A prejudice, however, would always linger that including illustrations with printed matter was somehow a concession to illiteracy, a

A Hoe color press used to print Sunday newspaper supplements.

bias that would particularly become attached to comic strips and comic books. If the readers had the pictures to look at, they wouldn't bother to read the text—at least, this was the fear. Also, contrary to popular belief, the comics did not thrive because of the immigrant readers who knew little English. A good command of the language was necessary to get the point of much comic strip humor—especially things like the street urchin dialect of *The Yellow Kid* or the mock-German dialect of *The Katzenjammer Kids.*

Another element that would make the controversy over illustrations a bit more "colorful" was the development of the color press for newspapers. As Frank Luther Mott determined in his history of American newspapers:

> Colored inserts were sometimes put into Sunday papers before the nineties, but the first regular color printing on a rotary newspaper press in America was done by the Chicago *Inter Ocean* for its Sunday supplement in 1892. The next year the New York *Recorder* installed a Hoe color press; the *World* followed soon, and the *Herald* in 1894. Sunday color supplements generally, however, did not go beyond four pages . . . until the New York *Journal* burst into many-hued splendor in 1896; after that color spread rapidly among the larger Sunday papers.[6]

William Randolph Hearst had acquired the New York *Journal* in 1895 and set about undermining Pulitzer's *World* by hiring the best talent in American journalism, regardless of cost. If the *World* had appeared outlandish in its use of illustrations and color in its Sunday supplements, Hearst would do them one better. In answer to the four pages of color in the *World* Sunday edition, Hearst issued on October 4, 1896, an eight-page comic supplement entirely in color which he proclaimed to be "eight pages of iridescent polychromous effulgence that makes the rainbow look like a lead pipe."[7]

Among the talented artists Hearst stole from Pulitzer for his supplement was Richard F. Outcault who had been drawing since 1894 for the *World* a series of panels called *Hogan's Alley* depicting the circus-like activities of tenement-house children in the back street slums of New York City. When the color-press man on May 5, 1895, added color to one of the panels called "At the Circus in Hogan's Alley," he selected a big-eared Oriental–looking urchin dressed in a dirty nightshirt and colored the shift blue. As the popularity of the feature increased, in order to make the urchin more

Wilhelm Busch, *Max und Moritz* (1865).

prominent, on January 5, 1896, the color-man gave him a bright yellow nightshirt. The character was an instant success, and soon everyone was talking about the "yellow kid." When Outcault moved to Hearst's *Journal* in 1896, he continued to draw adventures of the character under the title *The Yellow Kid* and soon changed the format into a sequence of panels with dialogue in balloons and thus in effect created the first comic strip as we know it today.

Outcault gave up the feature after a couple of years with Hearst to follow other interests, but the format he had originated was more fully developed by a young German immigrant named Rudolph Dirks, also hired by Hearst. In an attempt to create another "kid" oriented feature

Rudolph Dirks, self-portrait.

Cover, *Famous Funnies*, May, 1934.

that would duplicate the success of *The Yellow Kid*, which had inspired a profitable merchandising operation in toys, games, puzzles, magazines, and advertising, the comics editor Rudolph Block suggested that Dirks read *Max und Moritz*, a very popular children's book in verse about two devilishly mischievous boys by German poet and cartoonist Wilhelm Busch. Dirks was inspired to create *The Katzenjammer Kids*, one of the most successful features in comic strip history. Dirks established the practice, important in the development of the comic strip, of maintaining a set of central figures who on a consistent basis would appear in a set of adventures suitable to their characters. The reader, in other words, always knew what to expect when turning to the feature each Sunday—a successful formula for amusement. Dirks would never be known for innovation in his work, but he knew how to ply the formula time after time to the endless widespread approval of many readers. It should be noted that it was an illustrated book which directly influenced the creation of a comic strip which would remain in print for almost ninety years under the hands of several artists in both newspaper and comic book publications.

Almost from the start, the newspapers issued as promotional items reprint collections in cardboard covers of the most popular comic strips. The first of these was a collection of Outcault's

The Yellow Kid published in March of 1897, and it was followed by similar facsimile volumes devoted to *The Katzenjammer Kids, Buster Brown, Foxy Grandpa,* and *Mutt and Jeff.* These are precursors rather than actual comic books and were published occasionally rather than periodically on an established schedule. It was the idea of reprinting the colored Sunday funnies, however, that led directly to the production of the first comic book.

The Ledger syndicate began publishing a small broadside of their Sunday color comics on 7 by 9 inch plates in 1933. This was noticed by two employees at the Eastern Color Printing Company in New York, salesman Max C. Gaines and sales manager Harry I. Wildenberg, who figured that two such plates would fit a tabloid page, and this folded would produce a booklet about 7½ by 10 inches. They sold Proctor and Gamble on the idea of issuing as a promotional premium a 32 page collection of color newspaper reprints in this size, and thus 10,000 copies of *Funnies on Parade* in slick paper covers were printed. The success of the scheme led to additional one-shot publications, such as *Famous Funnies: A Carnival of Com-*

Jerry Siegel and Joe Shuster, creators of Superman, 1942.
Superman © DC Comics Inc. Used with permission.

ics, Century of Comics, and *Skippy's Own Book of Comics,* and these were issued in quantities of 100,000 to 500,000 copies.

The concept of give-away comic books was so popular that Max Gaines believed that young readers might pay at least ten cents for such books, just as they purchased the "Big Little Books" which also traded on popular comic strip characters. Early in 1934, Eastern Color printed 35,000 copies of *Famous Funnies, Series 1* with 64 pages of reprints of Sunday color strips. They sold out immediately in America's chain stores, so in May the first monthly comic magazine under the same title began. *Famous Funnies* would appear regularly thereafter for over 20 years through 218 issues with a circulation peak of nearly one million copies. Sensing a profitable spin-off from their comic strip titles, soon the syndicates were issuing their own reprint titles, such as *Popular Comics* from the News-Tribune, *Tip Top Comics* from United Features, and *King Comics* from Hearst's King Features.

It was Major Malcolm Wheeler-Nicholson's National Periodical Publications that developed the idea of publishing original material in this new periodical format with the appearance in 1935 of *More Fun.* At this point, except for the established reprint titles, the direct link between newspaper comics and comic books ended, and the new comics format developed a life of its own. *More Fun* was followed by *Detective Comics* in 1937 (which was to give the firm its initials "DC"), but it wasn't until the appearance of *Action Comics* in 1938, after Major Nicholson had sold the firm to Harry Donenfeld, that the character appeared who would assure the success of the comic book and establish the basic pattern for what would largely constitute the subject matter of thousands of comic books to come. It was Max C. Gaines again who discovered the material which had previously been submitted unsuccessfully to several newspaper syndicates. The creators were two high school students from Cleveland,

Ohio, writer Jerry Siegel and artist Joe Shuster. The character was Superman, who immediately captured the American imagination and became our first twentieth century folk hero, a perfect mythological figure for an age of technology in which man was methodically to step beyond every limitation on his intellectual and physical abilities and master the universe. Among the superheroes to follow in the pattern of Superman, only Batman, Captain Marvel, and Spider-Man would rival him in popularity, all of whom were earthbound and lacked the extra-terrestrial origin of the man of steel.

Heroes of superhuman strength have always been prominent figures in the literature and folklore of Western civilization, among them Ulysses, Hercules, Samson, Beowulf, and King Arthur. America has cherished its own breed of heroes, most of them products of the frontier experience when the psychological necessity of adjusting to a hostile environment required the projection of mythological figures larger than the environment itself. In the wake of Daniel Boone, whose individuality, bravery, strength, and guile seemed to reflect the emerging character of the American nation, came Davy Crockett, Mike Fink, Kit Carson, Deadwood Dick, Pecos Bill, Wild Bill Hickock, and Buffalo Bill, or in the black community John Henry, Railroad Bill, and Stackolee. It is important to note that these figures achieved national prominence not because of the persistence of folktales and oral traditions but because their exploits entered the pages of books, dime novels, almanacs, newspaper columns, and sheet music (and in some cases were largely created there). A large part of the heroic folklore in this century has survived because of the technology of print (and later film and television), and it might be argued that this print material is the proper folklore for an industrial society rather than the isolated oral traditions. Folklore purists would disagree with such a notion, however.

It was in the popular Crockett almanacs that Davy Crockett took on the lineaments of a hero of super-strength, as well as in spurious autobiographical accounts. It was there that he killed bears with his hands, spoke the language of animals, whipped his weight in wildcats, rode the lightning bolts, and even moved the very earth frozen on its axis one cold morning. His mythic life, as Richard M. Dorson has observed, is similar to the biographical pattern of epic heroes:

Cover, *The Crockett Almanac 1841.* Davy Crockett has a "Tussle with a Bear."

The Crockett universe portrays the customary masculine, individualistic, relatively barbaric society devoted to hunting, fighting, drinking and sporting; the narrative structure focuses on the career of a central hero, his conquests, courtships, adventures, nomadic travels, [remarkable] birth and [heroic] death.[8]

While the Crockett-Boone branch of heroes has been elevated to superbeing status from the level of ordinary humanity, comic book heroes begin already invested with their unusual abilities—Superman as a result of his origin on a planet where superior strength, x-ray vision, and the ability to fly was commonplace; Batman because of his excellent physical condition as an athlete and his keen ratiocinative skills; Captain Marvel because of an accidental encounter with the powers of the classical dieties; and Spider-Man as the result of being bitten by a radioactive spider during an experiment. They have moved away, however, from the masculine worlds of the epic and frontier societies, where drinking and hunting prevail, to the urban society where the impact of industrialism has created the threats of crime, poverty, alienation, and totalitarianism. Their conquests, courtships, adventures, and travels remain central, however.

The comic book heroes also tend to fit most of the classic patterns of heroism in Western culture. Superman, for example, belongs to what Roger D. Abrahams calls "the major type of American popular hero," that is "the outsider":

> . . . they exist apart from society because of the variance of their vision of what life should be from that of the city or town dweller [remember that Superman was raised by the Kent family on a farm where agrarian virtues prevail]; they must fabricate their own ethos and carry it around with them wherever they go. Because of their unbounded optimism, clear-sightedness, and essential egotism, whenever this ethos collides with society's, that of the hero prevails. . . . Whenever they enter a community, one can predict they will find its wound, and cleanse it before they leave. . . . They not only never marry, they never find the real heroic culmination in death. They are permanently stuck in the hero role.[9]

Batman partakes of the tradition of the vigilante hero who is motivated by a "cause" (in this case the brutal murder of his parents by a thief), thus "provoked into action by external pressure and not internal psychic need," and despite taking the law into his own hands retaining his "essential virtue."[10] Also like many literary heroes in American culture, he takes on a male companion, Robin the Boy Wonder, to share in his power and values. Given his anti-social attitudes and introspective insecurities, Spider-Man belongs to the trickster tradition among folk heroes. Even, as with Spider-Man, when the trickster's activities result in "benefits to the whole group, his actions can not be interpreted as providing a model for future conduct. He is a projection of desires generally thwarted by society."[11] It is interesting to note that the trickster figure in African folklore is often a spider. Most of the heroes of the world of comic books likewise fit these patterns which are as old as Western civilization. It seems obvious, then, that the comic books have continued to maintain and develop these patterns, translate them into forms more suitable to a post-industrial society, and educate young readers in

Spider-Man.
© Marvel Entertainment Group, Inc.

a significant part of their cultural heritage.

In addition to the illustrated book, the application of color printing in the newspaper to the comic strip, and the interest of Americans in mythic figures, one other technical development helped create a wider audience for visual narratives in America—that is the maturing of film as a form of entertainment. Comic strips and motion pictures followed parallel and mutually supportive paths of development in America. On December 25, 1895, just a week before Outcault's urchin in Hogan's Alley was to receive his first brightly colored yellow shirt, the Lumiére brothers in Paris arranged for the first showing to a paying audience of their films through a camera-projector they had developed. Four months later, on April 23, 1896, Thomas Edison demonstrated his Vitascope in New York by projecting films as the final "act" for a vaudeville show program. The public responded with amazement and an eagerness, almost insatiable, for further amusements reflected on the silver screen. In an effort to strike already familiar popular chords and bank upon proven formulas, film producers turned for inspiration to popular fiction, stage melodrama, theatrical entertainment, and graphic art.

Given the popularity of the Sunday comic supplements, it was natural then that they turned to comic strip characters as well for some of the early silent films. The first of a series of short films based on Frederick Burr Opper's strip *Happy Hooligan*, which began March 26, 1900, appeared that same year to be followed by another fifteen features between 1901 and 1903. Opper's *Alphonse and Gaston*, which first appeared in 1902, was filmed twice that year and three times in 1903 and *Maude the Mule*, also by Opper, once in 1906. Other popular comic strip characters to appear in these short films were Carl Edward Schultze's *Foxy Grandpa* in ten titles in 1902 and 1903, Richard F. Outcault's *Buster Brown* in eight titles in 1903 and 1904, and Rudolph Dirks' *The Katzenjammer Kids* in two titles in 1903. There was even a version in 1903 of that early important comic feature called *Trouble in Hogan's Alley*. These are the ones which happened to have survived, so many others were probably produced.[12] Since this was before the invention of animation, all of them featured live actors, and in two of them the cartoonists themselves appeared—Outcault in a 1904 *Buster Brown* short and Schultze in 1902 in a feature about the stage musical based on *Foxy Grandpa*.

The love affair of film with the comics would not end, of course, in 1904. Among the comic strips which would be adapted for the screen over the years were *Barney Google, Blondie, Buck Rogers, Dick Tracy, Ella Cinders, Flash Gordon, Joe Palooka, Li'l Abner, Prince Valiant, Red Ryder,* and *Terry and the Pirates,* some of them more than once in a series, such as the numerous *Blondie* films. Once the comic book had proven itself, its characters inspired a good many adventure serials shown in chapters at Saturday matinees, such as those based on Superman, Batman, Captain America, Captain Marvel, Spy Smasher, Vigilante, or Nyoka the Jungle Girl. The fascination continues with such productions in recent years as the three-part *Superman* series, *Popeye, Annie, Sheena, Batman,* and *Brenda Starr,* and such producers as William Friedkin, George Lucas, and Steven Spielberg have confessed that their cinematic visions were largely inspired by their early love of comic books.

Since film and comic art developed simultaneously, artists in both media had to solve the same problems in visual narrative on their own and without the aid of established precedent. Therefore, one can find in early comic strips panels and sequences that are filmlike in their use of perspective and point of view. For example, uses of panning, in which the camera remains in one place but pivots to follow an action, were frequently employed by comic artists long before it became commonplace in film. Traveling or tracking shots, in which the camera moved with the subject, and close-ups or cut-ins, in which a portion of the previous

Frederick Burr Opper, *And Her Name was Maude,* 1906 (detail). In the second of these two panels, it is as if Opper is moving to what in film would become known as a long shot, that is a wider view of the scene, so that we can see the outcome of Maude's actions.

Frederick Burr Opper, *And Her Name was Maude*, January 7, 1906 (detail). These two sequential panels demonstrate the use of a cut-in before it became stock-in-trade for the movie camera. A single portion of the frame is enlarged in the next.

scene is enlarged in the next as a point of focus, these too had their counterparts in techniques employed independently by comic artists. As John L. Fell has noted, in one remarkable sequence in that most remarkable of comic strips, *Little Nemo in Slumberland*, Winsor McCay resolved problems which cinematographers didn't even know yet they would have to confront with the introduction of aerial photography:

> In an airship adventure, Nemo's passage relative to the Statue of Liberty is documented by a view that poses extreme close-up against long shot as the camera draws off into a space independent of any visible foundation. In such a collection of drawings one finds the vision of an early cartoonist at its most stunning; he literally invents a place from which to view his adventure with the consistencies of an as yet nonexistent aerial camera shot.[13]

Because the comic strip is sharply limited in size and visual space, these experiments could not be continued and thus did not keep apace with innovations in film. The comic book, however, would pick up on these techniques and expand the repertoire of ways to manipulate visual narrative. But by then, the artist was clearly working under the influence of film

rather than independently. Thus comic book artists rely on the juxtaposition of sequential shots to create an effect, frequently use the ordinary traveling close-up, or employ slow-motion in a sequence to increase the dramatic impact of a scene. At their best, comic book artists carry the visual narrative into areas of innovation that the restricted camera cannot enter, except through animation, such as simultaneous continuities, or scenes that literally explode the strictures of the conventions of comic art. It is not surprising that student photographers and filmmakers now turn to comic books to learn the rudiments of their craft. The point here is that the mass market created for motion pictures by the film industry, which attuned audiences to stories told primarily through pictures, also looked to the other media for similar entertainment. Adventure and continuity comic strips, picture magazines, photogravure sections in newspapers, newsreels, and television were among the responses, but so was the comic book.

Considered in the context of these larger cultural and technological developments, the comic book, then, is a natural product of the times. Like the illustrated book, it provides stimulus to the imagination that mere words on

Winsor McCay, *Little Nemo in Slumberland* (detail). Note the camera angles employed by McCay as the airship approaches and passes the Statue of Liberty, achieving a cinematic reality before the motion picture camera had tried such a shot.

the printed page could never achieve. Like folklore, it gave new life to a tradition of heroic and mythic figures that the modern oral tradition cannot sustain in the face of mass communication. Insofar as these figures embody the traditions of Western culture, it has introduced generations of readers to symbolic ways of addressing the continuing problems of society and the philosophic questions of mankind. Like the comic strip and the motion picture, it pleases our visual sensibilities by bringing to life the kinds of dramatic conflicts that enable us to work out vicariously our internal frustrations. It is still an infant art form just beginning to realize its aesthetic potential, but the comic book has great promise in the century to come as a major creative opportunity for those talented people able to combine the skills of the artist with those of the storyteller, which da Vinci reminded us is the only satisfactory way to describe the experience of life.

1. Cited in David Bland, *A History of Book Illustration* (Cleveland: World Publishing Company, 1958), p. 14.

2. J. R. Harvey, *Victorian Novelists and Their Illustrators* (New York: New York University Press, 1971), p. 3.

3. Michael Steig, "Iconography of Sexual Conflict in *Dombey and Son*," *Dickens Studies Annual*, 1 (1970), 161.

4. Beverly R. David, "The Pictorial *Huck Finn*: Mark Twain and His Illustrator E. W. Kemble," in *Huck Finn Among the Critics*, ed. M. Thomas Inge (Frederick, Md.: University Publications of America, 1985), pp. 276-77, 280.

5. Robert H. Hirst, "Note on the Text," in *A Connecticut Yankee in King Arthur's Court*, ed. Bernard L. Stein (Berkeley: University of California Press, 1983), p. 479.

6. Frank Luther Mott, *American Journalism: A History of Newspapers in the United States Through 250 Years 1690 to 1940* (New York: Macmillan, 1941), p. 585.

7. Mott, p. 525.

8. Roger D. Abrahams, "Some Varieties of Heroes in America," *Journal of the Folklore Institute*, 2 (December 1966), 357.

9. Abrahams, p. 359.

10. Abrahams, p. 348.

11. Abrahams, p. 342.

12. Kemp R. Niver, *Early Motion Pictures: The Paper Print Collection in the Library of Congress* (Washington, D.C.: Library of Congress, 1985).

13. John L. Fell, *Film and the Narrative Tradition* (Norman: University of Oklahoma Press, 1974), p. 104.

Jerry Dumas, *Sam's Strip*, April 30, 1962.
All the characters out of the past of comic strip history came to visit *Sam's Strip* in 1962.
© King Features Syndicate, Inc.

Suggestions for Further Reading

COMIC STRIPS

Reference Works

The sound bibliographical and reference work that must precede historical and critical research has not been accomplished yet for the comics, but a few tentative efforts have been made and much good work is in progress. What should be a comprehensive and useful checklist of secondary data—the *International Bibliography of Comics Literature*, by Wolfgang Kempkes—is marred by inaccuracies, incomplete data, and inconvenience. The material is divided into eight general categories, such as histories of the development of comics, structure, readership, etc., and then subdivided by country of origin (Argentina, Australia, Belgium, Brazil, Germany, Finland, France, Great Britain, Italy, Mexico, the Netherlands, Austria, Portugal, Sweden, Switzerland, Spain, South Africa, Czechoslovakia, the USSR, and the United States). A subject cross-index in the first edition was inexplicably deleted in the revised edition, thus making it impossible to locate entries on specific artists or comics, the major use for a checklist. The book is, however, the only convenient source of information on criticism published outside the United States to 1974 and illustrates the extent to which the most comprehensive study of American comics has taken place abroad, especially in Italy, France, and Germany, rather than on native shores. As always, the most significant creators of American culture appear evident to Europe before we seem to be able to perceive them,

from Edgar Allan Poe and William Faulkner to Winsor McCay and George Herriman.

Randall W. Scott's *Comic Books and Strips: An Information Sourcebook* is an annotated checklist of almost 1,000 books about the comics, anthologies, and periodicals, as well as 44 libraries with significant holdings. It is invaluable and essential for any library, public or private, and one would hope it is slated for regular updates. Also essential for any library with an interest in popular culture is *Directory of Popular Culture Collections* by Christopher D. Geist and others, which indexes over 35 libraries with comic book and comic strip collections.

The main body of *The World Encyclopedia of Comics*, edited by Maurice Horn, consists of more than twelve hundred cross-referenced entries, arranged alphabetically, and devoted either to an artist, a writer, a comic strip title, or a comic book character, and prepared by an international group of contributors. Additional materials include a short history of the development of comic art, a chronology, an original analytic inquiry into the aesthetics of the comics by the editor, a history of newspaper syndication, a glossary, a selected bibliography, and several appendixes and indexes. Unfortunately, there are a number of typographical errors in the text and the critical comments are often biased. Nevertheless, with corrections, revisions, and updating, this work could be a chief authority among historians and commentators on the comics. Also relevant information will be found in Horn's *The World Encyclopedia of Cartoons*, similarly structured as the above, except here the almost twelve hundred entries deal with cartoonists, animators, editors, and producers, and the works they create in the fields of animation, gag cartoons, syndicated comic panels, editorial cartoons, caricature, and sports cartoons. The entries are supplemented with an overview of caricature and cartoons, a brief history of humor magazines, a world summary of animated cartoons, a chronology, a glossary, and a history of the humor periodicals *Puck*, *Life*, and *Judge*.

A new reference project initiated by Maurice Horn is the *Contemporary Graphic Artists* series to be issued on a regular basis by Gale Research Company. Each volume contains biographic, bibliographic, and critical assessments of present and past illustrators, animators, cartoonists, designers, and other graphic artists, but with an emphasis on comic artists. Much of the information has been obtained directly from the artists, many of whom provide comments on their own work. The first volume in 1986 contained an essay, "The Graphic Arts: An Overview," which defined the areas to be covered by the series.

In *Women and the Comics*, Trina Robbins and Catherine Yronwode, a comic book artist and editor respectively, provide a comprehensive catalog with brief commentary on the work of over five hundred women cartoonists and writers in America from 1901 to 1984. In a field thought to have been dominated by men, the authors find that almost from the start comic strips and later comic books have employed feminine talent extensively, although their names were concealed or lost to history. *Great Cartoonists and Their Art* is a collection of personal and biographical essays on comic strip and editorial artists whose work was collected over the years by cartoonist Art Wood. Wood includes quotations from the artists, background on the business, and the technical details of producing cartoons and comics for publication.

Will Eisner, a creator of the comic book and one of the most influential masters of comic art, discusses his ideas and theories on the practice of telling stories in graphic form in *Comics & Sequential Art*. Separate chapters, thoroughly illustrated by examples of his own work, treat imagery, timing, framing, and anatomy, and he discusses comics as a form of reading, learning, and teaching. Eisner views comics as a distinct artistic discipline and a literary-visual form, the development of which has been accelerated by advances in graphic technology and visual communication in this century. This is the best book ever written on the aesthetics of comic art. An engaging and witty overview of the various symbolic devices and shorthand visual images used by cartoonists is *The Lexicon of Comicana* by Mort Walker. While written tongue-in-cheek, the book is a valuable guide to the devices that make comic art distinctive.

Denis Gifford's *Encyclopedia of Comic Characters* contains entries on over 1,200 characters with notes on their creators, place of publication, beginning and ending dates, and description. Most of the characters are British, but quite a few Americans are included. *A Doonesbury Index* by Allan D. Satin is a comprehensive index to the characters, real people, topics, and themes that appeared in G. B. Trudeau's comic strip from 1970 through 1983. Future historians of politics and popular culture in the 1970s will find this extremely valuable.

Teachers wishing to use comics in an educational context will find some useful suggestions in *Cartoons and Comics in the Classroom*, edited by James L. Thomas. It must be used with caution as a reference, however, since it contains some inaccurate information about the history of comics and many of the articles are written with a degree of condescension for the art form. *The Art of the Comic Strip* by Shirley Glubok is written mainly for children as an introduction to the history of the art form. It is beautifully illustrated and contains historic sketches on over forty classic comic strips and artists. Bob Bennett's how-to guide, *Collecting Original Cartoon Art*, also contains estimates on the values of original comic strip drawings.

Research Collections

A once private collector, Bill Blackbeard, has turned his comprehensive collection of all known comic strips into a nonprofit research center that is open to the public, the San Francisco Academy of Comic Art. The academy can provide copies of sequential runs of comic strips to researchers and institutions for a fee, as well as authoritative information on all aspects of comic art and popular literature. The other major center for research is the Library for Communication and Graphic Arts at Ohio State University in Columbus. Begun with a gift from

Milton Caniff of his entire library, papers, and research files, under the direction of Lucy Caswell, the collection has grown rapidly with extensive gifts of papers, publications, and art from other cartoonists and their professional societies. The library also hosts major exhibitions and conferences on the comic arts. The Museum of Cartoon Art was established with the support of several individual artists, led by Mort Walker, and the professional cartoonist societies at the Town of Rye, Port Chester, New York, and the Cartoon Art Museum in San Francisco is receiving similar support. Both museums emphasize the collection of original art and provide important exhibitions and seminars open to the public.

Another extensive collection is found in the Popular Culture Library, a special division of the Bowling Green State University Library, Bowling Green, Ohio, and other large university libraries have begun to develop an interest in this area. Publisher Harry A. Chesler, Jr. gave to Fairleigh Dickinson University Library in Madison, New Jersey, his collection of materials including four thousand pieces of original art, the correspondence and records of the Chesler Syndicate, and a body of secondary literature. Comic artist Roy Crane deposited his scrapbooks and original art at the Syracuse University Library in Syracuse, New York. Collections devoted to primary and secondary materials in the areas of comic strips and political cartoons are located at Palomar College Library in San Marcos, California, Kenneth Spencer Research Library at the University of Kansas in Lawrence, James Branch Cabell Library at Virginia Commonwealth University in Richmond, and University of Virginia Library at Charlottesville. The best collection of Walt Disney comic books and strips is found in the Disney Studio Archives in Burbank, California (though not open to the public), but the Anaheim Public Library in California also has an impressive body of Disney material. Undoubtedly other collections exist or are being assembled throughout the country.

History and Criticism
It must be noted that because so little of the basic bibliographic and reference work has been completed, as indicated earlier, almost every single book to be discussed in the following pages abounds to one degree or another in errors and mistaken assumptions. Many authors assumed that the beginning date for a daily or

Sunday strip was the first appearance in their local newspapers, or the first date on which it was syndicated, whereas it may have begun months earlier. The syndicates themselves have kept very few records and even incomplete files of proof sheets for the strips they distribute. The most knowledgeable and meticulous scholar of the comics, Bill Blackbeard, is writing a history which will establish for the first time much of this factual information, but until his book appears all of the existing histories must be used with great caution. Omitted from discussion here are the many historical and appreciative studies of American comics published abroad in Europe or South America.

A History of American Graphic Humor, by William Murrell, was the first authoritative history of the development of pictorial satire and cartooning in America to include the comics. While he devotes only a few appreciative pages to the comic strip, the work is still valuable as a panorama of the forms of visual art that have influenced the comics. The earliest full-length book entirely devoted to American comic art was Martin Sheridan's *Comics and Their Creators* in 1942. Not actually an organized history, it consisted primarily of biographical sketches and interviews with the artists and writers of over seventy-five of the most popular newspaper comics, copiously illustrated with portraits and reproductions of the strips. It remains a useful resource for some of the primary data on the views and working habits of the cartoonists. The earliest full-scale history was *The Comics*, by Coulton Waugh, a practicing comic artist and devoted scholar of the subject. While many of his facts were faulty, Waugh attempted a comprehensive survey of the important movements and types of comic strips from *The Yellow Kid* through the first decade of the modern comic book. His insights into the reasons for the popularity of certain strips, his comments on the aesthetic principles behind them, and his early effort to define the medium make Waugh's pioneer effort of lasting interest, although he had little appreciation for the comic book as it had developed, and he appeared to accept without question some of the highbrow standards often applied to popular art by the self-appointed guardians of high culture.

The next effort on the part of a single author to chart the history of the medium was Stephen Becker's *Comic Art in America*, although his interests were broader than Waugh's in that he envisioned his book, according to its pretentious subtitle, as "A social history of the funnies, the political cartoons, magazine humor, sporting cartoons, and animated cartoons." Casting his net so broadly led to much superficiality, and his commentary is often derivative, but the volume is a useful storehouse of over 390 illustrations and sample sketches. The text is kept to an absolute minimum and the illustrations are at a maximum in *The Penguin Book of Comics*, by George Perry and Alan Aldridge, aptly described in its subtitle as "a slight history." Originally published in French in conjunction with an exhibition of comic art at the Louvre, and the joint product of six contributors headed by Pierre Couperie, *A History of the Comic Strip* is understandably uneven, yet it contains some of the most provocative comments yet ventured on the aesthetics, structure, symbolism, and themes in comic art. A general survey was undertaken by comic artist Jerry Robinson, *The Comics: An Illustrated History of Comic Strip Art*. Robinson provided a readable and interesting text complemented by thirteen original essays by eminent artists about the theories behind their work.

Though assembled as a catalog for an exhibition at the University of Maryland, Judith O'Sullivan's *The Art of the Comic Strip* contains a brief history with emphases on Winsor McCay, George McManus, George Herriman, and Burne Hogarth, a compilation of short biographies and bibliographic references on 120 comic artists, a chronology of important dates, and a bibliography. *Comics: Anatomy of a Mass Medium*, by Reinhold Reitberger and Wolfgang Fuchs, is a broad effort by two German scholars to relate the comics to their social context and developments in other mass media, but faulty secondary sources and inaccessible primary material led to an inordinate number of factual and other errors, which no one corrected in the process of translation. What appears to be the most ambitious effort yet undertaken to describe the "history of the comic strip" has yielded the first massive volume, *The Early Comic Strip*, by David Kunzle, which reaches the year 1825 before the comic strip as we know it actually begins. Kunzle traces the full development of narrative art in the European broadsheet which he sees as an antecedent to the comic strip as he defines it in the introduction. The complete corpus of reproductions of broadsheets in the over-sized volume makes it of greater interest to art historians than comic scholars, but it will be interesting to see how

this research is brought to bear on the American comic strip in the next volume, if it ever appears.

The short bookshelf of biographies of major comic artists is gradually expanding. Most early efforts took the form of brief personal memoirs or picture books in which the text was incidental to the illustrations. Examples of such promotional books are *Milton Caniff: Rembrandt of the Comic Strip* by John Paul Adams and *Charlie Brown, Snoopy and Me* by Charles M. Schulz and R. Smith Kiliper. As each anniversary of *Peanuts* has passed, Schulz has published volumes interlaced with autobiographical memoirs, such as *Charlie Brown & Charlie Schulz* by Lee Mendelson and Schulz (20th anniversary), *Peanuts Jubilee: My Life and Art with Charlie Brown and Others* by Schulz (25th), *Happy Birthday, Charlie Brown* by Mendelson and Schulz (30th), and *You Don't Look 35, Charlie Brown* by Schulz (35th). Walt Kelly's anthology *Ten Ever-lovin' Blue-eyed Years with Pogo* is another anniversary volume with significant autobiographical content. Basic bibliographic data about Kelly's published work is found in *The Walt Kelly Collector's Guide* by Steve Thompson.

Peter Marzio's *Rube Goldberg: His Life and Work* is a full-scale biographical account of Goldberg's versatile career and an interpretation of his art. Marzio achieves a sense of Goldberg's personality and character and provides a model for the kind of treatment other artists deserve. Goldberg's autobiography has been incorporated in Clark Kinnaird's *Rube Goldberg vs. the Machine Age*. Harold Davidson's *Jimmy Swinnerton: The Artist and His Work* is a beautifully designed and printed survey of the career of a major early cartoonist.

In *Krazy Kat: The Comic Art of George Herriman*, Patrick McDonnell, Karen O'Connell, and Georgia Riley de Havenon provide an overview of Herriman's life and career through an assemblage of unpublished letters, documents, photographs, and artwork for friends, as well as an extensive selection of *Krazy Kat* comic strips. There is still a good deal more to be said on Herriman, however. Joseph M. Cahn's *The Teenie Weenies Book: The Life and Art of William Donahey* reports on a little discussed artist. For more than 65 years, Donahey wrote and illustrated a color newspaper feature for the funny pages about a group of Lilliputian characters called *The Teenie Weenies*. The most lavishly produced biographical account of a comic artist we have is John Canemaker's *Winsor McCay: His Life and Art*. In the text, Canemaker emphasizes McCay's importance in American cultural history through his creation of *Little Nemo in Slumberland*, the most beautiful comic strip in the history of the form, and the production of *Gertie the Dinosaur*, which established the potential of the animated film long before Disney. The illustrations are stunning. A model of the way the work and life of a comic artist should be treated is found in Shelley Armitage's *John Held, Jr.: Illustrator of the Jazz Age*. She combines scrupulous research with a balanced critical appreciation for the way Held's cartoons and comic strips both reflected and influenced the fads, fashions, and movements of his times, and she does so without having to apologize for Held's popularity or denigrate the power of his artistic accomplishment.

Maurice Horn has published several thematic studies of the comics. His *Comics of the American West* is a heavily illustrated survey of the major Western comic strips and books and their basic symbolic themes, and his *Women in the Comics* surveys in a similar fashion the images and roles of women as reflected in the comics. A third book, *Sex in the Comics*, is an informal discussion of the presence of sexual behavior in comic strips and books of the mainstream and underground varieties. *Ethnic Images in the Comics*, edited by Charles Hardy and Gail F. Stern, is an exhibition catalog, but it contains more information than is available anywhere else in its seven essays on blacks, Jews, Asians, and other ethnic groups as portrayed in the comics. Another valuable exhibition catalog is *The Comic Art Show*, edited by John Carlin and Sheena Wagstaff, which is a comprehensive look at the influence of cartoons and comics on painting and the fine arts. It contains information not found elsewhere.

The History of Little Orphan Annie by Bruce Smith surveys the history of Harold Gray's famous orphan and her various permutations into a radio show, motion pictures, and the musical stage. Gray's political attitudes and the problems these caused are also discussed. Smith also assembled *The World According to Daddy Warbucks*, appropriately subtitled "Capitalist Quotations from the Richest Man in the World." Most of the quotations supporting free enterprise are culled from others, but occasionally Warbucks is quoted. *The Popeye Story* by Bridget Terry contains some background infor-

mation on E. C. Segar's comic strip, but its primary concern is the making of the motion picture. Charles Schulz's *Peanuts* is examined from a variety of theoretical perspectives— artistic, cultural, psychological, and political—in *The Graphic Art of Charles Schulz*, edited by Joan Roebuck, with essays by Roebuck, M. Thomas Inge, Elliott Oring, and Umberto Eco, and a memoir by Bill Mauldin. This was the catalog for an exhibition organized to celebrate the strip's 35th anniversary. The chronology and bibliography are especially useful. Mort Walker speaks out against his critics in *Miss Buxley: Sexism in Beetle Bailey?* with a good deal of disarming humor.

In *Backstage at the Strips*, Mort Walker provides an engaging insider's tour of the world of comic strip artists, how the strips are created, and who the people are who draw and read them. Ron Goulart's *The Adventurous Decade* is an informal and subjective history of the adventure comic strips during the 1930s when the American funnies came of age. The interviews Goulart conducted with living veterans of the period enrich the volume, which tends to adopt a studied controversial view in its critical judgments of the work of classic artists. In the catalog for the Smithsonian Institution's Bicentennial exhibition, *A Nation of Nations*, edited by Peter Marzio, there is an essay by M. Thomas Inge and Bill Blackbeard on the influences of Europe on the development of the comic strip and the later influences of the fully developed American comic strip and book on the culture of the world at large. An offshoot of interest in the comics is the large market for toys and merchandise based on the more popular characters, such as Mickey Mouse, Buck Rogers, Superman, or Little Orphan Annie. An extensive quantity of these mass-produced artifacts have been photographed and cataloged in Robert Lesser's *A Celebration of Comic Art and Memorabilia*.

Throughout the years the popular magazines, newspapers, and journals of commentary have published hundreds of articles and essays on the comics, many worthwhile, others superficial, and still others steeped in disdain for the subject. Much of this material is listed in the Kempkes bibliography. A useful anthology of some of the better essays is *The Funnies: An American Idiom*, edited by David Manning White and Robert H. Abel.

Several critics who have undertaken general assessments of popular culture have devoted portions of their studies to comic art. One of the earliest was Gilbert Seldes in his 1924 pioneer survey of the mass media, *The 7 Lively Arts*. Though somewhat apologetically, Seldes found some virtues in "The 'vulgar' comic strip" in one chapter of that title, but his essay on George Herriman and *Krazy Kat* was one of the first partly to define Herriman's unique genius. In *The Astonished Muse*, Reuel Denney finds the comics deeply rooted in the larger conventions and traditions of art and literature, especially naturalism, and Leo Lowenthal calls for more serious study of the comics in *Literature, Popular Culture, and Society*. One chapter of Charles Beaumont's *Remember? Remember?* praises the daily funnies for their beauty, imagination, communication, and general good to the world. Perhaps some of the most fruitful, provocative, and rational comments are found in Alan Gowans' *The Unchanging Arts*. Gowans recognizes the extent to which the popular visual arts play a functional part in the total context of society and finds the comics one of the century's major art forms. A social scientist who has specialized in writing about the subject is Arthur Asa Berger, whose books include *Li'l Abner: A Study in American Satire*, the first book-length study of a single comic strip; *The Comic-Stripped American*, a series of pieces on the way comics reflect our culture; and *Pop Culture*, a collection of essays with three on the comics.

A special category of interpretive books are the "gospel" studies. Robert L. Short began the trend with *The Gospel According to Peanuts* and followed the phenomenal success of that book with *The Parables of Peanuts*. Then came *The Gospel According to Superman* by John T. Galloway, Jr., *The Gospel According to Andy Capp* by D. P. McGeachy, III and *Good News for Grimy Gulch* by Del Carter (based on Tom K. Ryan's comic strip *Tumbleweeds*). These books basically are sermons or theological disquisitions illustrated by the comics in question and make little commentary of a significant sort on their meaning or value, except insofar as they are all concerned with the problems of human existence. Jeffrey H. Loria's *What's It All About, Charlie Brown?* is a similar kind of book which describes with frequent illustrations the philosophical and psychological meaning of *Peanuts*.

Most serious study of comic art seems to have focused on how it reflects or relates to society and the culture out of which it has grown. Only

now are we witnessing the development of a body of writing that attempts to assess the comics on their own terms, by measuring their worth against their own developed standards and aesthetic principles rather than by the irrelevant yardsticks of other related arts. A collection of essays mainly on comic book super-heroes helped initiate this development, *All in Color for a Dime*, edited by Dick Lupoff and Don Thompson. Many of the essays originated in a series of fan magazine articles and still bear the stylistic and judgmental marks of their origin. A second volume, also edited by Thompson and Lupoff, *The Comic-Book Book*, is a marked improvement in this regard. In style and judgment, many of these essays are distinguished. Although most of Maurice Horn's *75 Years of the Comics* is devoted to reprinting sample pages from an exhibition at the New York Cultural Center, his excellent ten-page introduction is one of the best efforts so far to define comic art as it relates to the other narrative arts and on its own internal principles. In *The Art of Humorous Illustration*, Nick Meglin has assembled appreciative, fully illustrated tributes to twelve illustrators, including comic artists Sergio Aragones, Jack Davis, Mort Drucker, Johnny Hart, and Arnold Roth. The purpose of *Moviemaking Illustrated: The Comicbook Filmbook*, by James Morrow and Murray Suid, is to teach the technical principles of filmmaking, but the textbook utilizes nothing but frames from Marvel comic books and thereby makes many valuable points about the complex sound and visual techniques of comic art. *The Art of the Comic Strip*, edited by Walter Herdeg and David Pascal, is noteworthy for its excellent choice of illustrations and the perceptive quality of the brief notes and commentary (originally a special issue of *Graphis* magazine). Also of interest is *The Very Large Book of Comical Funnies*, compiled by the staff of the *National Lampoon* as a good-natured satire on the plethora of historic and appreciative books about the comics but which in its own way displays an appreciative sense of what makes the comics special. In a similar category is *Mad Magazine*'s send up of "The Comics" as a *Mad Super Special* Number 36 (Fall 1981), which includes a feature in which several cartoonists draw the strip they would really like to do instead of the one they do every day— Charles Schulz, Walt Kelly, Ken Ernst and Allen Saunders, Mort Walker, and Mell Lazarus.

Academic criticism of a theoretical kind on the comics has only recently begun. "The Comics as Culture," edited by M. Thomas Inge, is a special issue of the *Journal of Popular Culture*, which includes essays on Walt Kelly, Milton Caniff, and the Tarzan comic strip, and an especially valuable article on "The Aesthetics of the Comic Strip" by Robert C. Harvey. Two other articles on the aesthetics of comic art to be recommended, and also from the *Journal of Popular Culture*, are "The Funnies, the Movies and Aesthetics" by Earle J. Coleman and "Comic Art: Characteristics and Potentialities of a Narrative Medium" by Lawrence L. Abbott.

The publication of fan magazines and amateur press publications about comic art began in the 1950s and reemerged in the 1960s as a significant development in the history of American magazines. Much of the pioneer scholarship about the comics first appeared in those pages, and extremely useful biographical and bibliographical information can be found there. A history of their development and a listing of titles would require more space than is available for this entire essay, and it would be almost impossible to assemble a file for back issues on most of them. The comments here will be restricted to only a few of the most professional, informative, and regularly published periodicals to which subscriptions are available.

The most widely circulated and read publication about the world of comic art is *Comic Buyer's Guide*, originated in 1970 by Alan L. Light (under the title *Buyer's Guide for Comics Fandom*). Krause Publications assumed ownership in 1983 and Don and Maggie Thompson became editors. In addition to advertisements for collectors, the weekly includes feature articles, news stories, columns, reviews, and a letters' column in which readers vigorously debate issues and controversies with the editors and each other. The second most popular is the *Comics Journal*, a monthly magazine with lengthy essays, in-depth interviews, review columns by leading commentators on the comics, and an aggressive editorial policy that often places the magazine in the center of controversy. Both the *Guide* and the *Journal* make for lively reading, but both contain a good deal more material about comic books than comic strips. This is not the case with the quarterly *Cartoonist Profiles*, which specializes in interviews with living comic strip artists and profiles on classic artists of the past. A wealth of professional and historic data is found in each issue. A source of reprints of classic strips of the past and ground-breaking essays on major artists is the magazine *Nemo: The Classic Comics Library*. A complete file of issues belongs in any research collection devoted to comic art.

Anthologies and Reprints
From the very beginning of the American comic strip in the 1890s, paperback collections of the most widely read titles were popular publications. Thus *The Yellow Kid*, *Foxy Grandpa*, *Buster Brown*, and *Mutt and Jeff* appeared in series of reprints, and in 1933 the first comic book, *Funnies on Parade*, was composed of reprints of Sunday and daily strips in color. Over the years various comics would find their way into paperback anthologies and less often into hardcover collections. Usually considered of ephemeral value, few copies survive and are considered collector's items. One of the first substantial anthologies of American cartoons, complete with historical introductions and annotations, was Thomas Craven's *Cartoon Cavalcade* in 1943. Interspersed among the chronologically arranged examples of political and gag cartoons filling over four hundred pages were selections from all the popular newspaper comic strips.

The one publisher who first initiated a program of reprinting classic comic strips in the most responsible format, in selected complete runs with authoritative introductions, was the late Woody Gelman of Nostalgia Press. Beginning with Alex Raymond's *Flash Gordon* in 1967, Gelman published one or more volumes a year in his series *The Golden Age of Comics*. He also issued a series of anthologies of selected daily strips entitled *Nostalgia Comics*. The ultimate result of his program is an extensive bookshelf of handsomely produced collections of the classic comic strips, preserved for convenient reading and future research.

The most ambitious reprint operation undertaken so far was the Classic American Comic Strips series by Hyperion Press of Westport, Connecticut, under the editorship of Bill Blackbeard. Series I contained twenty-two volumes in large format and in hardcover or paperback editions. Drawing on the archives of the San Francisco Academy of Comic Art, each volume contained complete sequential reprints from the first or peak years of selected daily and Sunday strips and an introduction by an authority on the subject of that volume. Unfortunately, the project was discontinued. Blackbeard, in collaboration with Martin Williams, also produced the most lavish general anthology to appear, *The Smithsonian Collection of Newspaper Comics*. This is an essential volume in any library for the general reader and researcher alike.

Several trade and paperback publishers have issued over the years collections of the most popular strips. Among them are Avon Books, Ballantine, Bantam, Dell, Fawcett, Grosset and Dunlap, Holt, Rinehart and Winston, New American Library, Pyramid Books, and Simon and Schuster. Andrews and McMeel specializes in reprint volumes. For a list of available titles, one should consult their catalogs as the books go in and out of print with unpredictable frequency. There are also a number of specialty publishers now who issue reprint series and volumes, such as Blackthorne, Dragon Lady Press, Fantagraphics Books, Kitchen Sink Press, and NBM (Nantier-Beall-Minoustchine Publishing Co.). The last firm has successfully seen into print a reproduction in twelve hardcover volumes of the complete run of Milton Caniff's *Terry and the Pirates*, the first such reprint project of a major long-run comic strip to reach completion. The series editor, Bill Blackbeard, is now managing a reprinting of Roy Crane's *Wash Tubbs and Captain Easy* in a similar format. Other comic strips which are to be reprinted in complete uniform sets, if the publishers succeed, include E. C. Segar's *Popeye* (Fantagraphics Books), Milton Caniff's *Steve Canyon* (Kitchen Sink Press), Harold Gray's *Little Orphan Annie* (Fantagraphics), Al Capp's *Li'l Abner* (Kitchen Sink), George Herriman's *Krazy and Ignatz* (Eclipse), and the complete comic strip and comic book work of Robert Crumb (Fantagraphics).

Two reprints of historically important comic strips should receive special note. Since 1926, school children in Texas have been taught their state history through *Texas History Movies*, a comic strip by Jack Patton and John Rosenfield, Jr., first published in the *Dallas Morning News* and later reprinted in numerous collections as textbooks, despite its use of ethnic stereotypes and racial slurs. Even today, *Texas History Movies* is available in a complete oversized reprint volume and in two abbreviated and edited editions (with the racism and offensive language removed). *Han Ola og han Per* was a Norwegian-American comic strip drawn by Peter Julius Rosendahl from 1918 to 1935 for the *Decorah-Posten*, a Norwegian language newspaper in Iowa. It has continuously been reprinted ever since in various newspapers. All 599 of the strips are collected in two volumes with historical and biographical introductions by the editors, Joan N. Buckley and Einar Haugen. The anthologies are in both Norwegian and English and provide a most unusual source for studying the assimilation of a major ethnic group in the American Midwest.

The number of anthologies of reprinted comic strips is so extensive that they cannot easily be discussed here. Instead the reader will find a separate checklist of these appended to the bibliography at the end of this essay. In most cases those I have selected include introductory appreciations, background essays, biographical notes, or other additional material which will be of interest to the reader and researcher.

COMIC BOOKS

Reference Works
While *The Comic Book Price Guide* by Robert M. Overstreet began in 1970 as a selling price reference for dealers and collectors, it has grown through annual revisions and expansions into the single most important source of information about the history of the comic book. A comprehensive listing of comic book titles from 1933 to the present, dates of first and last issues, publishing companies, and important artists have been supplemented with updated information on comic book collecting, fan publications, comic book conventions, a history of the development of comic books, and other special features. The text is copiously illustrated with comic book covers. Overstreet's *Guide* has also served to stabilize the vigorous market that has grown up around collectors and fandom. Although neither will serve as a substitute for Overstreet's *Guide*, collectors may use with profit Marcia Leiter's *Collecting Comic Books* or Mike Benton's *Comic Book Collecting for Fun and Profit*. The pamphlet, *A Guide to Collecting and Selling Comic Books* by Raymond Carlson, is of little consequence. There are several Overstreet imitations available, but

Charles Schulz, *Peanuts*, June 11, 1979.
© United Feature Syndicate, Inc.

they offer no competition. The underground comic book publishing phenomenon is thoroughly documented by Jay Kennedy in *The Official Underground and Newave Comix Price Guide*.

A standard source of biographical data on comic book artists and writers is *The Who's Who of American Comic Books* in four volumes, edited by Jerry Bails and Hames Ware. Conscientiously compiled and edited, each entry provides birth and death dates, pen names, art schools attended, major influences, and career data, including major publishers and comic book credits. Most of the information was obtained directly from the artists and writers themselves. At least two comic artists have been given comprehensive bibliographic treatment. Glenn Bray's *The Illustrated Harvey Kurtzman Index: 1939-1975*, catalogs Kurtzman's innovative work for comic books (he created *Mad*), magazines, newspapers, and films, with some two hundred examples of his art reprinted in an attractive, usefully arranged format. Donald M. Fiene's *R. Crumb Checklist of Work and Criticism* is a comprehensive and detailed annotated listing of practically everything underground cartoonist Robert Crumb has drawn (comic books, book illustrations, greeting cards, record covers, etc.) and everything written or drawn about him. There are a variety of indexes (titles, characters, autobiographical pieces, collaborations, etc.), a chronology of Crumb's life and career from 1943 to 1980, and numerous illustrations. Fiene's book is a model bibliographic effort for a diverse, productive, and elusive artist, probably one of the most influential of the last two decades.

The first volume of *The Encyclopedia of Comic Book Heroes* by Michael L. Fleisher contains over one thousand entries on every major and minor character to appear in the Batman stories, with one hundred pages alone devoted to the life and adventures of Batman himself. The second and third volumes provide similar coverage for Wonder Woman and Superman respectively. Although eight volumes were announced, only three were published. *The Encyclopedia of Superheroes* by Jeff Rovin is an alphabetically arranged catalog of information on more than 1,300 heroic figures and crime fighters from the comics, film, folklore, television, popular literature, radio, and computer games, with the great majority drawn from comic books. Each entry includes the hero's alter ego, first appearance, occupation when not fighting opponents, costume, weapons, biography, a characteristic quotation, and a commentary by Rovin, descriptive but often critical as well. While Rovin notes that superbeings and gods are as old as known history and found in all cultures, only those heroes are included in the encyclopedia who possess an extraordinary power, work for the common good rather than selfish reasons, are never vindictive, operate on earth, and assume an alter ego and a distinctive costume. Appendices provide data on superhero teams, obscure and minor figures, and foreign superheroes. There are illustrations and an index.

Also useful is Jerry Bails' *The Collector's Guide: The First Heroic Age*, an extensive effort "to list all costumed and super-heroes strips appearing from 1934 through 1947 in comic books, including reprints of newspaper strips and adaptations of heroes from pulps to radio." Publishers and artists are also listed. Complementing this volume is Howard Keltner's *Index to Golden Age Comic Books*, an alphabetically arranged index to approximately 98 percent of the "golden age" comic books of the

1940s and 1950s, with notes on publication dates, front cover and interior features, and other useful bibliographic data on over eight thousand issues of three hundred titles in the super-hero line.

The Full Edition of the Complete E. C. Checklist (Revised), by Fred von Bernewitz and Joe Vucenic, focuses on the life of one publisher, Entertaining Comics, generally regarded as the producers of the best drawn and most well written comic books published in America during the early 1950s. The contents of all issues are listed with biographical sketches of the main artists and writers who collaborated on the series. An index would have been useful. George Olshevsky's *Marvel Comics Index* is an extensive computerized project which in fourteen projected volumes will catalog all of the super-hero stories published in Marvel comic books since November 1961 (when the first issue of the *Fantastic Four* appeared). The first ten of the volumes are devoted to the Amazing Spider-Man, Conan and the Barbarians, the Avengers and Captain Marvel, the Fantastic Four (including the Silver Surfer and the Human Torch), Doctor Strange, Thor, the Incredible Hulk, Sub-Mariner, Captain America, and Iron Man. A synopsis of each character's history, information on artists and writers, and several cross-indexes are included. A quantity of artist, title, and publisher checklists have been published in full and fragmentary form in scattered fan magazines and separate pamphlets, but no one has undertaken to assemble a guide to this material.

Both Marvel and DC have published valuable illustrated guides to all the characters that populate their comic book stories: *The Official Handbook of the Marvel Universe* in eight squarebound paperback volumes, and *Who's Who: The Definitive Directory of the DC Universe* as a twenty-six issue comic book series. In an effort to place their characters in a larger chronological perspective, DC has also published a two-volume *History of the DC Universe* by Marv Wolfman and George Perez. Useful character and plot summaries, articles, and artist interviews are published in the issues of *Comics File Magazine*, each focused on specific figures, such as the X-Men, the Fantastic Four, Superman, and Spider-Man.

Although it is designed as a game book, there is a lot of information buried in *The Pow! Zap! Wham! Comic Book Trivia Quiz* by Michael Uslan and Bruce Solomon, with almost one hundred comic book covers reproduced. Other specialized reference items are *The Comic Book Custer* by Brian W. Dippie and Paul A. Hutton, an annotated checklist of the appearances of General George A. Custer in comic books and strips; and George Thomas Fisher's *The Classic Comics Index*, which indexes all authors, subjects, and topics covered in the 169-issue run of *Classics Illustrated* and related Gilberton publications. A thoroughly researched and invaluable guide to all the *Classics* series is *The Classics Handbook* by Charles Heffelfinger, now in its third edition. While there is much misinformation in *Cartoons and Comics in the Classroom*, edited by James L. Thomas, the book does reprint a few useful suggestions for using comic books in the teaching of reading, English, history, and languages. *The Penguin Encyclopedia of Horror and the Supernatural*, edited by Jack Sullivan, contains entries on comic books and artists Frank Frazetta and Gahan Wilson.

Publications with valuable professional and historic data include *Comics Feature*, a general interest magazine; *Amazing Heroes*, devoted to the superhero titles; and *Comics Interview*, which offers lengthy conversations with artists, writers, publishers, and creative people. John Benson's *Squa Tront* contains thoroughly researched and critically stimulating essays about the EC comic book titles. It appears on no regular schedule but is always more than worth the wait.

Research Collections

Most American libraries—public, private, and academic—never subscribed to or made any efforts to preserve comic books. They were viewed as ephemeral publications which catered to illiteracy and had little cultural or historic value. Only recently has this opinion changed, thus there are relatively few substantial collections to consult for research, and these have been built through the efforts of individuals who had the foresight to recognize their worth—not simply as investment items but as documents which relate to the cultural and social patterns of the twentieth century.

A leader in this development has been Randall W. Scott who singlehandedly built the invaluable Russel B. Nye Popular Culture Collection at Michigan State University and assembled over 40,000 comic books with another 2,000 on microfilm. Scott has also acquired a collection of reference books and extensive files of fan publications, journals, and materials related to the history and development of the comic book. Through his efforts, the Michigan State University Library has become the major research center for the comic book in the world, and since the publishers now automatically deposit their publications there, it is likely to remain so.

What should be a major resource—the Library of Congress—has lost a large part of its copyright deposit collection over the years either through neglect or lax security. Nevertheless, they claim to own 45,000 titles and now have a program for their preservation. Other extensive files include the Bowling Green State University Library, with more than 20,000 comic books; the San Francisco Academy of Comic Art (established by Bill Blackbeard as the major research center for the comic strip) with 10,000 issues; and the libraries at Northwestern University and the University of Pittsburgh with over 8,500 issues each. Collections of between 1,000 and 2,000 comic books are found in the libraries of California State University at Fullerton, the Comics Magazine Association of America, Southern Illinois University at Edwardsville, University of Maryland in Baltimore County, and University of Minnesota. Collections of underground comic books in excess of 2,000 issues are located at Iowa State University and Washington State University. The Library of Communication and Graphic Arts at Ohio State University, under the expert guidance of Lucy Caswell, has extensive holdings on the comic book work of Will Eisner, Milton Caniff, and others.

A useful guide to these and other collections is found in Randall W. Scott's survey "Comic Research Libraries," which includes the names of contacts, addresses, and phone numbers. This information is updated in the quarterly newsletter edited by Scott at Michigan State University, *Comic Art Collection*.

History and Criticism

Denis Gifford's *The International Book of Comics* is a fully illustrated, broad survey of the cultural and historic development of comic strips and comic books in America and Great Britain, from nineteenth-century caricature and humorous periodicals through the underground comix movement. This comparative approach demonstrates the degree to which influences have worked internationally in the shaping of comic art.

The first full-length volume on the comic book

was neither a history nor an appreciation. The purpose of *Seduction of the Innocent* by psychologist Frederic Wertham, published in 1954, was to prove that comic books, especially of the crime and horror variety, were a major contributor to juvenile delinquency. Although his data was scientifically invalid, Wertham's book upset many parent and teacher groups and added to the general hysteria of the McCarthy era, resulting in a congressional investigation chaired by Estes Kefauver. Wertham's book, therefore, remains of significant cultural and historic interest.

A summary and chronology of the institutional attacks on juvenile delinquency and its reputed causes in American popular culture on the part of governmental agencies, political groups, sociologists, intellectuals, and parents during the 1950s is found in James Gilbert's *A Cycle of Outrage*. Gilbert focuses in particular on the crusades against films and comic books, and he analyzes the arguments of Wertham and the Kefauver Senate Subcommittee. Gilbert finds their evidence inconclusive and contradictory. The report *Juvenile Delinquency*, issued by the U.S. Congress, Senate Committee on the Judiciary, has been made available in a reprint from Greenwood Press. Martin Barker's *A Haunt of Fears* is a study of the British campaign against comic books in the 1950s. Barker discovers that the campaign was originated and covertly sponsored by the Communist Party, that the comic books under question were primarily American imports, and that a large part of the campaign was inspired by nationalistic and anti-American sentiments. Comic books, along with American film and mass media, were viewed as seductive, corrupting influences on British culture during World War II. Barker provides thorough analyses of selected stories to demonstrate that the meanings were exactly opposite to the claims of the detractors but that they did seriously question the assumptions of the American and British society about the nature of life, the reality of childhood, and the roots of human behavior.

Before Wertham, Gershon Legman had issued early warnings about the baneful effect of violence in the comics in *Love & Death: A Study in Censorship* in 1949. Also in tune with Wertham are the comments of Gillian Freeman in *The Undergrowth of Literature*. Freeman fears that costumed super-heroes will inspire fantasies of fetishism and sadomasochism. A chapter of Ron Goulart's *The Assault on Child-*

hood traces how he feels that the comic book industry "ignored its potential and became preoccupied with murder, torture, sadism and storm-trooper violence." Wertham and all his alarmist colleagues are given a gentle and good humored debunking from the Canadian perspective of novelist Mordecai Richler in a short essay that gives its title to the book *The Great Comic Book Heroes and Other Essays.*

The first writer to inaugurate what he claimed would be a full-scale history of the comic book was James Steranko, himself a talented comic book artist. Volume 1 of *The Steranko History of Comics* finds that pulp fiction of the 1930s was the single most important source of inspiration to the development of the comic book and then traces the histories of Superman, Batman, Captain America, Captain Marvel, and the D.C. comic books. Volume 2 continues the coverage of Captain Marvel and related Fawcett superheroes, the Blackhawks and other airborne characters, Plastic Man and the Quality titles, and Will Eisner's Spirit. Encyclopedic in detail, there is more information in these two volumes than most readers can easily assimilate, but Steranko's contributors have a high regard for the distinctive qualities of comic book art and view it as a part and reflection of the total context of popular culture. Unfortunately, none of the promised following four volumes have appeared. Though primarily an anthology of selected stories, Jules Feiffer's *The Great Comic Book Heroes* has a lengthy introduction in which artist/author Feiffer reminisces about his days in the comic book industry and provides his personal commentary on the meaning of the superhero. Published as a catalog for an exhibition held at Ohio State University, M. Thomas Inge's *The American Comic Book* contains a brief history of the subject, an analysis of selected stories from the EC science fiction comic books, interviews with publishers Stan Lee and Jenette Kahn, and additional essays by Stan Lee, Will Eisner, and Ray Bradbury.

A single-volume history is *Comix: A History of Comic Books in America* by Les Daniels. Daniels provides a sensible outline of the major developments and reprints over twenty stories, four of them in color. His final chapter deals with the development of underground comic books, generally called "comix" to distinguish them from the traditional publications. Partly a radical rejection of the Comics Code Authority and partly a natural development of the counterculture underground press, comix provided ar-

tists with unrestricted freedom to write and draw to the limits of their imagination, something which has seldom been possible in comic art. While shameless obscenity and bad taste abound, several striking talents emerged from the movement—Robert Crumb remains the best known—and much highly original work was accomplished. Mark James Estren attempted to produce *A History of the Underground Comics,* which is difficult to accomplish because the publishing centers have ranged from California to the Midwest to New York, and the artists have never been eager to cooperate with researchers and critics. While much of his commentary is debatable, Estren has assembled an excellent cross-section of representative art by the major figures, many of them are allowed to speak for themselves through interviews and letters, and a useful checklist of underground titles by comix scholar Clay Geerdes concludes the volume. It is an engaging grab bag of reading matter about an important cultural development.

Ron Goulart's *Great History of Comic Books* is a richly detailed overview of the main trends and developments with attention to many often overlooked titles, characters, and artists. His breezy and personalized style belies the extensive research that goes into his writing about the comics. Focusing on the early pre-Superman years of the comic book, Charles Wooley's *History of the Comic Book 1899-1936* traces with meticulousness and careful research the development of the precursors to the modern comic book, its earliest form as a reprint publication for comic strips, and the beginning efforts to produce original material for comic book publication. In *The Comic Book Heroes,* Will Jacobs and Gerard Jones undertake an analysis of the contents and style of the comic book from 1956, the "silver age," to the present, with a major focus on the dominant publishers DC and Marvel. In chronologically arranged chapters, they examine the trends in superheroes and the artists and writers who have made the comic book into a creative medium of increasing breadth and sophistication. Although marketing problems and conservative editorial practices are causes for concern, they feel that comic books remain a significant force in mainstream entertainment.

Ron Goulart's *The Great Comic Book Artists* showcases the work of over 100 accomplished artists with a single page biographical and appreciative essay devoted to each. Fewer artists are treated but with fuller commentary and more extensive illustration in *Masters of Comic Book Art* by P. R. Garrick. A great deal of information about numerous comic book artists, along with full-color reproductions of forty classic covers, has been gathered in Richard O'Brien's *The Golden Age of Comic Books: 1937-1945*.

There are only two full-length books devoted to major figures in the comic book world. Frank Jacobs' *The Mad World of William M. Gaines* is partly a biography and partly a personal memoir about the publisher responsible for the distinguished EC line of comic books and later *Mad* magazine (which he began as a comic book). One half of Michael Barrier's *Carl Barks and the Art of the Comic Book* is biography and the remainder is an annotated bibliography of Bark's fine work, especially on the Donald Duck and Scrooge McDuck stories in the Disney comic books. Barks has emerged as a true master of visual narrative and satire. One of Barks' most notable creations was given his own biographical treatment in *An Informal Biography of Scrooge McDuck* by Jack Chalker. A related item is *How to Read Donald Duck: Imperialist Ideology in the Disney Comic* by Ariel Dorfman and Armand Mattelart. Originally published in South America and translated into English in 1975, this tract attempts to demonstrate how Disney comic books were used in Chile before Allende to promote capitalistic ideology. Actually the culprits were the translators who put words into the mouths of characters not contained in the originals from Disney studios.

In *Mythmakers of the American Dream*, Wiley Lee Umphlett takes a studied look at the way fiction, the comics, movies, and television have conditioned people of his generation to view the world in new and different ways. In a lengthy and thoroughly illustrated essay, Umphlett explores his thesis that "In a way that no other popular medium could, the comic book played on the conflict between our present condition and our longing for a more idealized existence even while offering fantasies that embodied our fear of the unknown." A little explored area is the direct influence of reading comic books on popular culture figures, although a few such influences have been noted. In *Danse Macabre*, Stephen King pays tribute to the EC comic books and the way they inspired his own fiction in the horror line. In their study of Mickey Spillane, *One Lonely Knight*, Max Allan Collins and James L. Traylor discuss Spillane's early work for the comic books, and Elaine Dundy, in *Elvis and Gladys*, identifies Captain Marvel, Jr., as a source of inspiration to Elvis Presley in his dress and appearance.

Superman at Fifty: The Persistence of a Legend, edited by Dennis Dooley and Gary Engle, gathers over two dozen appreciations and critical or historical estimates of the importance of the man of steel on the occasion of the fiftieth anniversary of his first appearance in *Action Comics*. *The New Comics*, edited by Gary Groth and Robert Fiore, reprints interviews with over 27 comic book artists and writers from the pages of *The Comics Journal*. Because they have been abbreviated here, the original lengthier versions remain essential resource material for the researcher.

Anthologies and Reprints
The reprinting of comic book material has occurred with much less frequency than with comic strips, possibly because of the expense of color reproduction which is necessary to do it properly. The first hardcover anthology of selected comic book stories was Jules Feiffer's *The Great Comic Book Heroes* in 1965, a best-selling volume which partly spurred the commercial nostalgia market development. One of the major comic book publishers, National Periodical Publications, devoted a special publication, *Famous First Edition*, to over-sized, full-color, facsimile reproductions of valuable first issues: *Action* No. 1, *Detective* No. 27, *Sensation* No. 1, and *Whiz Comics* No. 2, each of which introduced Superman, Batman, Wonder Woman, and Captain Marvel respectively, as well as *Batman* No. 1, *Superman* No. 1, *Wonder Woman* No. 1, *Flash Comics* No. 1, and *All Star Comics* No. 3. The first five of these were issued in hardcover editions by Lyle Stuart.

Michael Barrier and Martin Williams surveyed thousands of comic book stories to make their selection for *A Smithsonian Book of Comic-Book Comics* and the result is an excellent sampler of thirty-two stories which they feel show the comic book at its very best. Brief instructions helpfully place the stories in their historic and cultural perspectives.

Under the editorship of Stan Lee, Marvel Comics has released a series of popular square-bound paperback anthologies drawing together some of the best stories about selected superhero figures in full color. Among these are

Origins of Marvel Comics, Son of Origins of Marvel Comics, Bring on the Bad Guys, The Superhero Women, The Incredible Hulk, Marvel's Greatest Superhero Battles, The Amazing Spider-Man, Dr. Strange, The Fantastic Four, Captain America, The Invincible Iron Man, The Uncanny X-Men, and *Mighty Marvel Team-Up Thrillers.* DC has released a similar series focusing on genres, such as *Heart Throbs* edited by Naomi Scott, *America at War* and *Mysteries in Space,* both edited by Michael Uslan, as well as several hardcover volumes devoted to major figures, such as *Secret Origins of the DC Super Heroes,* edited by Dennis O'Neil; *Batman from the 30s to the 70s; Wonder Woman; Shazam! from the Forties to the Seventies;* and *Superman from the Thirties to the Seventies,* updated subsequently through the eighties. In 1971 a selection from the EC titles was published in an oversized volume as *Horror Comics of the 1950s,* edited by Ron Barlow and Bhob Stewart. A selection of *The Best of Archie* by John Goldwater is also available. A substantial number of collections from the underground comic books have been issued, and they will be found listed in the checklist at the end of this essay under anthologies.

Three major publication projects are underway to bring into print in oversized, hardcover volumes some of the classic works of comic book art. A complete set of all published titles in the EC comic book series has been issued by Russ Cochran Publisher, P.O. Box 469, West Plains, MO 65775, and the complete works of Carl Barks for the Walt Disney comic book titles and John Stanley for the *Little Lulu* series are coming from Another Rainbow Publishing, P.O. Box 2206, Scottsdale, AZ 85252. These are deluxe, slipcased volumes, printed on high quality paper, and shot in black and white from the original art. They also contain excellent historical and critical introductions and essays. All the sets are indispensable for research libraries.

Many of the major paperback publishers issue from time to time collections of comic book stories, as do the smaller alternative presses supplying collectors and comic book shops. The easiest way to find out about these is to obtain the catalogs of a major distributor, such as Bud Plant, P.O. Box 1689, Grass Valley, CA 95945.

Bibliography

COMIC STRIPS

Books and Articles

Abbott, Lawrence L. "Comic Art: Characteristics and Potentialities of a Narrative Medium." *Journal of Popular Culture*, 19 (Spring 1986), 155-76.

Adams, John Paul. *Milton Caniff: Rembrandt of the Comic Strip*. New York: David McKay, 1946.

Armitage, Shelley. *John Held, Jr.: Illustrator of the Jazz Age*. Syracuse, N.Y.: Syracuse University Press, 1987.

Beaumont, Charles. *Remember? Remember?* New York: Macmillan, 1963.

Becker, Stephen. *Comic Art in America*. New York: Simon and Schuster, 1959.

Bennett, Bob. *Collecting Original Cartoon Art*. Lombard, Ill.: Wallace-Homestead Book Company, 1987.

Berger, Arthur Asa. *The Comic-Stripped American*. New York: Walker & Co., 1973.

——. *Li'l Abner: A Study in American Satire*. New York: Twayne Publishers, 1970.

——. *Pop Culture*. New York: Pflaum/Standard, 1973.

Cahn, Joseph M. *The Teenie Weenies Book: The Life and Art of William Donahey*. La Jolla, Cal: The Green Tiger Press, 1986.

Canemaker, John. *Winsor McCay: His Life and Art*. New York: Abbeville Press, 1987.

Carlin, John, and Sheena Wagstaff, eds. *The Comic Art Show: Cartoons in Painting and Popular Culture*. New York: Fantagraphics Books, 1983.

Carter, Del. *Good News for Grimey Gulch*. Valley Forge, Pa.: Judson Press, 1977.

Coleman, Earle J. "The Funnies, the Movies and Aesthetics." *Journal of Popular Culture*, 18 (Spring 1985), 89-100.

Couperie, Pierre, et al. *A History of the Comic Strip*. Translated by Eileen B. Hennessey. New York: Crown, 1968.

Davidson, Harold. *Jimmy Swinnerton: The Artist and His Work*. New York: Hearst Books, 1985.

Denney, Reuel. *The Astonished Muse*. Chicago: University of Chicago Press, 1957.

Eisner, Will. *Comics & Sequential Art*. Tamarac, Fla.: Poorhouse Press, 1985.

Galloway, John T., Jr. *The Gospel According to Superman*. Philadelphia: Lippincott and A. J. Holman, 1973.

Geist, Christopher, Ray B. Browne, Michael T. Marsden, and Carole Palmer. *Directory of Popular Culture Collections*. Phoenix, Ariz.: Oryx Press, 1989.

Gifford, Denis. *Encyclopedia of Comic Characters*. Essex, England: Longman, 1987.

Glubok, Shirley. *The Art of the Comic Strip*. New York: Macmillan, 1979.

Goulart, Ron. *The Adventurous Decade*. New Rochelle, N.Y.: Arlington House, 1975.

Gowans, Alan. *The Unchanging Arts*. Philadelphia: Lippincott, 1971.

Hardy, Charles, and Gail F. Stern, eds. *Ethnic Images in the Comics*. Philadelphia: Balch Institute for Ethnic Studies, 1986.

Harvey, Robert C. "The Aesthetics of the Comic Strip." *Journal of Popular Culture*, 12 (Spring 1979), 640-52.

Herderg, Walter, and David Pascal, eds. *The Art of the Comic Strip*. Zurich, Switzerland: Graphis Press, 1972.

Horn, Maurice. *Comics of the American West*. New York: Winchester Press, 1977.

————. *75 Years of the Comics*. Boston: Boston Book & Art, 1971.

————. *Sex in the Comics*. New York: Chelsea House, 1985.

————. *Women in the Comics*. New York: Chelsea House, 1977.

————, ed. *Contemporary Graphic Artists*. Detroit: Gale Research Company, 1986-.

————, ed. *The World Encyclopedia of Cartoons*. New York: Chelsea House, 1981.

————, ed. *The World Encyclopedia of Comics*. New York: Chelsea House, 1976.

Inge, M. Thomas, ed. "Comics as Culture." *Journal of Popular Culture*, 12 (Spring 1979), 630-754. Special issue.

————, and Bill Blackbeard. "American Comic Art." In *A Nation of Nations*. Edited by Peter Marzio. New York: Harper and Row, 1976, pp. 600-609.

Kelly, Walt. *Ten Ever-lovin' Blue-eyed Years with Pogo*. New York: Simon and Schuster, 1959.

Kempkes, Wolfgang. *International Bibliography of Comics Literature*. Detroit: Gale Research Company, 1971. Revised edition. New York: R. R. Bowker/Verlag Dokumentation, 1974.

Kinnaird, Clark, ed. *Rube Goldberg vs. the Machine Age*. New York: Hastings House, 1968.

Kunzle, David. *The Early Comic Strip. History of the Comic Strip*, volume 1. Berkeley: University of California Press, 1973.

Lesser, Robert. *A Celebration of Comic Art and Memorabilia*. New York: Hawthorne Books, 1975.

Loria, Jeffrey H. *What's It All About, Charlie Brown?* New York: Holt, Rinehart and Winston, 1968.

Lowenthal, Leo. *Literature, Popular Culture, and Society*. Englewood Cliffs, N.J.: Prentice-Hall, 1961.

Lupoff, Dick, and Don Thompson, eds. *All in Color for a Dime*. New Rochelle, N.Y.: Arlington House, 1970.

McDonnell, Patrick, Karen O'Connell, and Georgia Riley de Havenon. *Krazy Kat: The Comic Art of George Herriman*. New York: Harry N. Abrams, 1986.

McGeachy, D. P., III. *The Gospel According to Andy Capp*. Richmond, Va.: John Knox Press, 1973.

Mad Magazine. "The Comics." *Mad Super Special Number 36*. Fall 1981. New York: E. C. Publications, 1981.

Marzio, Peter. *Rube Goldberg: His Life and Work*. New York: Harper and Row, 1973.

Meglin, Nick. *The Art of Humorous Illustration*. New York: Watson-Guptill, 1973.

Mendelson, Lee. *Charlie Brown & Charlie Schulz*. New York: World, 1970.

————, and Charles Schulz. *Happy Birthday, Charlie Brown*. New York: Ballantine Books, 1979.

Morrow, James, and Murray Said. *Moviemaking Illustrated: The Comicbook Filmbook*. New York: Hayden Book Co., 1973.

Murrell, William. *A History of American Graphic Humor*. 2 vols. New York: Whitney Museum of American Art and Macmillan, 1933 and 1938.

National Lampoon. *The Very Large Book of Comical Funnies*. New York: National Lampoon, 1975.

O'Sullivan Judith. *The Art of the Comic Strip*. College Park, Md.: University of Maryland, Department of Art, 1971.

Perry, George, and Alan Aldridge. *The Penguin Book of Comics*. New York: Penguin Books, 1969. Revised edition, 1971.

Reitberger, Reinhold, and Wolfgang Fuchs. *Comics: Anatomy of a Mass Medium*. Translated by Nadia Fowler. Boston: Little, Brown, 1972.

Robbins, Trina, and Catherine Yronwode. *Women and the Comics*. Guerneville, Cal.: Eclipse Books, 1985.

Robinson, Jerry. *The Comics: An Illustrated History of the Comic Strip*. New York: G. P. Putnam's Sons, 1974.

Roebuck, Joan, ed. *The Graphic Art of Charles Schulz*. Oakland, Cal.: Oakland Museum, 1985.

Satin, Allan D. *A Doonesbury Index: An Index to the Syndicated Daily Newspaper Strip "Doonesbury" by G. B. Trudeau, 1970-1983*. Metuchen, N. J.: Scarecrow Press, 1985.

Schulz, Charles. *Peanuts Jubilee: My Life and Art with Charlie Brown and Others*. New York: Holt, Rinehart and Winston, 1975.

————. *You Don't Look 35, Charlie Brown*. New York: Holt, Rinehart and Winston, 1985.

————, and R. Smith Kiliper. *Charlie Brown, Snoopy and Me*. Garden City, N.Y.: Doubleday, 1980.

Seldes, Gilbert. *The 7 Lively Arts*. New York: Harper and Brothers, 1924. Revised edition. Layton, Utah: Peregrine Smith and Sagamore Press, 1957.

Sheridan, Martin. *Comics and Their Creators*. Boston: Hale, Cushman & Flint, 1942.

Short, Robert. *The Gospel According to Peanuts*. Richmond, Va.: John Knox Press, 1964.

————. *Parables of Peanuts*. New York: Harper and Row, 1968.

Smith, Bruce. *The History of Little Orphan Annie*. New York: Ballantine Books, 1982.

————. *The World According to Daddy Warbucks*. Piscataway, N.J.: New Century Publishers, 1982.

Terry, Bridget. *The Popeye Story*. New York: Tom Doherty Associates, 1980.

Thomas, James L., ed. *Cartoons and Comics in the Classroom*. Littleton, Col: Libraries Unlimited, 1983.

Thompson, Don, and Dick Lupoff, eds. *The Comic-Book Book*. New Rochelle, N.Y.: Arlington House, 1973.

Thompson, Steve. *The Walt Kelly Collector's Guide: A Bibliography and Price Guide*. Richfield, Minn.: Spring Hollow Books, 1989.

Walker, Mort. *Backstage at the Strips*. New York: Mason/Charter, 1975.

————. *The Lexicon of Comicana*. Port Chester, N.Y.: Museum of Cartoon Art, 1980.

————. *Miss Buxley: Sexism in Beetle Bailey*. Bedford, N. Y.: Comicana Books, 1982.

Waugh, Coulton, *The Comics*. New York: Macmillan, 1947.

White, David Manning, and Robert H. Abel, eds. *The Funnies: An American Idiom*. New York: Free Press, 1963.

Wood, Art. *Great Cartoonists and Their Art*. Gretna, La.: Pelican Publishing Company, 1987.

Anthologies and Reprints

Blackbeard, Bill, ed. *Classic American Comic Strips*. 22 vols. Westport, Conn.: Hyperion Press, 1977. (Includes the following titles: Percy Crosby, *Skippy;* Billy De Beck, *Barney Google;* Clare Dwiggins, *School Days;* Harry Fisher, *A. Mutt;* Frank Godwin, *Connie;* Rube Goldberg, *Bobo Baxter;* George Herriman, *Baron Bean;* George Herriman, *The Family Upstairs;* Harry Hershfield, *Abie the Agent;* Harry Hershfield, *Dauntless Durham of the U.S.A.:* Clifford McBride, *Napoleon;* Winsor McCay, *Winsor McCay's Dream Days;* George McManus, *Bringing Up Father;* Gus Mager, Sherlocko the Monk; Dick Moores, *Jim Hardy;* Frederick Opper, *Happy Hooligan;* Richard Outcault, *Buster Brown;* Elzie C. Segar, *Thimble Theater, Introducing Popeye;* Cliff Sterrett, *Polly and Her Pals;* George Storm, *Bobby Thatcher;* Harry Tuthill, *The Bungle Family;* and Edgar S. Wheelan, *Minute Movies.)*

————, and Martin Williams, eds. *The Smithsonian Collection of Newspaper Comics*. Washington, D.C.: Smithsonian Institution Press, 1977.

————, and Malcolm Whyte, eds. *Great Comic Cats*. San Francisco: Troubedor Press, 1981.

Breathed, Berke. *Bloom County*. Boston: Little, Brown, 1983.

————. *'Toons for Our Times*. Boston: Little, Brown, 1984.

————. *Penguin Dreams and Stranger Things*. Boston: Little, Brown, 1985.

————. *Bloom County Babylon*. Boston: Little, Brown, 1986.

————. *Billy and the Boingers Bootleg*. Boston: Little, Brown, 1987.

————. *Tales Too Ticklish To Tell*. Boston: Little, Brown, 1988.

Briggs, Clare. *When a Feller Needs a Friend and Other Favorite Cartoons*. New York: Dover Publications, 1975.

Browne, Dik. *The Best of Hagar*. Bedford, N.Y.: Comicana Books, 1986.

Bushmiller, Ernie. *The Best of Ernie Bushmiller's Nancy*. Edited by Brian Walker. New York: Comicana/Henry Holt, 1988.

Caniff, Milton. *The Complete Dickie Dare*. Agoura, Cal.: Fantagraphics Books, 1986.

————. *Male Call*. Princeton, Wis.: Kitchen Sink Press, 1987.

————. *Milton Caniff's Steve Canyon*. Princeton, Wis.: Kitchen Sink Press, 1983-.

————. *Terry and the Pirates*. 12 vols. New York: Nantier-Beall-Minoustchine Publishing Co., 1984-1987.

————. *Terry and the Pirates*. Franklin Square, N.Y.: Nostalgia Press, 1970.

Capp, Al. *The Best of Li'l Abner*. New York: Holt, Rinehart and Winston, 1978.

————. *Li'l Abner*. Princeton, Wis.: Kitchen Sink Press, 1988-.

Crane, Roy. *Wash Tubbs and Captain Easy*. New York: Nantier-Beall-Minoustchine Publishing Co., 1987-.

Craven, Thomas, ed. *Cartoon Cavalcade*. New York: Simon and Schuster, 1943.

Crouch, Bill, ed. *Dick Tracy: America's Most Famous Detective*. Secaucus, N.J.: Citadel Press, 1987.

Crumb, Robert. *The Complete Crumb Comics*. Agoura, Cal.: Fantagraphics Books, 1987-.

———. *Fritz the Cat*. New York: Ballantine Books, 1969.

Davis, Jim. *Garfield Treasury*. New York: Ballantine Books, 1982.

———. *The Second Garfield Treasury*. New York: Ballantine Books, 1983.

Dille, Robert C., ed. *The Collected Works of Buck Rogers in the 25th Century*. New York: Chelsea House, 1969. Revised edition 1977.

Dirks, Rudolph. *The Katzenjammer Kids*. New York: Dover Publications, 1974.

Falk, Lee, and Phil Davis. *Mandrake the Magician*. Franklin Square, N.Y.: Nostalgia Press, 1970.

———, and Ray Moore. *The Phantom*. Franklin Square, N.Y.: Nostalgia Press, 1969.

Fleischer, Max. *Betty Boop*. New York: Avon Books, 1975.

Foster, Harold. *Prince Valiant*. 2 vols. Wayne, N.J.: Manuscript Press, 1982-1984.

———. *Prince Valiant*. Agoura, Cal.: Fantagraphics Books, 1985- .

———. *Prince Valiant in the Days of King Arthur*. Franklin Square, N.Y.: Nostalgia Press, 1974.

———. *Prince Valiant Companions in Adventure*. Franklin Square, N.Y.: Nostalgia Press, 1974.

Fox, Fontaine. *Toonerville Trolley*. New York: Charles Scribner's Sons, 1972.

Galewitz, Herb, ed. *Great Comics Syndicated by the New York Daily News and Chicago Tribune*. New York: Crown, 1972.

Garner, Philip, ed. *Rube Goldberg: A Retrospective*. New York: Delilah Books, 1983.

Gilmore, Donald H. (pseud.) *Sex in Comics*. 4 vols. San Diego, Cal.: Greenleaf Classics, 1971.

Gottfredson, Floyd. *Walt Disney's Mickey Mouse in Color*. New York: Pantheon/Another Rainbow, 1988.

Gould, Chester. *The Celebrated Cases of Dick Tracy, 1931-1951*. New York: Chelsea House, 1970.

———. *Dick Tracy, the Thirties, Tommy Guns, and Hard Times*. New York: Chelsea House, 1978.

Gray, Harold. *Arf! The Life and Hard Times of Little Orphan Annie*. New Rochelle, N.Y.: Arlington House, 1970.

———. *Little Orphan Annie*. Agoura, Cal.: Fantagraphics Books, 1987-.

Guisewite, Cathy. *The Cathy Chronicles*. Kansas City, Mo.: Sheed, Andrews, and McMeel, 1978.

Herriman, George. *Krazy & Ignatz: The Complete Kat Comics*. Forestville, Cal.: Eclipse Books, 1988-.

———. *Krazy Kat*. New York: Henry Holt, 1946.

———. *Krazy Kat*. New York: Grosset & Dunlap-Madison Square Press, 1969.

Hogarth, Burne. *Jungle Tale of Tarzan*. New York: Watson-Guptill Publications, 1976.

———. *Tarzan of the Apes*. New York: Watson-Guptill Publications, 1972.

Holbrook, Bill. *On the Fastrack*. New York: Putnam, 1985.

Howard, Greg. *Sally Forth*. New York: Fawcett Columbine-Ballantine Books, 1987.

Johnson, Crockett. [David Johnson Leisk.] *Barnaby*. New York: Henry Holt, 1943.

———. *Barnaby*. 6 vols. New York: Ballantine Books, 1985-1986.

Keller, Charles. *The Best of Rube Goldberg*. Englewood Cliffs, N.J.: Prentice-Hall, 1979.

Kelly, Mrs. Walt, and Bill Crouch, eds. *The Best of Pogo*. New York: Simon and Schuster, 1982.

———. *Pogo Even Better*. New York: Simon and Schuster, 1984.

———. *Outrageously Pogo*. New York: Simon and Schuster, 1985.

———. *Pluperfect Pogo*. New York: Simon and Schuster, 1987.

Lardner, Ring. *Ring Lardner's You Know Me Al*. New York: Harcourt Brace Jovanovich, 1979.

Larson, Gary. *The Far Side Gallery*. Kansas City, Mo.: Andrews, McMeel & Parker, 1984.

———. *The Far Side Gallery 2*. Kansas City, Mo.: Andrews, McMeel & Parker, 1986.

Lee, Stan. *The Best of Spider-Man*. New York: Ballantine Books, 1986.

MacNelly, Jeff. *The Very First Shoe Book*. New York: Avon Books, 1978.

———. *The Other Shoe*. New York: Avon Books, 1980.

———. *The New Shoe*. New York: Avon Books, 1981.

———. *On with the Shoe*. New York: Holt, Rinehart and Winston, 1982.

———. *A Shoe for All Seasons*. New York: Holt, Rinehart and Winston, 1983.

———. *The Shoe Must Go On*. New York: Holt, Rinehart and Winston, 1984.

————. *The Greatest Shoe on Earth.* New York: Holt, Rinehart and Winston, 1985.

————. *One Shoe Fits All.* New York: Henry Holt & Co., 1986.

————. *Too Old for Summer Camp and Too Young to Retire.* New York: St. Martin's Press, 1988.

Marlette, Doug. *Kudzu.* New York: Ballantine Books, 1982.

McCay, Winsor. *Daydreams and Nightmares: The Fantastic Visions of Winsor McCay.* Westlake Village, Cal.: Fantagraphics Books, 1988.

————. *Dreams of the Rarebit Fiend.* New York: Dover Publications, 1973.

————. *Little Nemo.* Franklin Square, N.Y.: Nostalgia Press, 1972.

————. *Little Nemo—1905-1906.* Franklin Square, N.Y.: Nostalgia Press, 1976.

————. *Little Nemo in the Palace of Ice and Further Adventures.* New York: Dover Publications, 1976.

McManus, George. *Bringing Up Father.* New York: Charles Scribner's Sons, 1973.

————. *Jiggs is Back.* Berkeley, Cal.: Celtic Book Company, 1986.

Moores, Dick. *Gasoline Alley.* New York: Avon Books, 1976.

Nostalgia Comics. 6 vols. Franklin Square, N.Y.: Nostalgia Press, 1971-1974.

Outcault, Richard F. *Buster Brown.* New York: Dover Publications, 1974.

Patton, Jack, and John Rosenfield, Jr. *Texas History Movies.* Collector's Limited Edition. Dallas, Tex.: Pepper Jones Martinez, 1970.

————. *Texas History Movies.* Abridged and revised. Dallas, Tex.: Pepper Jones Martinez, 1985.

————. *Texas History Movies.* Abridged and revised. Austin: Texas Historical Association, 1986.

Raymond, Alex. *Flash Gordon.* Franklin Square, N.Y.: Nostalgia Press, 1967.

————. *Flash Gordon in the Planet Mongo.* Franklin Square, N.Y.: Nostalgia Press, 1974.

————. *Flash Gordon in the Underwater World of Mongo.* Franklin Square, N.Y.: Nostalgia Press, 1974.

————. *Flash Gordon into the Water World of Mongo.* Franklin Square, N.Y.: Nostalgia Press, 1971.

Ripley, Robert L. *Ripley's Giant Believe It or Not!* New York: Warren Books, 1976.

Rosendahl, Peter J. *Han Ola og han Per.* Ed. Joan N. Buckley and Einar Haugen. Vol. 1. Oslo: Universitetsforlaget, 1984. Vol. 2. Iowa City: University of Iowa Press, 1988.

Schulz, Charles. *Peanuts Treasury.* New York: Holt, Rinehart and Winston, 1968.

————. *The Snoopy Festival.* New York: Holt, Rinehart and Winston, 1974.

Scott, Randall W. *Comic Books and Strips: An Information Sourcebook.* Phoenix, Ariz.: Oryx Press, 1988.

Segar, Elzie C. *The Complete E. C. Segar Popeye.* Agoura, Cal.: Fantagraphics Books, 1984-.

Smith, Sidney. *The Gumps.* New York: Charles Scribner's Sons, 1974.

Trudeau, G. B. *The Doonesbury Chronicles.* New York: Holt, Rinehart and Winston, 1975.

————. *Doonesbury's Greatest Hits.* New York: Holt, Rinehart and Winston, 1978.

————. *The People's Doonesbury.* New York: Holt, Rinehart and Winston, 1981.

————. *Doonesbury Dossier.* New York: Holt, Rinehart and Winston, 1984.

————. *Doonesbury Deluxe.* New York: Holt, Rinehart and Winston, 1987.

Unger, Jim. *The 1st Treasury of Herman.* Kansas City, Mo.: Andrews and McMeel, 1979.

————. *The Second Herman Treasury.* Kansas City, Mo.: Andrews and McMeel, 1980.

————. *Herman, the Third Treasury.* Kansas City, Mo.: Andrews and McMeel, 1982.

————. *Herman, the Fourth Treasury.* Kansas City, Mo.: Andrews, McMeel & Parker, 1984.

————. *Herman Treasury 5.* Kansas City, Mo.: Andrews, McMeel & Parker, 1986.

Walker, Mort. *The Best of Beetle Bailey.* Bedford, N.Y.: Comicana Books, 1984.

————. *The Best of Hi and Lois.* Bedford, N.Y.: Comicana Books, 1986.

Watterson, Bill. *Calvin and Hobbes.* Kansas City, Mo.: Andrews, McMeel & Parker, 1985.

————. *Something Under the Bed is Drooling.* Kansas City, Mo.: Andrews and McMeel, 1988.

Willard, Frank. *Moon Mullins: Two Adventures.* New York: Dover Publications, 1976.

Young, Dean, and Rick Marschall. *Blondie & Dagwood's America.* New York: Harper & Row, 1981.

Periodicals

Cartoonist Profiles. Fairfield, Conn., 1969-.

Comics Buyer's Guide. Iola, Wis., 1971-.

Comics Journal. Seattle, Wash., 1977-.

Nemo: The Classic Comics Library. Seattle, Wash., 1983-.

COMIC BOOKS

Books and Articles

Bails, Jerry, *The Collector's Guide: The First Heroic Age*. Detroit: Jerry Bails, 1969.
——, and Hames Ware, eds. *The Who's Who of American Comic Books*. 4 vols. Detroit: Jerry Bails, 1973-76.

Barker, Martin. *A Haunt of Fears: The Strange History of the British Horror Comics Campaign*. London: Pluto Press, 1984.

Barrier, Michael. *Carl Barks and the Art of the Comic Book*. New York: M. Lilien, 1981.

Benton, Mike. *Comic Book Collecting for Fun and Profit*. New York: Crown Publishers, 1985.

Bernewitz, Fred von, and Joe Vucenic. *The Full Edition of the Complete E.C. Checklist* (Revised). Los Alamos, N.M.: Wade M. Brothers, 1974.

Bray, Glen. *The Illustrated Harvey Kurtzman Index: 1939-1975*. Sylmar, Cal.: Glenn Bray, 1976.

Carlson, Raymond. *A Guide to Collecting and Selling Comic Books*. New York: Pilot Books, 1976.

Chalker, Jack. *An Informal Biography of Scrooge McDuck*. Baltimore: Mirage Press, 1974.

Collins, Max Allan, and James L. Traylor. *One Lonely Knight: Mickey Spillane's Mike Hammer*. Bowling Green, Ohio: Bowling Green State University Popular Press, 1984.

Daniels, Les. *Comix: A History of Comic Books in America*. New York: Outerbridge & Dienstfrey, 1971.

DC Comics. *The Greatest Superman Stories Ever Told*. New York: DC Comics, 1987.
——. *The Greatest Batman Stories Ever Told*. New York: DC Comics, 1988.
——. *The Greatest Joker Stories Ever Told*. New York: DC Comics, 1989.

Dippie, Brian W., and Paul A. Hutton. *The Comic Book Custer: A Bibliography of Custeriana in Comic Books and Comic Strips*. Publication No. 4 Brazos Corral of the Westerners, 1983.

Dooley, Dennis, and Gary Engle, eds. *Superman at Fifty: The Persistence of a Legend*. Cleveland, Ohio: Octavia Press, 1987.

Dorfman, Ariel, and Armand Mattelart. *How to Read Donald Duck: Imperialist Ideology in the Disney Comic*. Translated by David Kunzle. New York: International General, 1975.

Dundy, Elaine. *Elvis and Gladys*. New York: Macmillan, 1985.

Eisner, Will. *Comics & Sequential Art*. Tamorac, Fla.: Poorhouse Press, 1985.

Estren, Mark James. *A History of Underground Comics*. San Francisco: Straight Arrow Books, 1974.

Feiffer, Jules. *The Great Comic Book Heroes*. New York: Dial Press, 1965.

Fiene, Donald M. *R. Crumb Checklist of Work and Criticism*. Cambridge, Mass.: Boatner Norton Press, 1981.

Fisher, George Thomas. *The Classic Comics Index*. Nottingham, N.H.: Thomas Fisher Publishing, 1986.

Fleisher, Michael L. *The Encyclopedia of Comic Book Heroes*. Vol. I: *Batman*. Vol. II: *Wonder Woman*. Vol. III *Superman*. New York: Macmillan, 1976-.

Freeman, Gillian. *The Undergrowth of Literature*. London: Thomas Nelson and Sons, 1967.

Garrick, P. R. *Masters of Comic Book Art*. New York: Images Graphiques, 1978.

Gifford, Denis. *The International Book of Comics*. New York: Crescent Books, 1984.

Gilbert, James. *A Cycle of Outrage: America's Reaction to the Juvenile Delinquent in the 1950s*. New York: Oxford University Press, 1986.

Goulart, Ron. *Great History of Comic Books*. Chicago: Contemporary Books, 1986.
——. *The Great Comic Book Artists*. 2 vols. New York: St. Martin's Press, 1986, 1988.
——. *The Assault on Childhood*. Los Angeles: Sherbourne Press, 1969.

Groth, Gary, and Robert Fiore, eds. *The New Comics*. New York: Berkley Books, 1988.

Heffelfinger, Charles. *The Classics Handbook*. 3rd ed. Tampa, Fla.: Charles Heffelfinger, 1986.

Inge, M. Thomas. *The American Comic Book*. Columbus: Ohio State University Libraries, 1985.

Jacobs, Frank. *The Mad World of William M. Gaines*. New York: Lyle Stuart, 1972.

Jacobs, Will, and Gerard Jones. *The Comic Book Heroes: From the Silver Age to the Present*. New York: Crown Publishers, 1985.

Keltner, Howard. *Index to Golden Age Comic Books*. Detroit: Jerry Bails, 1976.

Kennedy, Jay. *The Official Underground and Newave Comix Price Guide*. Cambridge,

Mass.: Boatner Norton Press, 1982.

King, Stephen. *Danse Macabre*. New York: Everest House, 1981.

Legman, Gershon. *Love & Death: A Study in Censorship*. New York: Breaking Point, 1949. Reprint. New York: Hacker Art Books, 1963.

Leiter, Marcia. *Collecting Comic Books*. Boston: Little, Brown, 1983.

O'Brien, Richard. *The Golden Age of Comic Books: 1937-1945*. New York: Ballantine Books, 1977.

The Official Handbook of the Marvel Universe. 8 vols. New York: Marvel Comics Group, 1986-87.

Olshevsky, George. *Marvel Comics Index*. Vol. I: *the Amazing Spider-Man*. Vol. II: *Conan and the Barbarians*. Vol. III: *Avengers and Captain Marvel*. Vol. IV: *Fantastic Four*. Vol. V: *The Mighty Thor*. Vol. VI: *Heroes from Strange Tales*. Vol. VIIA: *Heroes from Tales to Astonish, The Incredible Hulk*. Vol. VIIB: *Heroes from Tales to Astonish, The Sub-Mariner*. Vol. VIIIA: *Heroes from Tales of Suspense, Captain America*. Vol. VIIIB: *Heroes from Tales of Suspense, Iron Man and Others*. Toronto, Canada: G & T Enterprises, 1975-.

Overstreet, Robert M. *The Comic Book Price Guide*. Cleveland, Tenn.: Overstreet Publications, 1970 (and subsequent annual editions).

Richler, Mordecai. *The Great Comic Book Heroes and Other Essays*. Toronto, Canada: McClelland and Stewart, 1978.

Robbins, Trina, and Catherine Yronwode. *Women and the Comics*. Guerneville, Cal.: Eclipse Books, 1985.

Rovin, Jeff. *The Encyclopedia of Superheroes*. New York: Facts on File Publications, 1985.

Scott, Randall W. "Comic Research Libraries." *Comic Art Collection*, No. 33 (2 February 1987), 5-7. Reprinted *The Comics Buyer's Guide*, No. 694 (6 March 1987): 51-52.

Steranko, James. *The Steranko History of Comics*. 2 vols. Wyomissing, Pa.: Supergraphics, 1970-72.

Sullivan, Jack, ed. *The Penguin Encyclopedia of Horror and the Supernatural*. New York: Viking, 1986.

Thomas, James L., ed. *Cartoons and Comics in the Classroom: A Reference for Teachers and Librarians*. Littleton, Col.: Libraries Unlimited, 1983.

Umphlett, Wiley Lee. *Mythmakers of the American Dream: The Nostalgic Vision in Popular Culture*. Lewisburg, Pa.: Bucknell University Press, 1983.

U.S. Congress. Senate Committee on the Judiciary. *Juvenile Delinquency: Comic Books, Motion Pictures, Obscene and Pornographic Materials, Television Programs*. Westport, Conn.: Greenwood Press, 1969.

Uslan, Michael, and Bruce Solomon. *The Pow! Zap! Wham! Comic Book Trivia Quiz*. New York: William Morrow, 1977.

Wertham, Fredric. *Seduction of the Innocent*. New York: Holt, Rinehart and Winston, 1954. Reprinted. Port Washington, N.Y.: Kennikat Press, 1972.

Who's Who: The Definitive Directory of the DC Universe. 26 issues. New York: DC Comics, March 1985-April 1987.

Wolfman, Marv, and George Pérez. *History of the DC Universe*. 2 vols. New York: DC Comics, 1986.

Wooley, Charles. *History of the Comic Book 1989-1936*. Lake Buena Vista, Fla.: Charles Wooley, 1986.

Anthologies and Reprints

Barlow, Ron, and Bob Stewart, eds. *Horror Comics of the 1950s*. Franklin Square, N.Y.: Nostalgia Press, 1971.

Barrier, Michael, and Martin Williams, eds. *A Smithsonian Book of Comic-Book Comics*. Washington, D.C.: Smithsonian Institution Press, 1981.

Batman from the 30s to the 70s. New York: Crown, 1971.

The Best of the Rip Off Press. 2 vols. San Francisco: Rip Off Press, 1973-74.

Boxell, Tim. *Commies from Mars—The Red Planet, The Collected Works*. San Francisco: Last Gasp, 1985.

The Carl Burks Library. 30 vols. Scottsdale, Ariz.: Another Rainbow Publishing, 1983-.

The Complete EC Library. 53 vols. West Plains, Mo.: Russ Cochran Publisher, 1979-1989.

Crumb, Robert. *Fritz the Cat*. New York: Ballantine Books, 1969.

———. *Head Comix*. New York: Ballantine Books, 1970.

———. *Robert Crumb's Carload o' Comics: An Anthology of Choice Strips and Stories—1968 to 1976*. New York: Bélier Press, 1976.

Donahue, Don, and Susan Goodrick, eds. *The Apex Treasury of Underground Comics*. New York: Quick Fox, 1974.

Goldwater, John. *The Best of Archie*. New York: Putnam, 1980.

Griffith, Bill, and Jay Kinney. *The Young Lust*

Reader. Berkeley, Cal.: And/Or Press, 1974.

Kurtzman, Harvey, and Will Elder. *Playboy's Little Annie Fanny.* 2 vols. Chicago: Playboy Press, 1966, 1972.

Lee, Stan. *The Amazing Spider-Man.* New York: Simon and Schuster, 1979.

———. *Bring on the Bad Guys.* New York: Simon and Schuster, 1976.

———. *Captain America.* New York: Simon and Schuster, 1979.

———. *Dr. Strange.* New York: Simon and Schuster, 1979.

———. *The Fantastic Four.* New York: Simon and Schuster, 1979.

———. *The Incredible Hulk.* New York: Simon and Schuster, 1978.

———. *The Invincible Iron Man.* New York: Marvel Comics, 1984.

———. *Marvel's Greatest Superhero Battles.* New York: Simon and Schuster, 1978.

———. *Mighty Marvel Team-Up Thrillers.* New York: Marvel Comics, 1985.

———. *Origins of Marvel Comics.* New York: Simon and Schuster, 1974.

———. *Son of Origins of Marvel Comics.* New York: Simon and Schuster, 1975.

———. *The Superhero Woman.* New York: Simon and Schuster, 1977.

———. *The Uncanny X-Men.* New York: Marvel Comics, 1984.

Leyland, Winston, ed. *Meatmen: An Anthology of Gay Male Comics.* San Francisco: G. S. Press, 1986.

The Little Lulu Library: First Series, 18 vols. Scottsdale, Ariz.: Another Rainbow Publishing, 1985-.

Lynch, Jay, ed. *The Best of Bijou Funnies.* New York: Links Books, 1975.

Marvel Comics. *Marvel Masterworks.* New York: Marvel Comics, 1987-. A continuing series of volumes reprinting complete runs of the contents of major titles, such as *The Amazing Spider-Man, The Fantastic Four,* *The X-Men, The Avengers,* etc.

O'Neil, Dennis, ed. *Secret Origins of the DC Super Heroes.* New York: Crown-Harmony Books, 1976.

Pekar, Harvey. *American Splendor.* Garden City, N.Y.: Doubleday Dolphin, 1986.

———. *More American Splendor.* Garden City, N.Y.: Doubleday Dolphin, 1987.

Scott, Naomi, ed. *Heart Throbs: The Best of DC Romance Comics.* New York: Simon and Schuster, 1979.

Shazam! from the Forties to the Seventies. New York: Harmony Books, 1977.

Superman from the Thirties to the Eighties. New York: Crown, 1983.

Superman from the Thirties to the Seventies. New York: Crown, 1971.

Sutton, Laurie S., ed. *The Great Superman Comic Book Collection.* New York: DC Comics, 1981.

Uslan, Michael, ed. *America at War: The Best of DC War Comics.* New York: Simon and Schuster, 1979.

———, ed. *Mysteries in Space: The Best of DC Science Fiction Comics.* New York: Simon and Schuster, 1980.

Wonder Woman. New York: Holt, Rinehart and Winston, 1972.

Wrightson, Berni. *The Reaper of Love and Other Stories.* Westlake Village, Cal.: Fantagraphics Books, 1988.

Periodicals

Amazing Heroes. Seattle, Wash., 1983-

Comic Art Collection. East Lansing, MI, 1979-

The Comics Buyer's Guide. Iola, WI, 1971-

Comics Feature. Canoga Park, CA, 1980-

Comics File Magazine. Canoga Park, CA, 1986-

Comics Interview. New York, NY, 1983-

Comics Journal. Seattle, Wash., 1977-

Squa Trout. New York, 1986-

Index